Liberty, Property, and the Foundations of the American Constitution

SUNY Series in the Constitution and Economic Rights

Ellen Frankel Paul, Editor

Liberty, Property, and the Foundations of the American Constitution

edited by
Ellen Frankel Paul *and*
Howard Dickman

State University of New York Press

Published by
State University of New York Press, Albany

For information, address State University of New York Press, State University Plaza, Albany, N.Y., 12246

Library of Congress Cataloging in Publication Data
Liberty, property, and the foundations of the American Constitution /
    edited by Ellen Frankel Paul, Howard Dickman.
        p.   cm. — (SUNY series in the Constitution and economic rights)
    Includes index.
    ISBN 0-88706-914-2.   ISBN 0-88706-915-0 (pbk.)
    1. Right of property—United States—History. 2. United States—
Constitutional history. I. Paul, Ellen Frankel. II. Dickman, Howard. III. Series.
JC605.L53 1988
323.4'6—dc19
                                                            88-11614
                                                              CIP

10 9 8 7 6 5 4 3 2 1

Contents

Acknowledgments

The editors wish to acknowledge the generous support of the National Endowment for the Humanities (Ref: GB-20081-86), and especially the encouragement of the Bicentennial Division and the Division of Public Programs. Additional support was received from the Bowling Green State University Office of University Relations, the College of Arts and Sciences, and the Graduate College. Many individuals at the Social Philosophy and Policy Center, Bowling Green State University provided invaluable assistance in the preparation of this volume; they include: Assistant Project Director Kory Tilgner, Jeffrey Paul, Fred D. Miller, Jr., Dan Greenberg, Terrie Weaver and Tamara Sharp.

Preface

GORDON S. WOOD

The American Revolution was a great turning point in the economic history of the United States. Almost overnight, it seems, the American economy was transformed. The aftermath of the Revolution saw a great release and expansion, a virtual explosion, of energy. The population and productivity of America grew as never before. Americans took the Declaration of Independence seriously, and more of them than ever before were off in the pursuit of happiness. "There is not upon the face of the earth a body of people more happy or rising into consequence with more rapid stride, than the inhabitants of the United States of America," Charles Thomson, the secretary of the Confederation Congress told Thomas Jefferson in 1786. "Population is increasing, new houses building, new lands clearing, new settlements forming, and new manufacturers establishing with a rapidity beyond conception."

The suddenness of the transformation was breathtaking. In 1760 there were only thirteen insignificant colonies of scarcely two million monarchical subjects huddled along a strip on the Atlantic coast, living on the very edges of the British empire and the civilized world. By the early decades of the nineteenth century ten million or so enterprising citizens spanned half a continent; their huge, pulsating, independent, commercial republic was well on its way to becoming a capitalistic world power.

Such an explosive transformation is not easily explained. Some commentators believe that the formation of the Constitution in 1787 was itself principally responsible for this sudden release of energy and enterprise. Certainly the Constitution helped create a political and legal environment conducive to commercial expansion. It made possible a national market and the uniform regulation of trade with foreign states. But it is people, lots of them, who create economic "miracles," not political leaders or legal institutions. No constitution, no legal or political institutions, could ever have created, or restrained, the popular energies that burst forth in the aftermath of the American Revolution. America suddenly emerged a prosperous, scrambling, enterprising society not because the Constitution was created, or because a few leaders like Alexander Hamilton formed a national bank, but rather because hundreds of thousands of ordinary people began working harder to make money and "get ahead."

In this massive release of energy, which can rightly be called the "American Miracle," the Constitution and the federal and state governments mattered only insofar as they got out of the way of the surging, enterprising population. Even when governments managed to get in the way, they were usually overwhelmed by powerful popular forces, by people's newly released aspirations to move, to do business, and to make money. In the years following the Revolution, the federal government made repeated efforts to control the spread of settlement westward. In order to fill up America's vast space in an orderly manner, the government priced the land high, limited the credit available, and kept the plots that could be bought large in size. But people-on-the-move simply ignored these restrictions. They swarmed around the speculative holdings of land companies, squatted where they wanted, or preempted land and refused to pay for it. Consequently, over the next half century or so the national government was repeatedly forced to lower prices, expand credit, and decrease the size of plots of land that could be purchased. It did so in a desperate effort to catch up with what people were already doing. Finally, in 1862, the goverment threw up its hands and simply gave the western land away free to anyone who would settle on it.

Such a mobile, entrepreneurial people treated the restrictions of the Constitution no differently. Article I, Section 10 of the Constitution, as several of the contributors to this volume point out, prohibited the states from emitting bills of credit, but such a technical legal restraint could never have held back the burgeoning forces of popular enterprise. The people wanted money, and so they pressed their state legislatures to charter banks, hundreds of them, which in turn emitted the paper money the people wanted and needed for their commercial activities.

The reader will find contained in this volume a lively debate over the extent to which the Constitution is or was intended to be an endorsement of what would later be called capitalism. In my own view, probably the best that we can say is that the Constitution did not prevent its development. It is always dangerous in writing history to presume that what happened in the past was intended. We know that the United States by the middle of the nineteenth century developed into a massively capitalistic and prosperous nation. But could the Founding Fathers have anticipated this development? Certainly, most of the Founders hoped that the United States would become a great and wealthy commercial republic, though both Jefferson and James Madison expected commerce, by which they meant international trade, to be ancillary to agriculture. But none of them, including Hamilton, clearly foresaw the scrambling, individualistic, acquisitive, democratic business society that suddenly emerged in the early nineteenth century.

Certainly the Founders had economic ideas, and they had what soon would be called 'political economies'. They were well aware of commerce, by which they commonly meant overseas trade. They believed in the importance of such commerce, saw it as a major agent in the refining and civilizing of people, and were generally eager to use the power of government to promote its growth. They were also aware of manufacturing, but they were often suspicious of it, some, like Jefferson and Madison, more than others. Manufacturing that involved the labor of adult males drew such workers from agriculture and the countryside and brought them into cities, where they became dependent wage earners and thus ripe for economic and political manipulation by wealthy men. Increased productivity in such circumstances was far less important than the workers' loss of independence. The Revolutionary leaders were interested more in the virtue of the populace than in its prosperity. Economics was as yet inconceivable apart from morality.

Nearly all of the Founders' economic concerns were different from ours, for they were set within a moral context that we have almost totally lost. Where we measure our society's health by its GNP, its unemployment figures, or its inflation rate, the Revolutionary leaders measured theirs by its virtue, by the extent to which the people were willing to sacrifice their private interests to the public and to forego the consumption of luxuries. Wealth, commerce, and prosperity were important, but they had to be considered in terms of their moral effects on the character of the American people. We can never understand the different eighteenth century economic world until we understand its preoccupation with morality.

The Founders were no utopian reformers who expected people to become different from what they were. They knew that most people had interests, which Madison defined "in the popular sense" as the "immediate augmentation of property and wealth." Some American leaders in 1775-76 had hoped that Americans could transcend their selfish interests, but this hope proved illusory. Their experience after 1776 had taught them otherwise: most people, for example, would not serve in the army or supply troops with food and clothing unless it was in their interests to do so. The Founding Fathers, therefore, were not dreamers. They recognized the prevalence of self-interest in society, accepted this reality with a cold eye, and sought in the federal Constitution of 1787 to construct their political system accordingly.

The Founders ultimately accepted the natural self-interestedness of human beings. This was, of course, the understanding of human nature out of which capitalism developed. What distinguished the framers, however, from later defenders of capitalism is that they clung to the traditional classical hope that there were some disinterested few, some patrician gentry, in the society who were capable of standing above the marketplace and acting as impartial umpires over the competing interests. We have often pictured Hamilton, for example, as a prototypical booster of American capitalism. But this is misleading. Hamilton was willing to allow most people their interests and profits, but it was fame and honor he wanted for himself and for the United States. Hamilton was a traditional aristocrat, not a businessman. Although he thought that most people were selfish and intent on material gain, and thus incapable of noble and disinterested acts, he did not want to be one of them. In the 1790s, he refused to make speculative killings in land or banking as everyone else was doing, "because," as he put it in one of his sardonic moods, "there must be some *public fools* who sacrifice private to public interest at the certainly of ingratitude and obloquy—because my *vanity* whispers I ought to be one of those fools and ought to keep myself in a situation the best calculated to render service." Hamilton clung as long and as hard to this traditional aristocratic conception of public leadership as anyone in post-Revolutionary America.

The Founders' attitude towards property was also as much traditional as it was modern, as much moral as it was commerical. They tended to see property less as a means of aggrandizing profits and more as a source of personal independence. Of course, the Founders' meant by property generally what we mean today—land and tangible goods. But they also meant by property whatever gave a person independence. Thus, in the case of an artisan, a skill or craftmanship was part of his property. Those persons who were without property, such as women and servants, were considered dependent, and they could be justifiably denied the vote because they presumably lacked wills of their own.

The Americans' right to property was one of those rights and liberties of which the English-speaking world was very proud and protective. From time immemorial Englishmen had thought that their peculiar history and their common law made their rights and liberties more secure than those of other peoples. Throughout English history, in a series of successful struggles that began with Magna Charta in 1215 and continued up through the Bill of Rights of 1689, Englishmen had managed to place fences between their rights and liberties and the encroaching rights and prerogatives of the king. The early modern world still had not worked out a clear and distinct separation of private from public, and therefore the king's power to govern the realm was often still thought of as his by virtue of his prerogatives—that bundle of patrimonial private rights adhering in the king because he was the leading landowner and wealthiest member of the realm. Much of medieval English history in fact could be considered as a continual setting of boundaries between the king's personal right to rule and the people's personal right to their lives and property. By the eighteenth century most Englishmen had come to describe this relationship between king and people in terms of a kind of private contract between two parties who had competing rights and mutual obligations; the considerations for this contract from the two parties were protection and allegiance.

The Revolution and the disavowal of the king and the creation of republican states suddenly changed all this for Americans. Republican government was not something to form a contract with; it could no longer be thought of as the prerogative or private patrimonal right of a king. Now, in a republic, government had to be the public power, based on the consent of the whole citizenry—the commonwealth. Good republicans like James Madison had not expected that this new public power of the whole people, especially as represented in the new state legislatures, would pose any danger to the private rights of the people, particularly their right to their property. Kings had threatened the people's right to their property, but legislatures that represented the people had not. How could the people tyrannize over themselves? In 1776 it seemed impossible. But experience during the decade following 1776 convinced many American leaders that such popular tyranny was indeed quite possible. By the middle 1780s, many American leaders thought that the major crisis of the Revolution was at hand. This apprehension was based on their growing realization that the greatest danger to the personal rights and liberties of the people, including their right to property, came from factional majorities of the people themselves. Such threats to individual liberties by legislative majorities were no minor vexation. Such threats struck at the heart of what the Revolution was about. For, said Madison, they "brought into question the fundamental principle of republican government, that the majority who rule in such governments are the safest guardians both of public and private rights."

Many Americans in the decades following the creation of the Constitution became increasingly convinced that they must protect their rights, especially rights to property, from legislative majorities. In the famous Supreme Court case of *Calder* v. *Bull* (1798), Justice Samuel Chase argued that "there are certain vital principles in our free Republican government, which will determine and overrule an apparent and flagrant abuse of legislative power." Among the acts which exceeded legislative authority was "a law that takes property from A. and gives it to B." In a series of subsequent decisions, the Supreme Court took the traditional common law protection of individual property rights against the power of the king and used it against the power of the new, popular republican legislatures. The judges called these protections "vested rights"—a notion that the great constitutional historian, Edward S. Corwin, called "the basic doctine of American constitutional law." As Chancellor James Kent put it in his *Commentaries on American Law* (1826), a statute "affecting and changing vested rights is very generally considered in this country as founded on unconstitutional principles, and consequently inoperative and void." Not legislatures, but only courts, it seemed, could change and transfer "vested rights"; and in time the ancient English phrase that no person shall be deprived of his property "without due process of law" came to be confined exclusively to judicial proceedings.

Much of subsequent American history, including that of our own time, has been involved with the judicial delineation of private rights that are immune from governmental majoritarian tampering. In the course of two hundred years the nature of these private rights has changed, the constitutional justifications of their defense have repeatedly shifted, and property as a personal right has lost much of the primacy it had for the Founders. But compared to people elsewhere, including even Englishmen from whom we inherited our preoccupation with private property, we Americans have remained remarkably suspicious of the public's power to take and use our personal property.

The essays contained in this volume address the important connections between property and liberty, and they do so at the time of the Founding. What intellectual forces shaped the thought of our Founders? How did they envision America's economic future? What constitutional mechanisms did they design to make our economic rights secure? The essays that follow address these questions, and together they may help us understand why economic liberty held such a central place in America's political culture.

"The Rights of Property, and the Property in Rights"[1] The Problematic Nature of 'Property' in the Political Thought of the Founders and the Early Republic

MICHAEL KAMMEN

Students of the formative era in American government have long assumed that liberty and property were closely intertwined concepts in the Founders' political thought. Scholars have frequently acknowledged, moreover, that the obligation to protect private property was perceived as a prime responsibility of government. Advocates of the Constitution argued in 1787-88 that their newly proposed regime would enhance the protection of liberty as well as property. In *Federalist* No. 1, where Alexander Hamilton offered a prospectus for the entire series, he anticipated "the additional security, which its adoption [i.e., the proposed constitution] will afford to the preservation of [republican] government, to liberty and to property."[2]

In *Federalist* No. 2, moreover, John Jay reminded readers that members of the Continental Congress in 1774-75 had been "individually interested in the public liberty and prosperity. . . ." He then observed that "every succeeding Congress, as well as the late Convention, have invariably joined with the people in thinking that the prosperity of America depended on its Union. To preserve and perpetuate it, was the great object of the people in forming that Convention, and it is also the great object of the plan which the Convention has advised them to adopt."[3]

In 1788, when Hugh Williamson (one of North Carolina's delegates to the Philadelphia Convention) made an appeal for ratification to the freemen of Edenton and Chowan County, he offered hope for the "prospect of better times" and asserted that the delegates "imagined that we had been securing both liberty and property on a more stable foundation."[4]

There is even iconographic evidence to corroborate this optimistic mood. Surely it is neither a coincidence nor a chronological quirk that in the year 1789 Benjamin West, the American painter who had removed to England in order to further his vocational ambitions, produced an oil painting titled "Genius Calling Forth the Fine Arts to Adorn Manufactures and Commerce."[5]

Similarly, but at the level of popular culture where we can surmise broad distribution and high public visibility, a broadside that ran through numerous

1

Benjamin West, *Genius Calling Forth the Fine Arts to Adorn Manufactures and Commerce*, 1789. By permission of The Fine Arts Museums of San Francisco, Gift of Mr. and Mrs. John D. Rockefeller 3rd.

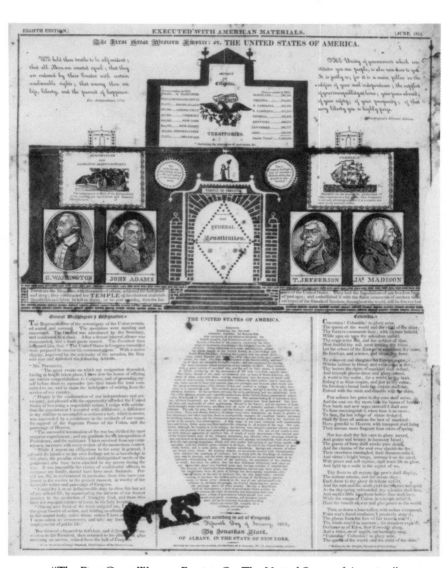

"The First Great Western Empire: Or, The United States of America."

imprints early in the nineteenth century bore the title, "The First Great Western Empire: Or, The United States of America." Above portraits of Washington, Adams, Jefferson, and Madison, which flank a Temple of Freedom inscribing the Federal Constitution, two vignettes are paired. One designates AGRICULTURE AND DOMESTIC MANUFACTURES as "the immoveable pillars of the Independence of our country," while the other lauds COMMERCE as a "strong support to our national edifice."[6]

For more than a full generation following 1789—i.e., for at least four decades—preachers and writers reinforced the common belief that an efficacious connection existed. In 1795, for example, a New England clergyman named Henry Ware enumerated the blessings of "private prosperity," "industry and enterprize," and the attractive prospect that a "comfortable subsistence" was within reach of everyone. "Our constitutions of government," he explained, are "the source of most of our social and domestic felicity."[7]

Ware's plural use of constitutions is noteworthy because it offers a prescient anticipation of the great polemic that occurred in 1819 following the Supreme Court's nationalistic ruling in the case of *McCulloch v. Maryland*. Whereas Judge Spencer Roane of the Virginia Court of Appeals ascribed American prosperity to the state governments (and hence to *their* constitutions), Chief Justice John Marshall, writing under several pseudonyms, alluded often to the federal government's interest in "public prosperity"; and began his "Friend of the Constitution" essays by affirming that "the prosperity of the American people [is] inseparable from the preservation of this government...."[8]

Even before the new government had been implemented, then, as well as several decades into the nineteenth century, the assumption came to be widely shared that constitutional revision in 1787 served to enhance the protection of private property as well as to promote public prosperity. Anticipatory declarations of principle appeared intermittently from the pre-Revolutionary crisis onward. In 1768 a writer in the *Boston Gazette* made the Lockean assertion that liberty and property were so closely linked that one of them could not possibly survive without the other. Speaking at the dedication of a Liberty Tree in Providence, Rhode Island that same year, a Son of Liberty (Silas Downer) developed a similar contention.[9]

Throughout the 1770s and into the subsequent decade, acquisition and protection of property were tightly tied to the preservation of liberty and notions concerning the pursuit of happiness. We frequently encounter statements in which two or all three of these concepts are treated as being inextricably linked—once again, an outlook that appears to be Lockean in derivation.[10]

Finally, when we look at the early state constitutions, most of which prohibit the taking of private property without just compensation, along with the oft-cited last clause of the Fifth Amendment ("nor shall private property be taken for public use, without just compensation."), there would appear to be a clear-cut case supporting the inseparability of private property and personal liberty in American constitutionalism, not to mention the sacredness of private property in the minds of many if not most of the Framers.[11]

Owing to quite an array of historical sources, however, unsettling complexities and ambiguities appear on every side. They give one pause, at least, in attempting to render a conclusive judgment about the "watertight" character of the case for liberty and property as a coherent concept in the thought of the Framers' generation. Consequently, I would like to explore some of these complexities. Although I intend to concentrate primarily on the period from the 1770s to the 1830s, in a concluding section I shall suggest that these ambiguities persist through the century and a half that has elapsed *since* the Charles River Bridge case (1837).[12] Indeed, they are compounded by outright changes in American social and economic activity—alterations that are ultimately reflected in constitutional thought, but that seem less startling if we acknowledge the Preamble to be an integral and meaningful part of the U.S. Constitution.

It may be helpful if I provide the reader initially with a simple listing of major points that will be covered. Because of their chronological overlap, I acknowledge an element of arbitrariness in their sequence of presentation:

I. Ideological ambiguities of republicanism as a value system;

II. Assumptions concerning the socio-economic implications (actual and potential) of American exceptionalism;

III. Plausible consequences of changes that were occurring in western European political thought during the last third of the eighteenth century;

IV. Peculiar silences in the Convention of 1787 and in the Constitution itself;

V. Ambiguities in Antifederalist discourse and in the *Federalist* as well;

VI. Madisonian assumptions and assertions, especially during the years from 1787 until 1792.

I. Ideological Ambiguities of Republicanism as a Value System

The emergence of republicanism as an ideological value system from the 1770s onward has not exactly suffered from scholarly neglect over the past two decades.[13] Certain vital aspects of that value system, however, bear directly on the matter at hand and therefore require brief recitation. The American revolutionaries developed a clear calculus for personal and social morality.

Avarice, luxury, extravagance, grandeur, and "a rage for profit and commerce," qualities attributed to Georgian England, were bad. Frugality, simplicity, industry, enterprise, "prudence, virtue and economy" were good.

Once the War for Independence ended, however, the polarization of positive versus negative values took a somewhat different form, and consequently the social tensions that preoccupied American republicans likewise took a somewhat different form. On July 4, 1783, for example, John Warren, Boston's most prominent physician, articulated the widely shared apprehension that an excess of liberty would lead to economic inequality of a sort deleterious to the public good. Although a commonwealth should ideally facilitate the pursuit of commercial gain, he argued, acquisition of property and the achievement of prosperity tended to stratify society. When "the riches of the state become accumulated in the coffers of a few," republican egalitarianism (equality of condition) would inevitably be lost. "The passions of the great almost invariably extend to the body of the people, who to gratify an unbounded thirst for gain, are ready to sacrifce every other blessing to that...."[14] His wife, Mercy Otis Warren, echoed these plaintive sentiments in her *History of the American Revolution*, published in 1805.

In essence, cultural assumptions in post-Revolutionary America acknowledged a dualism inherent in the close nexus of liberty and property. Republicanism required austerity, restraint, and simplicity in social circumstances. Yet freedom would be conducive to enterprise, prosperity, and hence to significant degrees of inequality. At some point, possibly imminent, the two sets of values, incarnate as social forces, could collide. John Adams conveyed the dilemma in the form of a rhetorical query to Thomas Jefferson in 1819: "Will you tell me how to prevent riches from becoming the effects of temperance and industry? Will you tell me how to prevent riches from producing luxury? Will you tell me how to prevent luxury from producing effeminacy intoxication extravagance, Vice and folly?" Jefferson had no response.[15]

The fulfillment of Revolutionary aspirations for individual liberty could lead—inded, had already led—to the acquisition of private property beyond any reasonable degree consistent with republican values. What ought to be done? Few could say, or would, because this contradiction was one of the most perplexing in the young republic; and the imperatives of law pertaining to private property were at odds with the ethos of civic virtue and Sam Adams's ideal of a Christian Sparta.

II. Socio-economic Implications of American Exceptionalism

As early as 1776, however, Adams and Jefferson, independently of one another, had wistfully contemplated a solution made conceivable by the distinctive circumstances of American geography and demography. In his draft of a constitution for Virginia, Jefferson proposed that fifty acres of land be given to every grown man who lacked real property. Although his proposal was not adopted, the abundance of land available at that time, coupled with the widely shared stake-in-society concept, made it appear quite plausible.[16]

Throughout his life, in fact, Jefferson retained that commitment to using property as a means of averting socio-economic dependence (and thereby disseminating liberty). He perceived the alternatives in stark form: "*economy and liberty, or profusion and servitude.*" Phrased differently, the options were frugality with freedom for all, or extremes of wealth and poverty with unfreedom for the many. His disciples recurred frequently to "the principles of a just and equal distribution."[17]

Similarly, in 1776 John Adams advocated making "the acquisition of land easy to every member of society" in order to enhance the prospect of achieving equal opportunity, liberty, and public virtue.[18] And in 1814, writing to Jefferson from Quincy, he conveyed a sense of the inevitable in troubled tones: "as long as Property exists, it will accumulate in Individuals and Families. . . .So sure as the Idea and the existence of PROPERTY is admitted and established in Society, Accumulations of it will be made, the Snow ball will grow as it rolls." Why was the accumulation of property in families and individuals problematic? Because it encouraged aristocracy which was antithetical to republicanism.[19]

When we concentrate upon the years 1787-88, and connect this issue directly to the new Constitution of the United States, we encounter several points of view. One, however, predominates across ideological lines. Noah Webster, a Federalist, insisted that "an equal distribution of property is the *foundation* of a republic." He even sounded a variation on the Jefferson-Adams theme of 1776: "Let the people have property, and they *will* have power."[20]

The most prolific among Antifederalist pamphleteers, "Centinel" (possibly Samuel Bryan of Pennsylvania), also writing in October 1787, took the very same position: a free republican government could only exist "where property is pretty equally divided."[21]

Although a majority of the polemicists on both sides, then, seemed to echo David Hume's dictum that "the natural equality of property favors liberty" (1752), Alexander Hamilton articulated the obverse position that "an inequality [of property] would exist as long as liberty existed, and that it would unavoidably result from that very liberty itself."[22]

III. Changes in Western European Political Thought

Many of those who have written about assumptions concerning property in America at the time of the Founding tend to provide an exegesis upon Locke's views of property in the *Second Treatise* and then leap directly to 1787 in a rather unhistorical way, as though no changes or modifications intervened that might have affected the attitudes of the Founders.[23]

I would like to suggest the likelihood that in key respects Locke's influence as a political theorist in America diminished between 1776 and 1787. References to him in all of the basic texts that date from 1787-88 are exceedingly scant, and the citations that do occur are quite perfunctory.[24] Locke had been invaluable, after all, as a philosopher of the circumstances under which revolution could be justified. I think it reasonable to assume, however, that he would not have envisioned republicanism as an ideology or as a mode of government. He also had a strong preference for legislative bodies and for weak executives—just the opposite of the felt need in America in 1787.[25]

Some writers have recognized that Locke's understanding of "property" was exceedingly comprehensive, referring not so much to things in themselves but to the act or conditions of possession.[26] The Founders often conflated property with life, liberty, and estate (which was Lockean, to be sure); but several of the most important ones, such as James Madison, extended the definitional scope of "property" more broadly still, as we shall see momentarily.

Finally, regarding John Locke, property, and the Constitution, it seems to me that much too little attention has been given to the fluidity and conflicts within western European views of property as of the 1770s and '80s. In France, for example, we now know that precisely in 1786-87 a major public debate arose between advocates of the "national interest," led by Controller General Calonne, who proposed various fiscal reforms to Louis XVI, and members of the Assembly of Notables who fought to preserve "privilege" in the form of fiscal exemptions. They resisted the idea of paying taxes in proportion to their property holdings.[27] Calonne's concept of national interest is similar, in many ways, to the American notion that I shall cite below—familiarly known as being "affected with a public interest."

Even more germane to our focus here, however, is the recent elucidation by scholars of a shift in the theoretical justification of the origins of property that took place in Scottish thought during the eighteenth century.[28] Over a period of three generations, a shift occurred from the moral justification of private property by means of natural law (the key texts being Locke's *Second Treatise* [1689], Francis Hutcheson's *Short Introduction to Moral Philosophy* [1747] and *A System of Moral Philosophy* [1755]) towards a theory that sought to identify the historical origins of private property (the key texts being Adam Smith's *Lectures on Jurisprudence* [1762, 1766] and John Millar's *Of the Origin of the Distinction of Ranks* [1771]). Millar does not even deal with the moral aspect of how private property, and its unequal distribution, could be justified; and Smith's *Wealth of Nations* says little about the origin and legal status of property.

In view of our new awareness of the impact of Scottish Enlightenment ideas upon American political thought, especially during the final quarter of the eighteenth century,[29] it seems reasonable to reassess the relative importance of Locke on property in relation to subsequent sources of influence. The quest for a new science of politics lay at the core of the Enlightenment in America. We know that that quest was dynamic rather than static.

IV. Property and Liberty in the Convention and the Constitution

When we come to the great debate concerning the embryonic Constitution in 1787-88, we find that both sides expressed concern about the protection of property under the new government. At several points "Publius" reassures his readers that property will become more secure if the new regime is approved (see *Federalist* Nos. 1, 5, 70, and 85). He may well have been proleptic on this score, though more because of the social composition of the judiciary, the fiscal policies pursued at the time, and the various laws that were approved, than because of anything to be found in the Constitution beyond the final clause of the Fifth Amendment. Justice William Paterson's opinion in the case of *Vanhorne's Lessee v. Dorrance* (1795)[30] is commonly cited as a representative position from the first decade under the Constitution: "the right of acquiring and possessing property," he declared, "and having it protected, is one of the natural, inherent, and unalienable rights of man."

Although I acknowledge that Paterson's view may have been widely shared, I must nonetheless notice that in the significant case of *Ware v. Hylton* (1796),[31] John Marshall and Patrick Henry, arguing the case on behalf of the Virginia debtors, insisted that British creditors did not require compensation, and that state law (which in this instance flouted property rights) was controlling. I suspect that Marshall and Henry had a significant number of sympathizers, as did their successors two decades later in the case known as *Martin v. Hunter's Lessee* (1816),[32] in which Virginia refused to permit heirs to the Fairfax lands to resume control of a huge estate that had been confiscated during the War for Independence.

Be that as it may, my point here is quite simply that Farrand's four volumes of *Records of the Federal Convention* are amazingly silent concerning the status and protection of property per se. They contain considerable discussion, of course, concerning property qualifications for congressmen and other officials, or the propriety of freehold property for electors; but little pertaining to government's role in safeguarding private property.

Equally significant, and perhaps even more so, the Preamble to the Constitution—its clearest statement of underlying assumptions and values—never mentions property. It does mention liberty and justice, of course, as well as domestic tranquility.[33] We know that many of the Framers believed that domestic tranquility depended upon the contentment contingent upon a widespread and roughly equal distribution of property.[34] Even so, the Preamble simply remains mute on the subject of property. If the Lockean vision conflated most other values under an expansive conception of "property," then perhaps the Framers were less than full-blooded Lockeans. We cannot be sure; but I regard it as a possibility that requires serious consideration.

V. Property and Liberty During the Ratification Debate

Although Antifederalists frequently expressed the formulaic regard for liberty and property as a biform yet singular concept, they persistently conveyed a deep concern that class conflict would intensify in the United States if the Constitution were adopted, because property belonging to the lower classes would be increasingly at risk. The "Essays of John DeWitt," published at Boston late in 1787, put it this way:

> The great object throughout, is the acquisition of property and power, and every possible opportunity has been embraced to make ample provision for supplying a redundancy of the one, to exercise the other in its fullest extent. They ["men of ambition"] have engrossed to themselves the riches of America, and are carefully silent what use they intend to put them to.[35]

Most strikingly, a number of Antifederalists insisted that human rights took precedence over property rights, and that the proposed Constitution offered prosperity at the sacrifice of liberty. An anonymous catechism that appeared at Boston in 1787 included this extract:

Q. What ought to be the object of government?

A. The welfare of the governed.

Q. How is such a government to be obtained?

A. By forming a constitution which regards men more than things.[36]

One of the most penetrating and forceful Antifederalists, writing as "A [Maryland] Farmer," summed up the outlook of many by asserting that "the unequal division of property silently and gradually undermines" liberty and equality, two of the most vital props of republicanism.[37]

VI. Madisonian Political Economy: 1787 - 1792

The originality and sustained nature of James Madison's thoughts on liberty, property, and the Constitution oblige us to give his views special consideration. Although it is difficult to ascertain just how representative his writings may have been, they clearly became influential. Madison's views were unquestionably the most insightful, and it is equally evident that between 1787 and 1792 they acquired greater complexity and became more subtly nuanced.

In *Federalist* No. 10, published on November 22, 1787, Madison took a deterministic position comparable to the one that Hamilton had presented to the Convention in June. Property rights developed from "the diversity in the faculties of men."

The protection of these faculties is the first object of Government.[38] From the protection of different and unequal faculties of acquiring property, the possession of different degrees and kinds of property immediately results.[39]

Subsequently, in this, the best known of all the *Federalist* papers, Madison proclaimed the unequal distribution of property to be so long-standing in nature as to be normative; and he concluded with the judgment that "a rage. . . .for an equal division of property" would be a "wicked project," though one that was less likely to arise within the extended sphere of the newly proposed government.[40]

In *Federalist* No. 54, Madison made the unexceptionable observation that "Government is instituted no less for the protection of the property, than of the persons of individuals." He proceeded to add a plea for the selection of propertied persons to office: "The rights of property are committed into the same hands with the personal rights. Some attention ought therefore to be paid to property in the choice of those hands."[41]

On March 29, 1792, however, Madison published in *The National Gazette* an essay, titled "Property," that is every bit as extraordinary as the preceding views were commonplace. The essay is virtually unprecedented. It dramatically expands the meaning and scope of "property." Whereas property in John Locke's usage had been broad but rather indeterminate, Madison's articulation is both comprehensive and very explicit. It would not be, in my opinion, an overstatement to call it visionary. It certainly required a leap of empathy and imagination.

> In its larger and juster meaning, [property] embraces every thing to which a man may attach a value and have a right; and *which leaves to every one else the like advantage.*
> In the former sense, a man's hand, or merchandise, or money is called his property.
> In the latter sense, a man has property in his opinions and the free communication of them.
> He has a property of peculiar value in his religious opinions, and in the profession and practice dictated by them.
> He has property very dear to him in the safety and liberty of his person.
> He has an equal property in the free use of his faculties and free choice of the objects on which to employ them.
> In a word, as a man is said to have a right to his property, he may be equally said to have a property in his rights.

Madison concluded this analysis with the pronouncement that "conscience is the most sacred of all property," and he devoted the remainder of his essay to constitutional responsibilities that followed from such an expansive vision of property.

Government is instituted to protect property of every sort; as well that which lies in the various rights of individuals, as that which the term particularly expresses. This being the end of government, that alone is a *just* government, which *impartially* secures to every man, whatever is his *own*.... That is not a just government, nor is property secure under it, where the property which a man has in his personal safety and personal liberty, is violated by arbitrary seizures of one class of citizens for the service of the rest.... That is not a just government, nor is property secure under it, where arbitrary restriction, exemptions, and monopolies deny to part of its citizens that free use of their faculties, and free choice of their occupations, which not only constitute their property in the general sense of the word; but are the means of acquiring property strictly so called.... If there be a government then which prides itself on maintaining the inviolability of property; which provides that none shall be taken *directly* even for public use without indemnification to the owner, and yet *directly* violates the property which individuals have in their faculties; nay more, which *indirectly* violates their property in their actual possessions, in the labor that acquires their daily subsistence, and in the hallowed remnant of time which ought to relieve their fatigues and soothe their cares, the inference will have been anticipated, that such a government is not a pattern for the United States. If the United States mean to obtain or deserve the full praise due to wise and just governments, they will equally respect the rights of property, and the property in rights: they will rival the government that most sacredly guards the former; and by repelling its example in violating the latter, will make themselves a pattern to that and all other governments.[42]

It seems to me unfortunate that Justice Paterson's narrower understanding of property, elaborated in *Vanhorne's Lessee v. Dorrance* (1795), promptly became central to our canon of orthodox constitutional interpretation, while Madison's broader view did not. It is unfortunate because Madison's 1792 schematization of property is not only consistent with the Bill of Rights, but with the spirit of the Preamble as well. Justice Paterson's definition, by contrast, is "merely" consistent with the Fifth and Fourteenth Amendments.

Balancing the rights of property and the individual's property in rights emerged as one of Madison's lifelong preoccupations. By the 1820s he felt a deepening concern for the impact of equal and universal suffrage on the protection of property (in the narrower and more traditional sense). He took solace, however, from a gratifying aspect of American distinctiveness: "the universal hope of acquiring property"—in marked contrast to Europe.[43]

Madison's final judgment on the problem of striking a balance between the rights of property and the property in rights leaned in favor of the latter because doing so would maximize human freedom. "If the only alternative," he wrote,

be between an equal and universal right of suffrage for each branch of the Government, and a confinement of the entire right to a part of the citizens, it is better that those having the greater interest at stake, namely, that of property and persons both, should be deprived of half their share in the Government, than that those having the lesser interest, that of personal rights only, should be deprived of the whole.[44]

Madison's ambivalence concerning property as a social, political, and constitutional issue strikes me as an appropriate culmination to the problematic complexities that existed at the dawn of the creation of American political culture. I would like to conclude, however, with a coda that acknowledges not merely the persistence, but the actual *deepening* of those ambiguities that we have had under surveillance.[45]

Conclusion

At first glance, the Federal Constitution's injunction that private property may not be "taken for public use without just compensation" would appear to be matched by similar safeguards in the various state constitutions.[46] Nevertheless, during the initial decades following independence, it was laxness or outright deviance by the states concerning due compensation for confiscated property that caused serious fiscal and judicial problems for the national government.[47]

Writing in *Federalist* No. 7 (and then once again in No. 85), Alexander Hamilton complained about the state's cavalier treatment of property in diverse pieces of legislation. Among the virtues of the new Constitution, he claimed, were the precautions that it provided against the repetition of "practices on the part of the state governments which have undermined the foundations of property and credit." Under the Articles of Confederation, the crucial powers of commercial regulation and taxation—hence the control of property—had remained solely with the states. Redistribution of this power to a national government in 1789 inevitably added a new area of ambiguity. Examples come readily to mind: the impact of national treaties (e.g., the Peace Treaty of 1783 with Great Britain) on state laws, such as Virginia's law of 1777 relieving debtors, or the activities of a national bank are just two of the most obvious.[48]

Alexander Hamilton's "Defence of the Funding System" (July 1795) combined a relentless critique of the states with foreboding for those who doubted the damage that state selfishness and laxness might cause. "Adieu to the security of property," he warned, "adieu to the security of liberty." It was no accident, Hamilton admonished, that the Constitution prohibited the states from coining money, emitting bills of credit, making anything but gold and silver coin as legal tender in payment of debt, and passing any law that impaired the obligation of contracts. He also asserted that assumption of the entire public debt by the national government had parried "a severe blow to the general security of property."[49]

In view of the material already covered, along with Hamilton's aggressively nationalistic program (not to mention his solicitude for the protection of property) and John Marshall's nationalistic decisions, especially those pertaining to the contracts clause (not to mention Marshall's inhibiting the states from interfering with property rights), one is tempted to reaffirm categorically Willard Hurst's assertion that "those who framed and adopted the Constitution accepted the private market as a central institution in the social order—so central that, without substantial controversy, they wove provisions affecting its care into the structure of government."[50]

Nevertheless, a sufficient number of exceptions, constraints, and special circumstances emerged from the conditions of early national political economy that the respect owed to private property became, if anything, even more ambiguous than it had been during the later eighteenth century. Perhaps I can make this point most effectively by itemizing a few examples.

- When Chief Justice John Marshall, in the major case of *McCulloch v. Maryland* (1819), conceded "that the power of taxing the people and their property is essential to the very existence of government," he surely diminished the "sacredness" of private property and personal liberty by just a bit.[51]

- In the great debate over slavery, even as early as the 1790s, antislavery polemicists cited Blackstone's trinity of "primary articles" that "every man is entitled to enjoy": the rights of personal security, personal liberty, and private property. Where human beings were regarded as property, however, abolitionists insisted that that third element in the trinity should receive "an inferiour consideration."[52]

- During the quarter century preceding the American Civil War, Chief Justice Roger B. Taney, along with many of the state courts, narrowed the customary meaning of "property," because doing so seemed to be in the best interest of national economic growth. The scarcity of capital, in particular, caused judges to constrict significantly the definition of a "taking."[53]

On the basis of these as well as numerous other instances, I want to suggest several possible conclusions. Above all, that American attitudes toward private property have not been held, nor have they evolved, in an intellectual vacuum. They have varied with changes in political circumstance and with the imperatives of a volatile marketplace.[54]

The notion of the sanctity of private property that prevailed during the period from 1776 to 1789, owed much to two sets of variables. First, the particular pre-Revolutionary experience with arbitrarily invalidated land titles, seizures of property by actions of escheat (the reversion of property to the state or sovereign by reason of a breach of condition), the forcible quartering of troops, and the profound resentment of taxation without consent.[55] And second, the ubiquitous concern for the protection of property at that time was predicated upon a widely shared assumption, or desire, that property would be broadly and equitably distributed in republican America.[56]

Half a century later—in 1837, let us say—American regard for private property had been partially tempered by growing recognition of the public interest as a collectivity, and by negative experiences with monopolies and corporations that served the needs of an elite few rather than the democratic many.[57]

The most thorough and persuasive scholarship on the so-called age of laissez faire in political economy, the final quarter of the nineteenth century, demonstrates a similar degree of realism and pragmatism rather than the perpetuation of ideological purity for its own sake. In 1874 Justice Samuel Miller, who had written the majority opinion in the *Slaughterhouse Cases*, acknowledged that "it may not be easy to draw the line in all cases so as to decide what is a public purpose in this sense and what is not."[58] Justice Stephen J. Field, supposedly a paragon of laissez-faire, strenuously defended the states' police power, even at the risk of undermining or actually taking private property. Field conceded, in fact, that state governments had numerous grounds for subjecting property rights to varying degrees of public inter-ference.[59]

A second broad conclusion that I wish to suggest is a highly speculative and revisionist one. A recent work asserts that the "general welfare" rationale for a "taking" (or for "takings") is of comparatively recent vintage. Another asserts that the concept of a business "affected with a public interest" dates from 1877.[60] Perhaps they are correct in a technical sense; but it seems to me that what is really at stake here is the very old question of whether the Preamble is a justiciable part of the U.S. Constitution, and if so, to what degree?[61]

Judge Spencer Roane of Virginia, that forceful spokesman for states' rights, proclaimed back in 1819 that "the preamble is no part of the constitution. If it were, it would carry to congress all powers which are conducive to 'the general welfare'...."[62] Roane recognized his enemy—and correctly identified its adverse implications for his ideological stance. But I believe that he was wrong. The Preamble has enjoyed a place in American constitutionalism ever since Chief Justice John Jay incorporated it, itemized, in his opinion in *Chisholm v. Georgia* back in 1793.[63]

Chief Justice John Marshall did so, as well, in his opinion for the Court in *McCulloch v. Maryland* (1819). He felt sufficiently justified in doing so that he reiterated that deployment of the Preamble in his essays by "A Friend of the Constitution," first printed in the *Alexandria Gazette* in the summer of 1819. The government and the Constitution, he declared, derived their authority from the people and were ordained "in order to form a more perfect union, establish justice, insure domestic tranquility, and secure the blessings of liberty to themselves and to their posterity."[64]

Obviously, the Preamble is more attractive to a nationalist, like Marshall, who believes that the federal government must have broad powers. Even so, the conclusion seems inescapable that the Preamble *is* part of the Constitution, that it *does* count in American jurisprudence, and that it does not mention property. To my way of thinking, those simple facts could assist us in clarifying some of the more knotted conflicts between property and liberty on the one hand, and the general welfare or public interest on the other.[65]

It is customary to acknowledge that Franklin D. Roosevelt's New Deal inaugurated a new era in American constitutionalism. Those who disapprove, or who doubt the legitimacy of that governmental transformation, may ruefully recall an aphorism written by Lorenz von Stein in 1852: "whenever constitution and government become involved in serious conflict it is always the government which overcomes the constitution."[66]

Be that as it may, ever since Roosevelt's second administration, constitutional scholars have urged and sought new approaches to American property law. They contend, for example, that the protection of property must be justified by utilitarian considerations, that social needs should affect our decisions pertaining to property rights, and that individual interests ought to prevail only where they enhance the general interest.[67]

My concluding suggestion, therefore, is that these emphases are not entirely new. They are consistent with the Preamble to the United States Constitution. Their roots will be found in such major decisions of the Jacksonian era as the Charles River Bridge case. And, above all, they are altogether consonant with James Madison's prescription for wise and just governments: namely, that they must "equally respect the rights of property, and the property in rights."

Notes

1. Madison, *Property* (1792), in 6 THE WRITINGS OF JAMES MADISON 103 (G. Hunt ed. 1906).

2. THE ORIGINS OF THE AMERICAN CONSTITUTION: A DOCUMENTARY HISTORY 129 (M. Kammen ed. 1986).

3. *Id.* at 133, 134.

4. Williamson, *Remarks on the New Plan of Government*, in ESSAYS ON THE CONSTITUTION OF THE UNITED STATES PUBLISHED DURING ITS DISCUSSION BY THE PEOPLE, 1787-1788 405 (P. Ford ed. 1892).

5. In the M.H. de Young Museum, San Francisco, Calif. (gift of Mr. and Mrs. John D. Rockefeller, 3rd).

6. The broadside, prepared by Jonathan Clark of Albany, appears to have had eight printings in 1812 alone. A copy is located in the Library of Congress, Prints and Photographs Division, Washington, D.C.

7. H. WARE, THE CONTINUANCE OF PEACE AND INCREASING PROSPERITY A SOURCE OF CONSOLATION AND JUST CAUSE OF GRATITUDE TO THE INHABITANTS OF THE UNITED STATES 9, 20 (1795); SULLIVAN, THE HISTORY OF LAND TITLES IN MASSACHUSETTS 347 (1801). *See also* the

assertion by Congressman Richard Bland Lee (1794) quoted in M. KAMMEN, A MACHINE THAT WOULD GO OF ITSELF: THE CONSTITUTION IN AMERICAN CULTURE 41 (1986).

8. JOHN MARSHALL'S DEFENSE OF McCULLOCH v. MARYLAND 29, 127, 129, 155, 212 (G. Gunther ed. 1969).

9. M. JENSEN, THE AMERICAN REVOLUTION WITHIN AMERICA 74 (1974); AMERICAN POLITICAL WRITING DURING THE FOUNDING ERA, 1760-1805 6-7, 101 (C. Hyneman & D. Lutz eds. 1983).

10. See, Ethan Allen to Zebulon Butler, Oct. 27, 1785, quoted in ONUF, THE ORIGINS OF THE FEDERAL REPUBLIC: JURISDICTIONAL CONTROVERSIES IN THE UNITED STATES, 1775-1787 70 (1983); ADAMS, THE FIRST AMERICAN CONSTITUTIONS: REPUBLICAN IDEOLOGY AND THE MAKING OF THE STATE CONSTITUTIONS IN THE REVOLUTIONARY ERA 190, 193-194 (1980).

11. Id. at 190-94, 217; R. EPSTEIN, TAKINGS: PRIVATE PROPERTY AND THE POWER OF EMINENT DOMAIN esp. 9-31 (1985).

12. Charles River Bridge v. Warren Bridge, 11 Peters 420 (1837).

13. See, 37 AMERICAN QUARTERLY 461-598 (1985), s special issue devoted to the theme of "Republicanism in the History and Historiography of the United States."

14. Bushman, *Freedom and Prosperity in the American Revolution*, in LEGACIES OF THE AMERICAN REVOLUTION 78, 80-81 (L. Gerlach, ed.). See also, Cato's Letters, reprinted in Boston's Independent Advertiser, Jan. 25, 1748, quoted in Nash, *Also There at the Creation*, 44 WILLIAM AND MARY QUARTERLY 602, at 607 (1987); and the words of an anonymous writer in the Cumberland Gazette [N.H.], April 27, 1786: "Equality of property is the life of a Republican Government." Quoted in ONUF, *supra* note 10, at 35.

15. Adams to Jefferson, Dec. 21, 1819, in THE ADAMS-JEFFERSON LETTERS: THE COMPLETE CORRESPONDENCE OF THOMAS JEFFERSON AND ABIGAIL AND JOHN ADAMS 551 (L. Cappon ed. 1959).

16. 1 THE PAPERS OF THOMAS JEFFERSON 362 (J. Boyd ed. 1950); B. BAILYN, VOYAGERS TO THE WEST: A PASSAGE IN THE PEOPLING OF AMERICA ON THE EVE OF THE REVOLUTION 542 (1986). For similar proposals in 1776 and 1783, see E. FONER, TOM PAINE AND REVOLUTIONARY AMERICA 123-124 (1976); and R. BLOCH, VISIONARY REPUBLIC: MILLENNIAL THEMES IN AMERICAN THOUGHT, 1756-1800 98 (1985).

17. See D. BOORSTIN, THE LOST WORLD OF THOMAS JEFFERSON 198-199 (1960); Atwater, *A Sermon* (1801), in 2 Hyneman & Lutz, *supra* note 9, at 1178; Katz, *Thomas Jefferson and the Right to Property in Revolutionary America*, 19 J. L. & ECON., 467-88 (1976). See, Jefferson's letter to Madison, October 28, 1785: "Whenever there is in any country, uncultivated lands and unemployed poor, it is clear that the laws of property have been so far extended as to violate natural right. The earth is given as a common stock for man to labor and live on." 8 Boyd, *supra* note 16, at 682.

18. Adams to James Sullivan, May 26, 1776, in 9 THE WORKS OF JOHN ADAMS 376-78 (C. Adams ed. 1854). In 1780, when Adams wrote the Massachusetts constitution, he deliberately retained a property qualification and the voters approved. See, THE POPULAR SOURCES OF POLITICAL AUTHORITY: DOCUMENTS ON THE MASSACHUSETTS CONSTITUTION OF 1780 35, 37-39 (O. & M. Handlin 1966). Referring to the need for property to be separately represented in legislative bodies, Adams wrote the following in his DISCOURSE ON DAVILA....(1790): "Property must be secure, or liberty cannot exist." 6 Adams, *supra*, at 280.

19. Adams to Jefferson, July 16, 1814, in 2 Cappon, *supra* note 15, at 437-38. Curiously enough, in 1831 Tocqueville reached the conclusion that in the United States "riches will tend more and more to become equal." *See*, SCHLEIFER, THE MAKING OF TOCQUEVILLE'S DEMOCRACY IN AMERICA 263-64 (1980).

20. [Webster], *An Examination into the leading principles of the Federal Constitution proposed by the late Convention held at Philadelphia. . . .* (Philadelphia, 1787), *in* PAMPHLETS ON THE CONSTITUTION OF THE UNITED STATES, PUBLISHED DURING ITS DISCUSSION BY THE PEOPLE, 1787-1788 60, 61 (1888).

21. *Letters of Centinel*, in 2 THE COMPLETE ANTI-FEDERALIST 139 (H. Storing ed. 1981).

22. Hamilton's speech in the Convention, June 26, 1787, in 424 THE RECORDS OF THE FEDERAL CONVENTION OF 1787 (M. Farrand ed., 2nd ed. 1937). David Hume's observation appeared in *The Idea of a Perfect Commonwealth*, ESSAYS: MORAL, POLITICAL, AND LITERARY 512, 528 (E. Miller ed. 1985). In 1786 a Pennsylvania author insisted that different degrees of liberty and industry resulted in "inequality of property." Quoted in FONER, *supra* note 16, at 196.

23. *See*, EPSTEIN, *supra* note 11, at 9-16, 162-64; E. PAUL, PROPERTY RIGHTS AND EMINENT DOMAIN 3, 8, 76-77, 199-212 (1987); P. LARKIN, PROPERTY IN THE EIGHTEENTH CENTURY WITH SPECIAL REFERENCE TO ENGLAND AND LOCKE chaps. 3-5 (1930).

24. *See, e.g.*, the indexes to the seven volumes that have appeared to date of THE DOCUMENTARY HISTORY OF THE RATIFICATION OF THE CONSTITU-TION (M. Jensen, J. Kaminski, & G. Saladino eds.). Locke is never mentioned, moreover, in the 85 numbers of the FEDERALIST!

25. *See* Post, *Jeffersonian Revisions of Locke: Education, Property-Rights, and Liberty*, 47 JOURNAL OF THE HISTORY OF IDEAS 147 (1986); D. EPSTEIN, THE POLITI-CAL THEORY OF THE FEDERALIST 72-74; Ogden, *The State of Nature and the Decline of Lockian Political Theory in England, 1760-1800*, 46 AMERICAN HISTOR-ICAL REVIEW 21-44 (1940); W. SCOTT, IN PURSUIT OF HAPPINESS: AMERI-CAN CONCEPTIONS OF PROPERTY FROM THE SEVENTEENTH TO THE TWENTIETH CENTURY 33 (1977).

26. *See*, B. ACKERMAN, PRIVATE PROPERTY AND THE CONSTITUTION 26-27 (1977); A. RYAN, PROPERTY AND POLITICAL THEORY 14-48 (1984); L. HYDE, THE GIFT: IMAGINATION AND THE EROTIC LIFE OF PROPERTY 94 (1983).

27. Gruder, *A Mutation in Elite Political Culture: The French Notables and the Defense of Property and Participation, 1787*, 56 JOURNAL OF MODERN HISTORY 598 (1984). *See*, R. RUTLAND, THE BIRTH OF THE BILL OF RIGHTS, 1776-1791 102, 106 (2nd ed. 1983), where quotations from 1786 indicate an (unLockean) differentiation in America between property rights and personal liberty.

28. Bowles, *The Origin of Property and the Development of Scottish Historical Science*, 46 JOURNAL OF THE HISTORY OF IDEAS 197-209 (1985). *See also*, J. GUNN, BEYOND LIBERTY AND PROPERTY: THE PROCESS OF SELF-RECOGNITION IN EIGHTEENTH-CENTURY POLITICAL THOUGHT, esp. chs. 5-7 (1983).

29. *See*, G. WILLS, INVENTING AMERICA: JEFFERSON'S DECLARATION OF INDEPENDENCE (1978), passim; G. WILLS, EXPLAINING AMERICA: THE FEDERALIST 15-20, 64-71 (1982); Coram, *Political Inquiries. . . .(1791)* in 2 Hyneman & Lutz, *Inquiry Into the Origin of Property; supra* note 9, at 766-783, and Howe, *European*

Sources of Political Ideas in Jeffersonian America, 10 REVIEWS IN AMERICAN HISTORY 28 (1982).

30. 2 U.S. 304, 310 (1795).

31. 3 U.S. 199 (1796).

32. 14 U.S. 304 (1816).

33. Notice also that in *Federalist* No. 23, where Alexander Hamilton expands upon the Preamble and declares "the principal purposes to be answered by Union," he does not mention the protection of property. *See*, THE FEDERALIST at 146-147 (J. Cooke ed. 1961).

34. *See*, FONER, *supra* note 16, at 39-40; D. McCOY, THE ELUSIVE REPUBLIC: POLITICAL ECONOMY IN JEFFERSONIAN AMERICA 28, 130 (1980). Although most Americans were strenuously attached to "property" during the later eighteenth century, a large majority defined property as the product of visible labor. *That* is what was sacred, and of which an individual should not be deprived.

35. 4 Storing, *supra* note 21, at 29. *See also*, 3 *id.* at 118; 5 *id.* at 56, 77-78; and 4 COMMENTARIES ON THE CONSTITUTION: PUBLIC AND PRIVATE 200, 364-65 (J. Kaminski & G. Saladino eds. 1986).

36. *Serious Questions Proposed to All Friends to the Rights of Mankind, with Suitable Answers* (1787), in 2 Hyneman & Lutz, *supra* note 9, at 703. *See also, Letter from a Delegate Who Has Catched Cold* (June 18, 1788), in 5 Storing, *supra* note 21, at 269.

37. "Essays by a Farmer" (April 4, 1788), *id.* at 55.

38. In *Federalist* No. 52, however, Madison proclaimed that "Justice is the end of government. It is the end of civil society. It ever has been, and ever will be pursued, until it be obtained, or until liberty be lost in the pursuit." Cooke, *supra* note 32, at 352. In *Federalist* No. 70, Hamilton conflated the protection of property and the security of liberty as a unified objective. *Id.* at 471.

39. *Id.* at 58.

40. *Id.* at 59, 65.

41. *Id.* at 370. See, however, the note that Madison added to the speech he gave at the Philadelphia Convention on August 7, 1787: "Persons and property being both essential objects of Government, the most that either can claim, is such a structure of it as will leave a reasonable security for the other," 2 Farrand, *supra* note 21, at 204, esp. n. 17.

42. 6 Hunt, *supra* note 1, at 101-03.

43. 3 Farrand, *supra* note 22, at 450-51.

44. 11 THE PAPERS OF JAMES MADISON 283 (R.Rutland & C. Hobson eds. 1977). For specific manifestations of this dilemma at the state constitutional conventions held in Massachusetts in 1820 and New York in 1821, see SCOTT, *supra* note 25, at 75-76. Thomas Jefferson remained far more sanguine than Madison concerning the future clout of legislators who would safeguard property. *See*, Jefferson to John Adams, Oct. 28, 1813, in 2 Cappon, *supra* note 15, at 388, 391.

45. *See*, Catherine Drinker Bowen to John Powell, Dec. 21, 1965: "We can never recapture the Founders conception of property"; and William Sloane to Bowen, April 23, 1964: "This business about the mystique of property is indeed a tough thing.... The most general and universal conception of property that I have ever met around the world stems from ownership of land, and in 1787 we were a land-owning, land-living, and land-oriented culture. I would guess that there weren't very many people in the states in 1787 whose notion of property went very far beyond tangibles, beyond specific things—

houses, tools, furnishings, land, flocks and so on, and that the corporation share of stock was hardly present in most minds. I wonder if it isn't a lot simpler and therefore more of a mystique just because of that." Bowen Papers, box 37, Library of Congress, Manuscript Division, Washington, D.C.

46. *See, e.g.,* the Ohio constitution of 1851 (as amended), Art. I, § 19 (which is taken from Ohio's original 1802 constitution, Art. VIII, § 4): "Private property shall ever be held inviolate, but subservient to the public welfare. . . . Where private property shall be taken for public use, a compensation therefor shall first be made in money, or first secured by a deposit of money; and such compensation shall be assessed by a jury, without deduction for benefits to any property of the owner." *Ohio,* in CONSTI-TUTIONS OF THE UNITED STATES: NATIONAL AND STATE 3-4 (1986).

47. *See,* ONUF, *supra* note 10, at 35, 50, 54, 87; Foner, *supra* note 16, at 145, 170-171.

48. *Brutus* (March 6, 1788), in 4 Kaminski & Saladino, *supra* note 35 at 330; Bruchey, *The Impact of Concern for the Security of Property Rights on the Legal System of the Early American Republic,* WIS. L. REV., 1135-58 (1980); J. NELSON, Jr., LIBERTY AND PROPERTY: POLITICAL ECONOMY AND POLICYMAKING IN THE NEW NATION, 1789-1812 (1987).

49. Hamilton, *The Defense of the Funding System* (July 1795), in 19 THE PAPERS OF ALEXANDER HAMILTON 32, 47 (H. Syrett, ed. 1973).

50. J. HURST, LAW AND MARKETS IN UNITED STATES HISTORY: DIFFERENT MODES OF BARGAINING AMONG INTERESTS 12 (1982).

51. Gunther, *supra* note 8, at 44.

52. Dwight, *An Oration, Spoken Before the Connecticut Society, for the Promotion of Freedom and the Relief of Persons Unlawfully Holden in Bondage* (1794), in 2 Hyneman & Lutz, *supra* note 9 at 888-89. *Cf. id.* at 859, 866, 870; and Oakes, *From Republicanism to Liberalism: Ideological Change and the Crisis of the Old South,* 37 AMERICAN QUARTERLY 551 at 566, 569.

53. *See* McGurdy, *Justice Field and the Jurisprudence of Government-Business Relations: Some Parameters of Laissez-Faire Constitutionalism, 1863-1897* 61 JOURNAL OF AMERICAN HISTORY 970 at 975, 988-89 (1975).

54. *See generally,* B. SCHWARTZ, A COMMENTARY ON THE CONSTITU-TIONS OF THE UNITED STATES, Part II, THE RIGHTS OF PROPERTY (1965), and Louis D. Brandeis's famous dissent in *Truax v. Corrigan,* 257 U.S. 312, 376 (1921): ". . .in the interest of the public and in order to preserve the liberty and the property of the great majority of the citizens of a State, rights of property and the liberty of the individual must be remoulded, from time to time, to meet the changing needs of society."

55. By way of acknowledging a time-specific context, it should also be noted that the list of capital crimes in Great Britain during the 1770s and '80s approached 200—almost all of them offenses against property. As desperate unemployment and human privation caused an increase in "anti-social" behavior, Parliament sought to "make *every* kind of theft. . .an act punishable by death." *See,* B. BAILYN, VOYAGERS TO THE WEST: A PASSAGE IN THE PEOPLING OF AMERICA ON THE EVE OF THE REVOLUTION 279-95, esp. 292 (1986).

56. *See Civis,* Charleston Columbian Herald, Feb. 4, 1788, in 4 Kaminski & Saladino, *supra* note 35, at 26; R. WIEBE, THE OPENING OF AMERICAN SOCIETY: FROM THE ADOPTION OF THE CONSTITUTION TO THE EVE OF DISUNION 146 (1984).

57. *See,* S. KUTLER, PRIVILEGE AND CREATIVE DESTRUCTION: THE CHARLES RIVER BRIDGE CASE (1971); Kutler, *John Bannister Gibson: Judicial Restraint and the 'Positive State',* 14 J. PUBLIC L. 181, esp. at 195-96 (1965); WIEBE, *supra* note 55, at 242-43; Kulik, *Dams, Fish, and Farmers: Defense of Public Rights in Eighteenth-Century Rhode Island,* in THE COUNTRYSIDE IN THE AGE OF CAPITALIST TRANSFORMATION (S. Hahn & J. Prude, eds. 1985).

58. Loan Association v. Topeka, 87 U.S. 655, 644 (1874); Scheiber, *State Law and 'Industrial Policy' in American Development, 1790-1987,* 75 CALIF. L. REV. at 418 (1987).

59. *See,* McCurdy, *Field and the Jurisprudence of Government-Business Relations,* *supra* note 53, at 973-74, 980, 986-87, 992-94, 1003; Benedict, *Laissez-Faire and Liberty: A Re-Evaluation of the Meaning and Origins of Laissez-Faire Constitutionalism,* 3 LAW AND HISTORY REVIEW 293 (1985). For a much more critical view of private property articulated during the later nineteenth century, see J. KLOPPENBERG, UNCERTAIN VICTORY: SOCIAL DEMOCRACY AND PROGRESSIVISM IN EUROPEAN AND AMERICAN THOUGHT, 1870-1920 397 (1986); P. AVRICH, THE HAYMARKET TRAGEDY 109, 115 (1984).

60. PAUL, *supra* note 23, at 4-5; McCurdy, *supra* note 53, at 995. *Cf.,* Scheiber, *Public Rights and the Rule of Law in American Legal History,* 72 CALIF. L. REV. 217 (1984).

61. *See* J. STORY, 1 COMMENTARIES ON THE CONSTITUTION OF THE UNITED STATES § 460-462 (1833); Jacobson v. Massachusetts, 197 U.S. 11, 22 (1905). Justice John Marshall Harlan, who wrote the Court's opinion in *Jacobson,* cited Story's discussion but ignored its self-aware ambiguity, particularly in the passage from section 460 of the COMMENTARIES: There is no reason why, in a fundamental law "an equal attention should not be given to the intention of the framers, as stated in the preamble. And accordingly we find, that it has been constantly referred to by statesmen and jurists to aid them in the expostion of its provisions."

62. Roane, *"Hampden" Essays* (June 1819), in Gunther, *supra* note 8, at 142. I have heard a milder version of the same view attributed to Justice Hugo Black.

63. 2 U.S. 419 (1793), conveniently accessible in THE SUPREME COURT AND THE CONSTITUTION: READINGS IN AMERICAN CONSTITUTIONAL HISTORY 5 (S. Kutler ed. 1977).

64. 17 U.S. 316 (1819), accessible in Kutler, *id.* at 51. For Marshall's use of the Preamble in his essays, *see* Gunther, *supra* note 8, at 160. It is noteworthy, for comparative purposes, that in Canadian constitutionalism the preamble to the North American Act of the 1860s became crucial to major interpretations of individual rights prior to the 1982 Charter of Rights and Freedom.

65. *See, The Landholder,* Connecticut Current, March 10, 1788, in Kaminiski & Saladino, *supra* note 35, at 367. "Those who wish to enjoy the blessings of society must be willing to suffer some restraint of personal liberty, and devote some part of their property to the public that the remainder may be secured and protected."

66. Koselleck, *Historical Prognosis in Lorenz von Stein's Essay on the Prussian Constitution,* in R. Koselleck, FUTURE'S PAST: ON THE SEMANTICS OF HISTORICAL TIME 64 (1985).

67. Philbrick, *Changing Conceptions of Property in Law,* 86 U. PA. L. REV. 691 (1938); Powell, *The Relationship Between Property Rights and Civil Rights,* 15 HASTINGS L. J. 135 (1963); Reich, *The New Property,* 3 THE PUBLIC INTEREST 57 (1966).

Everyone may not entirely agree with him, but Powell's assertions deserve serious consideration, *viz*: (1) "The content of the term 'property right' has greatly changed in the past two centuries" (at 139); (2) "The history of the law of private ownership has witnessed simultaneously a playing-down of absolute rights and a playing-up of social concern as to the use of property" (at 149) and (3) "Property rights cease when civil rights involving the public welfare are at stake" (at 152).

Moral Philosophy and the Framing of the Constitution
ANDREW J. RECK

I. On Adams's Sources

Two lasting contributions to political philosophy were published during the constitution-making period of the United States, which stretches from the Declaration of Independence in 1776 to the establishment of the federal Constitution in 1789. Both appeared in the same year—1787—and both evince the pervasive influence of philosophy on the theory and conduct of politics.

The first is the less well-known but, for its time, highly influential *Defence of the Constitutions of Government of the United States of America,*[*] by John Adams.[1] The first volume of Adams's *Defence* was published in London in early 1787 (where Adams was then serving as the American envoy). Two American editions appeared shortly thereafter, and excerpts were printed in American newspapers, even while the Constitutional Convention was in session. While Adams's *Defence* is his account of the philosophers and historians, ancient and modern, who shaped the thinking of the framers of the states' constititutions, it also furnishes the philosophical background of the Federal Constitution. He expounded the principles of classical republicanism, elucidating their articulation by such philosophers as Plato, Aristotle, Cicero, Harrington, Sidney, Locke, Hume, Montesquieu, and Price, and by such historians as Polybius and Machiavelli.[2] Adams maintained that the best constitution is the mixed polity in which democracy, aristocracy, and monarchy—representing the fixed order or ranks of men in society—are incorporated in a delicate system of checks and balances.

A.O. Lovejoy has singled Adams out as "the principal American exponent" of the late eighteenth century theory of man.[3] To support his political theory, Adams maintained that:

> [T]he first inquiry should be, what kind of beings men are? You and I admire the fable of Tristram Shandy more than the Fable of the Bees, and agree with Butler

---

[*]Cited throughout the text as *DC*.

23

rather than Hobbes. It is weakness rather than wickedness, which renders men
unfit to be trusted with unlimited power. (DC at 127)

Adams viewed the passions as being unlimited by nature, and judged that, if
restricted artificially, they atrophy. He pointed to three so-called aristocratic
passions as central to the political process: love of gold, love of praise, and
ambition. These passions threaten to dominate and absorb all others, and they
are so devious that they wreak their effects while hidden from the sight of the
men they drive. The remedy Adams recommended was to balance them
through a system of checks. He elucidated:

> Men should endeavor at a *balance* of affections and appetites, under the
> monarch of reason and conscience, within, as well as at a balance of power
> without. If they surrender the guidance for any course of time to any one
> passion, they may depend upon finding it in the end, a usurping, domineering,
> cruel tyrant. (DC at 128)

Political power is similar to the passions from which it springs. If allowed to
go unchecked, it results in tyranny. For absolute power is destructive in the
same way that the domination of a single passion is. However, political stability
and progress rest upon the equilibrium of competing passions or rival interests,
so that "the commonwealth, being equally *poised* and *balanced*, like a *ship* or a
waggon [sic], acted upon by *contrary powers*, might long remain in the same
situation. . ." (DC at 169) Lovejoy has aptly dubbed this political mechanism
"the method of counterpoise—accomplishing desirable results by balancing
harmful things against one another."[4]

Adams admired the mixed polity as a singular achievement within the
broad sweep of history. It had originated in ancient republican Rome; it had
developed historically into the British constitution of King, Lords, and
commons; and it was being expressly formulated on rational grounds and
embodied in the constitutions of the American states. For Adams, as for many
of his readers, classical republicanism, with its mixed polity that mirrored the
nature of man, balanced the orders of men. It, thus, required bicameralism,
with a higher chamber for the nobility and a lower chamber for representatives
of the people. In the republican political order, moreover, the rule of law and
the security of liberties and rights resulted from the dynamic equilibrium of the
ranks of men, in the American experiments to be additionally buttressed by
written constitutions with explicit Bills of Rights. Essential to the efficacy of
classical republicanism is civic virtue, a quality best represented by the
aristocracy, which Adams, like Thomas Jefferson, conceived to be natural
rather than hereditary, and manifest in persons who possess meritorious
qualities of wisdom, experience, and virtue. Natural aristocrats are therefore
best able to transcend the passions of the moment and to subordinate private
and factional interests to the public good.

II. On the *Federalist Papers*

The second and certainly more famous contribution to political philosophy is the *Federalist Papers*,* published originally as anonymous contributions to newspapers by Alexander Hamilton, James Madison, and John Jay.[5] This work argued the case for the ratification of the Constitution of the United States, expounding its principles, justifying its provisions, and striving to persuade its readers to vote for ratification. Unlike Adams' *Defence*, the *Federalist Papers* did not offer translations and comments on philosophers and historians, nor was its gaze fixed on the state constitutions. Nevertheless, the arguments of the *Federalist* are often adorned by notions drawn from the philosophers whose doctrines Adams had so ably explicated.

Thus, for example, in *Federalist* No. 9, Hamilton turns the tables on those who cite the authority of Montesquieu to deny that a republic can govern a large expanse of territory. Instead he uses Montesquieu's conception of a confederate republic to contend that the very size of the proposed American union would both guarantee liberty within its borders and be a bulwark of security against foreign adversaries. (FP No 9 at 71-76)

And, to consider a passage examined by Morton White,[6] in *Federalist* No. 31, Hamilton, justifying the hotly opposed provision that the federal government have a national power of taxation, invoked the then prevalent moral epistemology to be found in the writings of such thinkers as John Locke and Jean-Jacques Burlamaqui. As Hamilton declared in his vigorous and lucid prose:

> In disquisitions of every kind there are certain primary truths, or first principles, upon which all subsequent reasonings must depend. These contain an internal evidence which, antecedent to all reflection or combination, commands the assent of the mind. Where it produces not this effect, it must proceed either from some disorder in the organs of perception, or from the influence of some strong interest, or passion, or prejudice. Of this nature are the maxims in geometry that the whole is greater than its parts; that things equal to the same are equal to one another; that two straight lines cannot enclose a space; and that all right angles are equal to each other. Of the same nature are these other maxims in ethics and politics, that there cannot be an effect without a cause; that the means ought to be proportioned to the ends; that every power ought to be commensurate with its object; that there ought to be no limitation of a power destined to effect a purpose which is itself incapable of limitation. And there are other truths in the two latter sciences which, if they cannot pretend to rank in the class of axioms, are yet such direct inferences from them, and so obvious in themselves, and so agreeable to the natural and unsophisticated dictates of common sense that they challenge the assent of a sound and

---

*Cited in text as FP.

unbiased mind with a degree of force and conviction almost equally irresistible. (*FP* No. 31 at 193)

Hamilton was quick to concede that in abstract subjects such as geometry man reaches the theorems more easily than in the sciences of morals and politics. Although some of the theorems in the former are often at variance with and always remote from common sense, they do not arouse man's unruly passions. Hamilton admitted:

> Though it cannot be pretended that the principles of moral and political knowledge have, in general, the same degree of certainty with those of mathematics, yet they have much better claims in this respect than to judge from the conduct of men in particular situations.... The obscurity is much oftener in the passions and prejudices of the reasoner than in the subject. Men, upon too many occasions, do not give their own understanding fair play; but, yielding to some untoward bias, they entangle themselves in words and confound themselves in subtleties. (FP No. 31 at 194)

The authors of the *Federalist* shared with Adams the conviction that passions and interests must be checked, balanced, or kept in equilibrium if a rational polity safeguarding liberty and administering justice is to prevail, although they may have blurred those nice distinctions of moral philosophy between reason and passion as motives and as cognitions. Nevertheless, their interpretation of politics was grounded in a theory of human nature which, as A.O. Lovejoy has demonstrated in his book, *Reflections on Human Nature*, was derived from the literature and philosophy of the seventeenth and eighteenth centuries.

In *Federalist* No. 51, James Madison, expatiating on the separation of powers and the safeguards for liberty provided in the Constitution, eloquently expressed the Founders' conception of human nature as it related to government. He wrote:

> Ambition must be made to counteract ambition. The interest of man must be connected with the constitutional rights of the place. It may be a reflection on human nature, that such devices should be necessary to control the abuses of government. But what is government itself but the greatest of all reflections on human nature? If men were angels, no government would be necessary. If angels were to govern men, neither external nor internal controls on government would be necessary. In framing a government which is to be administered by men over men, the great difficulty lies in this: you must first enable the government to control the governed; and in the next place oblige it to control itself. A dependence on the people is, no doubt, the primary control on the government; but experience has taught mankind the necessity of auxiliary precautions. (FP No. 51 at 323)

Again in *Federalist* No. 55, James Madison, while defending the decision of the Convention to keep the House of Representatives a reasonably small body in order to avoid the unruliness of large popular assemblies, commented on the nature of man as it bears upon politics. He said:

> As there is a degree of depravity in mankind which requires a certain degree of circumspection and distrust: So there are other qualities in human nature which justify a certain portion of esteem and confidence. Republican government presupposes the existence of these qualities in a higher degree than any other form. Were the pictures which have been drawn by the political jealousy of some among us, faithful likenesses of the human character, the inference would be, that there is not sufficient virtue among men for self-government; and that nothing less than the chains of despotism can restrain them from destroying and devouring one another. (FP No. 55 at 346)

The Founders embraced a political theory which separated powers within the federal government and which divided powers between the states and the national government. This theory offered an intricate system of checks and balances consonant with human nature. Nevertheless, commentators on the Federal Constitution and its justification in the *Federalist Papers* have discerned a departure from the classical republicanism represented by John Adams in *A Defence*.[7] Classical republicanism rests on a balance of the ranks of men and depends heavily on virtue, while, it is argued, the federal republic the *Federalist Papers* justifies attends to the balance of the conflicting interests in society and, although it does not disregard virtue, looks to compromise and checks to guarantee political stability and safeguard liberty. The *Federalist Papers* shows, perhaps unintentionally, how the modern republicanism it espouses, while its roots were nurtured in classical republicanism, represents a departure in politics. But despite the differences, the underlying theme remains the same: the political order reflects the nature of man.

III. On the Debates at the Convention

A third major source for ascertaining the influence of philosophy on the framing of the Constitution is the records of the debates in the Convention of 1787. They furnish the contemporary student a truly excellent opportunity to witness the clash of political philosophies as the founding fathers formulated the document that persists today as the core of the Constitution of the United States. While there are several reports of the Constitutional Convention, the most complete, informative, and insightful record is *The Debates in the Federal Convention of 1787*,* as reported by James Madison,[8] a statesman who has been hailed as the "father of the Constitution."[9] Madison's notes were first published in 1840.

---

*Cited in text as MN.

The contents and direction of the debates confirm the commonplace of scholarship that Montesquieu was the main philosopher who influenced the thinking of the American statesmen and politicians of the era. Montesquieu is mentioned twice by Madison; first, in respect to the Lycian confederacy, which was based on the proportional representation of its member (MN at 130); and second, on the separation of powers. (MN at 397) He is also cited by Edmund Randolph on the topic of suffrage (MN at 354), and, in the notes taken by Robert Yates, a delegate from New York, Montesquieu is invoked by Pierce Butler of South Carolina to caution on the corruption that results from entrusting persons with too much power and without checks.[10]

As regards the use and mention of the philosophers in these debates, however, the student will be struck by the paucity of references, especially by comparison to the numerous citations of philosophers in the pamphlet literature of the American revolutionary era from 1763 to 1776. And unfortunately for the reputation of philosophy in matters of practical politics, the delegate who most indulged in explicit philosophizing was Luther Martin of Maryland. In behalf of the rights of states and their equal representation in the legislature, Martin paraded many of the political theorists—Locke, Vattel, Priestley—who had inspired the pamphleteers of the American revolution;[11] his exhortation to the Convention on June 27 lasted "more than three hours." (MN at 289) Exhausted, he requested permission to continue his speech the next day and he did so, "with much diffuseness and considerable vehemence." (MN at 290) Of Martin, William Pierce, a delegate from Georgia, opined: "This Gentleman possesses a good deal of information, but he has a very bad delivery, and so extremely prolix, that he never speaks without tiring the patience of all who hear him."[12] In mitigation of the slur against the influence of philosophy on practical politics, it may be pertinent to recall that Luther Martin departed before the Convention ended and returned to Maryland to strenuously oppose ratification.

Although philosophy was present in the debates at the Convention, its presence was not conspicuous. Unlike Adams in A Defence of the Constitutions and even less so than the authors of the Federalist Papers, the delegates at the Convention, excepting Luther Martin, did not indulge in scholarly disquisitions on philosophers' opinions and their possible application to the resolution of the issues at hand. Yet, delegates expounded competing philosophies without making the attributions scholarship might demand. Indeed, they ingeniously triumphed over the conventional wisdom of the established philosophers when they extended republican government over the wide expanse of American territory, and when they adopted the Great Compromise, which, by providing equal representation of the states in the Senate and proportional representation in the House, seemed to resolve the conflict over sovereignty by dividing it between the federal government and the states.[13]

IV. On Forrest McDonald's Interpretation

The historian, Forrest McDonald, in his comprehensive study of the intellectual origins of the constitution, *Novus Ordo Seclorum*,* has discussed the usages of the theories of the philosophers by the Framers, treating some thinkers whom Adams had neglected or deliberately ignored, such as Mandeville, Hutcheson, and Bolingbroke.[14] McDonald has divided the republican ideology that shaped the thinking of the Americans at the time the Constitution was framed into two schools: "One, the more nearly classical, may be described as puritan; the other, more modern, may be described as agrarian." (*NOS* at 70) Both schools shared several attitudes in common, but the most crucial, according to McDonald, was "preoccupation with the mortality of republics.... The vital—that is, life-giving—principle of republics was *public virtue*." (*NOS* at 70) Puritanical republicanism differed from the agrarian variety, he continued, in "that the former sought a moral solution to the problem of the mortality of republics (make better people), whereas the latter believed in a socio-economic-political solution (make better arrangements)." (*NOS* at 71)

The neatness of McDonald's intellectual taxonomy is confounded by the actual complexity of the documentary material. Some framers, for example James Madison, traversed intellectual pathways that criss-crossed the two types of republican ideology. Indeed, what emerges is eclecticism: sometimes unconscious, as when the participants in the framing and establishment of the Constitution merely appealed to the moral and practical judgments that were accepted by their peers; sometimes deliberate, as when they sought to render their own reasoning comprehensive and coherent; sometimes opportunistic, as when they seized the moment to make the best case for their own point of view or faction; and sometimes innovative, as in the doctrine of shared sovereignty. Yet it is evident that the legacy of philosophical reflection on politics and history, extending back to the ancients such as Plato, Aristotle, Polybius, and Cicero, revived by Machiavelli during the Renaissance, and perpetuated by the moderns such as Harrington and Montesquieu, informed their deliberations as they struggled to stave off what they perceived as the disintegration of American polity under the Articles of Confederation and to erect a new polity which would endure for the ages.

V. Liberty and Property

Essential to the existence of a republic is the preservation of liberty.[15] Originally the idea of liberty signified the autonomy of a state, its freedom from

---

*Cited in text as *NOS*.

domination by another state so that it could make its own laws and determine
its own course of action. In modern times this classic notion, expressed by Plato
and Aristotle, was transformed to include the liberties of the members of a
state, the security of their rights within the framework of law and social
institutions. Concern with individual liberties and rights came to the forefront
of social consciousness during the seventeenth and eighteenth centuries. The
American Revolution, following the British Revolution of the seventeenth
century and succeeded by the French and other democratic revolutions in the
late eighteenth and nineteenth centuries, was fought on behalf of individual
liberties as well as the right of the American states to determine their own
future. As the Constitution came forth from the Convention, it was
remarkably silent with regard to such individual liberties, mainly because it was
assumed that the individual states afforded sufficient guarantees in their own
constitutions. However, as the Constitution advanced toward ratification, it
became necessary for its proponents to agree to provide for a Bill of Rights.

The delegates to the Convention were undeniably concerned with the
preservation of rights, and during the twentieth century historians have been
equally concerned about the degree to which the American Framers were
obsessed with the preservation of property rights. The most influential work to
expatiate on the Founders' concern for the preservation of property as the
stimulus to their erection of the Constitution is, of course, Charles Beard's *An
Economic Interpretation of the Constitution* (1913). Beard's thesis concentrated
on the form of property he called "personalty"—namely, the paper instruments
issued by the Congress and the States during the revolutionary war and its
aftermath to finance the military and the governments. Held by individuals,
the market value of this paper had fallen far below nominal value in the years
prior to 1787, and it had been acquired by speculators. He sought to expose the
interests of the Framers in this kind of property and to suggest that they favored
the establishment of the federal government because they would profit from
the redemption of these paper instruments at full value.[16] Beard's interpretation has been examined by more recent historians who have impugned his
methodology as well as his conclusions.[17] One critic has pointedly and correctly
declared: "To say that the Constitution was designed in part to protect
property is true; to say that it was designed only to protect property is false; and
to say that it was designed only to protect *personalty* is preposterous."[18]

The regard for property, widespread among the Framers, although by no
means reducible to Beard's interpretation, bears centrally upon the topic of
economic rights. The Framers viewed the protection of property in its various
forms to be a legitimate end of government in accord with sound Lockean
principles. And on sound Harringtonian principles (principles invoked by
Adams both during and after the American Revolution), they construed the
balance of property to be a fundamental determinant of the structure of a
polity. The outcry against the Stamp Act (1765) and other revenue-raising
measures imposed by the British Parliament on the American colonists in the

1760s was raised in the name of property rights; it invoked the lessons of John Locke that no one could enjoy a property right if his property could be taken from him without his consent (no taxation without representation).[19] But this grievance over the violation of property rights was itself assimilated to a long list of complaints against the British mercantilist policy that shackled American commerce and industry.

Although some Americans, including some Framers, had expressed the belief that the sole justification for government is the protection of property, the prevailing opinion was that liberty is paramount. In this context economic rights signify not merely that one's property be protected, but that one be free to pursue happiness by one's own choice of career, occupation, or business. The direction of this side of the American belief about economic rights was toward free enterprise and, in contrast to mercantilism, toward free trade. Of course, it would be a mistake to infer that at the time the Constitution was framed and ratified the Americans had embraced the theory of the free market which Adam Smith had, with modification, proposed in the previous decade. Still, the Constitution did establish the existence of a free market for commerce within and among the American states. As regards international commerce and domestic industry, Alexander Hamilton, in formulating American policies during the early years of the federal republic, relied heavily on the transitional political economy of the Scotsman, Sir James Steuart—a political economy which retained mercantilist features for the sake of protecting young domestic industries in the first stages of development. (*NOS* at 119-123) Paradoxically perhaps, even protectionism can be invoked in the name of free enterprise, since it makes possible the development of young industries that would otherwise be stifled by foreign competition.

During the early days of the American republic, property took many forms besides land, just as the idea of economic rights covers more than just property. The insights of the thinkers of the Scottish Enlightenment were stimulated by the pioneering essays of David Hume, who had eloquently delineated the contributions of commerce and industry to progress in the arts and the sciences and to the advance of liberty. These insights had nurtured the reflections of the Framers, especially Hamilton and Madison. In this regard, Madison's mentor, John Witherspoon, himself a signer of the Declaration of Independence and a president of the Congress of the United States of America under the Articles of Confederation, had earned a reputation in Scotland as a religious leader and philosopher of common sense before being called in 1766 to the post of president of the College of New Jersey (later Princeton). Year after year he delivered lectures on moral philosophy, in which he drew upon and recommended further readings in Francis Hutcheson, David Hume, Lord Kames, Adam Smith, and Thomas Reid.[20] Witherspoon epitomized the role of the Scottish Enlightenment in shaping the American mind during the era of the revolution and the formation of the federal republic.

VI. On the Great Compromise

At the Constitutional Convention, several memorable speeches reflected the teachings of the Scottish Enlightenment, perhaps nowhere more obviously than when the speakers appealed to concrete factuality in opposition to theoretical abstractions. So James Wilson, himself of Scottish origin, rose to speak against the New Jersey plan proposed by William Paterson. This plan would have retained the principle in the Articles of Confederation that the states have equal representation in the federal legislature. Wilson argued:

> as all authority was derived from the people, equal numbers of people ought to have an equal no. of representatives, and different numbers of people different numbers of representatives. This principle had been improperly violated in the confederation, owing to the urgent circumstances of the time.... We have been told that each State being sovereign, all are equal. So each man is naturally sovereign over himself, and all men are therefore naturally equal. Can he retain his equality when he becomes a member of Civil Government? He can not. As little can a Sovereign State, when it becomes a member of a federal Govnt. (MN at 183-184)

Paterson had invoked the abstract principle of the equal sovereighty of the individual states, having been stirred by the fear (which also motivated his supporters) that the small states such as his own would be swallowed by the large states, unless they were all equally represented. When a compromise was first proposed—granting the states equal representation in one chamber of the legislature, and proportional representation in the second, it immediately incited the opposition of the backers of the Virginia plan, which had been offered by Edmund Randolph and amended in the Committee of the Whole. This plan, which served as the basic document for the composition of the Constitution, originally provided that the representation of the states be proportional. So James Wilson rhetorically questioned:

> Can we forget for whom we are forming a Government? Is it for *men*, or for the imaginary beings called *States*? Will our honest constituents be satisfied with metaphysical distinctions? Will they, ought they to be satisfied with metaphysical distinctions? (MN at 307)

Fortunately, of course, for the success of the Convention and the establishment of the Constitution (and saving America from the perils of Balkanization), compromise prevailed. For this outcome incalculable credit belongs to Benjamin Franklin, who embraced the proposition of equal representation of the states in one chamber of a bicameral legislature in contradiction with his own commitment to unicameralism and in opposition to his colleagues from his own State of Pennsylvania. Franklin introduced his formulation of the Great Compromise by means of the following remarks, which not only underscore the clash between economic rights and liberty but also constitute as clear and succinct a statement of the theory of compromise in ethics and politics as is to be found in all the writings of all the philosophers.

> The diversity of opinion turns on two points. If a proportional representation takes place, the small States contend that their liberties will be in danger. If an equality of votes is to be put in its place, the large States say their money will be in danger. When a broad table is to be made, and the edges of the planks do not fit, the artist takes a little from both, and makes a good joint. In like manner here both sides must part with some of their demands, in order that they may join in some accomodating proposition. (MN at 313)

VII. Hamilton's Speech at the Constitutional Convention

Traces of the influence of David Hume and other Enlightenment thinkers are apparent in Hamilton's notorious speech of June 18. Contending that in the present situation the people would gravitate toward their states at the expense of a national government, Hamilton identified "five great & essential principles necessary for support of Government": (1) an "active & constant interest in supporting it," (2) the "love of power," (3) the "habitual attachment of the people," and (4) "*force by which may be understood a coertion of laws or coertion of arms*," and (5) "influence...not...corruption, but a dispensation of those regular honors & emoluments, which produce attachment to the Govt." (MN at 216-217) Dismayed at the prospect of extending the republican form of government over the wide expanse of territory occupied by the states, Hamilton judged that costly inducements would be necessary to lure "representatives from the extremes to the center of the community." (MN at 220) Thus he advised that the states be consolidated under the general government, although he refrained from actually proposing their abolition because public opinion would not have supported it. Reflecting the influence of Hume as historian, Hamilton praised the British constitution of King, Lords, and commons "as the best in the world; and...he doubted much whether anything short of it would do in America." (MN at 220) This British constitution, he held, united public strength with individual security—i.e., order with liberty. He praised the Lords as a noble institution both for the stability it imparted to the nation and for its commitment to the national interest, which stemmed in large part from the fact that its own property interests weighed against its participation in radical change. Hamilton also esteemed the institution of an hereditary King. With that office came great personal emoluments, which served to bind the King's interest to the national interest, rendering him immune from foreign corruption. Thus, the constitution both conferred independence upon the King and limited him in such ways as to enable him to govern effectively without threatening the security of his subjects. The British mixed polity, therefore, had the capacity to withstand corrupting foreign influences and to balance the rival internal interests that produce political instability and strife. As Hamilton explained:

> In every community where industry is encouraged, there will be a division of it into the few and the many. Hence separate interests will arise. There will be debtors & creditors & c. Give all power to the many, they will oppress the few. Give all power to the few, they will oppress the many. Both therefore ought to have power, that each may defend itself against the other.... To the proper adjustment of it the British owe the excellence of their Constitution. (*MN* at 221)

Aware that the American people were so devoted to republican principles that they would not embrace a government with an hereditary nobility and a monarch, Hamilton sketched a model of government in which what he deemed the vices of democracy could be curtailed. However, even this model of government, he was cognizant, "went beyond the ideas of most members" of the Convention, and was unlikely to be adopted by the people "out of doors." (*MN* at 223) So Hamilton threw his support behind the Virginia Plan as it was proceeding through the Committee of the Whole.

VIII. Challenges at the Constitutional Convention

Hamilton's attitude toward the British constitution and its appropriateness to the American situation did not go unchallenged. A delegate who expressed a social and political philosophy in opposition to Hamilton's was Charles Pinckney, whose own plan had fallen stillborn. In his speech of June 25, Pinckney cited the American situation as manifesting "a greater equality, than is to be found among the people of any other country," and he reflected that this equality would continue because of the immensity of the uncultivated lands and the opportunities for industry. (*MN* at 267) Although he esteemed the constitution of Great Britain "to be the best Constitution in existence," he did not think that it could or should be introduced into our system. The British system rested on a division of classes, ranks, or orders of men: Crown, Nobility, and People. By contrast, the United States, with its pervasive equality, does not have three orders, ranks, or classes: it has but one. As Pinckney exclaimed, "this is the order of Commons." (*MN* at 273) So it would be folly to fashion a government with three organs, like the British government, designed to represent three orders or ranks of people, for in America "two...[of these organs—king and Lords] have nothing to represent." (*MN* at 273) Although Pinckney did distinguish classes among the American people, his distinctions were based on function rather than on birth or wealth. The three classes he differentiated were the professional class, the commercial class, and the landed interest. Hailing from South Carolina, Pinckney naturally favored the landed interest. This group, he said, consists of "the owners and cultivators of the soil, who are and ought ever to be the governing spring in the system." (MN at 272) Pinckney continued:

> These three classes, however distinct in their pursuits, are individually equal in the political scale, and may be easily proved to have but one interest. The dependence of each on the other is mutual. The merchant depends on the planter. Both must in private as well as public affairs be connected with the professional men; who in their turn must in some measure depend upon them. Hence it is clear from this manifest connection & the equality which I before stated exists, and must for the reasons then assigned, continue, that after all there is one, but one great and equal body of citizens composing the inhabitants of this Country among whom there are no distinctions of rank, and very few or none of fortune. (MN at 272)

As the debate in the convention pivoted on the conflict between the large states and the small states over representation, Madison invoked the authority of Montesquieu for having esteemed the Lycian confederacy as the best because it proportioned the voice of each member according to its importance. Madison summarized his speech thusly:

> that the States were divided into different interests not by their difference of size, but by other circumstances; the most material of which resulted partly from climate, but principally from the effects of their having or not having slaves. These two causes concurred in forming the great division of interests in the United States. It did not lie between the large & small States: It lay between the Northern & Southern, and if any defensive power were necessary, it ought to be mutually given to these two interests. (MN at 310-311)

Later, in debating the qualifications for members of the Legislature, Madison spoke out against the proposal that landed wealth be required of those who would be elected to the legislature. In anticipation of the interest group theory of politics later expounded by him in *Federalist* No. 10, Madison affirmed:

> It was politic as well as just that the interests & rights of every class should be duly represented & understood in the public Councils. It was a provision everywhere established that the Country should be divided into districts & representatives taken from each, in order that the Legislative Assembly might equally understand & sympathize, with the rights of the people in every part of the Community. It was not less proper that every class of citizens should have an opportunity of making their rights be felt & understood in the public councils. The three principal classes into which our citizens were divisible were the landed, the commercial, & the manufacturing. The 2d. & 3d. class, bear as yet a small proportion to the first. The proportion however will daily increase. (MN at 461)

IX. On *Federalist* No. 10

Whatever reservations such Framers as Hamilton and Madison had concerning the constitution as it isssed from the Convention, they vigorously supported it through the process of ratification because as Franklin declared as the Convention was about to close, the Framers thought "a general Government necessary for us," and they doubted that a better form would be proposed by another convention or "for a course of years." (*MN* at 739) As Franklin put the matter, "I consent...to this Constitution because I expect no better, and because I am not sure that it is not the best." (*MN* at 740)

In the *Federalist*, the authors did not indulge in extensive speculations about economic rights and the nature and function of private property as a human right, as a foundation of society, and as a force in politics. They were too preoccupied with the immediate task of elucidating and defending the provisions of the Constitution against the arguments of the Antifederalists. It is remarkable that, given the occasional character of its origin as letters to newspapers, the *Federalist* still has universal appeal to students of republicanism and federalism.

Hamilton's argument for a vigorous government with a strong national defense as the guardian of freedom and prosperity figures prominently in the rhetoric of American politics to this day. And he was sufficiently clearsighted to apprehend that this implied that the national government must exercise extensive powers of taxation, for as he affirmed, "money is, with propriety, considered as the vital principle of the body politic; as that which sustains its life and motion and enables it to perform its most essential functions." (*FP* No. 30 at 188)

Madison, who by heritage might have been expected to adhere to the primacy of property in land as the bulwark of republican government, formulated in *Federalist* No. 10 a theory of politics focused on the balancing of multiple interests. Madison deemed an advantage of the national government to lie in "its tendency to break and control the violence of faction." (*FP* No. 10 at 77) As affairs stood in 1787, rival parties or factions in individual states rendered government unstable, and injustice resulted when, in disregard of the public good, even a majority transgressed the rights of a minority. Madison defined a faction as:

> a number of citizens, whether amounting to a majority or a minority of the whole, who are united and actuated by some common impulse of passion, or of interest, adverse to the rights of other citizens, or to the permanent and aggregate interests of the communtiy. (*FP* No. 10 at 78)

He stipulated that there are "two methods of curing the mischiefs of faction: the one, by removing its causes, the other by controlling its effects." (*FP* No. 10 at 78)

To remove the causes of faction required either (1) the destruction of "the liberty essential to its existence," or (2) "giving to every citizen the same opinions, the same passions, and the same interests." (FP No. 10 at 78) As regards liberty, Madison remarked that it "is to faction what air is to fire, an aliment without which it instantly expires," but that liberty is also "essential to political life." (FP No. 10 at 78) Hence, it would be as wholly unwise to eliminate liberty in order to eliminate faction as it would be to annihilate air—essential to animal life—in order to extinguish fire. Nor is it practical to strive to transform human nature so that all men share the same opinions, passions and interests. As Madison explained:

> As long as the reason of man continues fallible, and he is at liberty to exercise it, different opinions will be formed. As long as the connection subsists between his reason and his self-love, his opinions and his passions will have a reciprocal influence on each other, and the former will be objects to which the latter will attach themselves. The diversity in the faculties of men, from which the rights of property originate, is not less an insuperable obstacle to a uniformity of interests. The protection of these faculties is the first object of government. From the protection of different and unequal faculties of acquiring property, the possession of different degrees and kings of property immediately results; and from the influence of these on the sentiments and views of the respective proprietors ensues a division of the society into different interests and parties. (FP No. 10 at 78)

Since the causes of faction, on Madison's analysis, are "sown in the nature of man," it is impossible to eradicate them, and the upshot is that society is divided into parties each bent on the furtherance of its own interests at the expense of the common good. Whereas classical republicanism, represented by John Adams in A *Defence*, conceived society to be divided into ranks or classes of men as high (royalty), middle (aristocracy), and low (democracy), and looked to balance these orders, Hamilton and Madison construed divisions of society to spring in part from the possession and non-possession of property and the forms and functions property assumes. As Madison said:

> the most common and durable source of factions has been the various and unequal distribution of property. Those who hold and those who are without property have ever formed distinct interests in society. Those who are creditors, and those who are debtors, fall under a like discrimination. A landed interest, a manufacturing interest, a mercantile interest, a moneyed interest, with many lesser interests, grow up of necessity in civilized nations, and divide them into different classes, actuated by different sentiments and views. The regulation of these various and interfering interests forms the principal task of modern legislation and involves the spirit of party and faction in the necessary and ordinary operation of government. (FP No. 10 at 79)

Since the causes of faction are and ought to be ineradicable, Madison esteemed the structure of the proposed national government as the mechanism to mitigate and control the undesirable effects of faction. He looked to the system of checks and balances, the division of powers, and the territorial expanse of the American government to safeguard individual rights and the common good. Madison expected that the representative character of the American government, operating over a large territory, would render it unlikely—indeed, impossible—for a faction, even if a majority, to usurp control of the government, trampling the rights of others and violating the common good.

Madison's *Federalist* No. 10 has been the centerpiece of numerous learned commentaries. Beard singled it out as "the most philosophical examination of the foundations of political science," and he claimed that it asserted, "in no uncertain language, the principle that the first and elemental concern of every government is economic."[21] But as Robert E. Brown has shown in his critique of Beard, Madison grounded the causes of faction in the nature of man, of which the acquisition of property and the diversity of its forms and functions is but one expression, so that it is wrong to describe the father of the Constitution as an "economic determinist."[22]

Garry Wills, who has surveyed the pronouncements of the leading commentators on *Federalist* No. 10,[23] contends that what Madison's political philosophy, as incorporated in the Constitution, "prevents is not faction, but action. What he protects is not the common good but delay as such."[24] There is much to be said for this criticism, although it rests on the assumption that the ideals of individual rights and of "the permanent and aggregate interests of the community"—i.e., the common good—are unknowable. Actually Wills, following Robert Dahl, calls them "unknown." But only if they are unknowable, rather than simply "unknown," would the criticism hold. For if they are unknown, postponing action could be methodologically correct until an inquiry could be conducted to come to know them. Be that as it may, there is no doubt that the representative character of the national Congress and the continental expanse of the territory militate against hasty actions spawned by passing passions, and against the quick aggrandizement of any local interests even when these, in coalition with others, constitute a majority.

Conclusion

Eighteenth century moral philosophy, which centered on liberty and economic rights and their bearing on early American politics, turned on the issue of special interests vs. the general good. The Framers looked to the system of checks and balances, and the division of powers between the national government and the states, to achieve the common good and protect individual liberty. To accomplish the same end, Jean-Jacques Rousseau, the philosopher who most influenced the French Revolution, invoked the notion of a general will. The Americans avoided the trap of hypostatizing such a metaphysical entity by concentrating upon refining political mechanisms. In this way, it could be argued, we avoided the menace of totalitarian democracy.

Virtue, Montesquieu had taught, is the principle—and the human passion—which sets republican government in motion. The Founding Fathers concurred, with reservations. Other passions, they acknowledged, also move republics. Given the diversity of passions, interests, and faculties in human nature, the Founders were disposed to tolerate and even respect the expression of these differences. They were interested in the establishment of a government which would permit and promote the fullest expression of liberty consistent with law. While they could not have anticipated the remarkable development of the American continent by the spread of industrialism during the nineteenth century, they were disposed during their time to promote the rights of property and free enterprise, so far as these were compatible with the general good. Meanwhile, they believed that unless individual, class, local, or sectional interests are kept in dynamic equilibrium, there is no escape from the Polybian cycle of corruption, decline, and extinction. The bulwark against instability and revolution they erected is the Constitution, with its system of checks and balances and the division of powers. Despite its seeming stillness, the Constitution, in securing rights and aiming toward the common good, is the pilot of an ever-moving, ever-changing society.

Whether or not virtuous men take the helm of government, the Constitution inclines, so the Founders hoped, in the direction of virtue. Ultimately, the virtue essential to republican government is patriotism—in the words of Montesquieu, the favorite of the Founders, "the love of our country."[25] Patriotism is, Montesquieu and the Framers surmised, a political virtue, primary to civic humanism, but it is also "conducive to a purity of morals," which is reciprocally supportive of republican virtue.[26] Patriotism transcends the satisfaction of particular passions and local interests and addresses itself to the preservation of individual rights and the general good.

The Framers devised many mechanisms to assure that in large measure the most virtuous—i.e. patriotic—citizens would occupy positions of political leadership, and that transient interests and passions would be filtered out so that public policy would aim at the general good. These mechanisms included: the representative character of the government, drawing members of Congress from the far reaches of the country; the electoral college for the selection of the president; the independent judiciary; and the bicameral legislature with members of the Senate elected by the states and serving terms thrice as long as members of the House of Representatives. While some of these mechanisms have been modified over the years by constitutional amendments, the basic structure persists.

The moral philosophy embraced by the Framers of the Constitution tenuously synthesizes the polarities of virtue and interest.[27] The first is fundamental to the existence of republican polity in the classical sense, while the other is indispensable to the exercise of individual rights, including economic rights. Blended together, they formed the basis for the prospering of the American experiment in self-government.

Notes

1. 1 J. ADAMS, A DEFENCE OF THE CONSTITUTIONS OF GOVERN-MENT OF THE UNITED STATES OF AMERICA (1787).

2. *See* my paper, *The Philosophical Background of the American Constitution(s)*, in AMERICAN PHILOSOPHY 273 (M. Singer ed. 1986).

3. A. LOVEJOY, REFLECTIONS ON HUMAN NATURE 33-34 (1961).

4. *Id.* at 39.

5. THE FEDERALIST PAPERS (C. Rossiter ed. 1961).

6. M. WHITE, THE PHILOSOPHY OF THE AMERICAN REVOLUTION 88*ff.* (1978).

7. *See* G. WOOD, THE CREATION OF THE AMERICAN REPUBLIC 1776-1787 562, 605-615 (1969); and J. POCOCK, THE MACHIAVELLIAN MOMENT 523*ff.* (1975).

8. In this paper I will use the edition of Madison's notes published in DOCUMENTS ILLUSTRATIVE OF THE FORMATION OF THE UNION OF THE AMERICAN STATES (Government Printing Office, 1927).

9. I. BRANT, JAMES MADISON, FATHER OF THE CONSTITUTION 1787-1800 (1950). Madison has also been called the "philosopher of the Constitution." *See* E. BURNS, JAMES MADISON, PHILOSOPHER OF THE CONSTITUTION (1938).

10. *Secret proceedings and debates of the convention assembled at Philadelphia, in the year 1787, for the purpose of forming the Constitution of the United States of America.* From the notes taken by the late Robert Yates Esq., Chief Justice of New York (Albany, 1821), in DOCUMENTS, *supra* note 8, at 800.

11. *See* my paper, *Natural Law in America Revolutionary Thought*, 30 REVIEW OF METAPHYSICS 686 (1977).

12. *Notes of Major William Pierce (Ga.) in the Federal Convention of 1787*, DOCUMENTS, *supra* note 8, at 103.

13. *See* my paper, *Philosophy in the Debates at the U.S. Constitutional Convention of 1787*, to be published by Greenwood Press in CONSTITUTIONALISM: PHILO-SOPHICAL PERSPECTIVES (A. Rosenbaum ed.).

14. F. MCDONALD, NOVUS ORDO SECLORUM (1985).

15. For an analysis of the concept of a republic, *see* my paper, *The Republican Ideology*, in IDEOLOGY AND THE AMERICAN EXPERIENCE 73-96 (J. Roth & R. Whittemore eds. 1986).

16. C. BEARD, AN ECONOMIC INTERPRETATION OF THE CONSTI-TUTION OF THE UNITED STATES (1913). An introduction by Beard was added to the 1935 printing to disclaim the alleged Marxian origin of the volume.

17. R. BROWN, CLARLES BEARD AND THE CONSTITUTION (1956), and F. MCDONALD, WE THE PEOPLE (1958).

18. BROWN, *id.* at 111.

19. *See* my paper, *The Philosophical Background of the American Revolution*, 5 SOUTHWESTERN JOURNAL OF PHILOSOPHY 179 (1974).

20. H. MAY, THE ENLIGHTENMENT IN AMERICA 62-64 (1976).

21. BEARD, *supra* note 16, at 156.

22. BROWN, *supra* note 17, at 20.

23. G. WILLS, EXPLAINING AMERICA: THE FEDERALIST xiii-xxx (1981).

24. *Id.* at 195.

25. MONTESQUIEU, THE SPIRIT OF THE LAWS BK. V, Ch. 20, at 40.

26. *Id.*

27. *See* Thomas, *Politics as Language*, THE NEW YORK REVIEW OF BOOKS 36-39 (February 26, 1986). This article reviews J. POCOCK, VIRTUE, COMMERCE, AND HISTORY, CHIEFLY IN THE EIGHTEENTH CENTURY (1986); *see also* J. DIGGINS, THE LOST SOUL OF AMERICAN POLITICS: VIRTUE, SELF-INTEREST, AND THE FOUNDATIONS OF LIBERALISM (1984).

The Great Fence to Liberty:
The Right to Property in the American Founding

EDWARD J. ERLER

> *If the United States mean to obtain or deserve the full praise due*
> *to wise and just governments, they will equally respect the rights*
> *of property and the property in rights.*[1]

James Madison

I. The Contemporary View of Property Rights

In a speech delivered on August 8, 1986, Justice William Brennan described the constitutional revolution which had been occasioned by the passage of the Fourteenth Amendment to the United States Constitution. From the point of view of practice, the Fourteenth Amendment is, the Justice noted, "perhaps our most important constitutional provision—not even second in significance to the original basic document itself."[2] The cause of Justice Brennan's hyperbole was not difficult to discern: in his view, the Fourteenth Amendment has "served as the legal instrument of the egalitarian revolution that transformed contemporary American Society."[3] At the heart of this egalitarian revolution, the Justice continued, was an "ever-growing concern for 'life and liberty' as the really basic rights which the Constitution was meant to safeguard. The earlier stress upon the protection of *property* rights against governmental violations of due process gave way to one which increasingly focused upon *personal* rights. Under the new approach, the Fourteenth Amendment would at last become (as its framers intended) the shield of individual liberties throughout the nation."[4] Attentive listeners no doubt quickly noted that the Justice had failed to mention that the Fourteenth Amendment's due process clause included—in addition to life and liberty—the right to property.

Justice Brennan did not explain why he did not consider the right to property a personal right, or why he considered the right to property incompatible with the existence of personal rights. Perhaps he didn't think it

43

[Handwritten note:] Property rights exist at the expense of human rights; human rights therefore can be protected only to the extent that the right to property is diminished or extinguished

"That is not a just gov't, nor is property secure under it, where the property which a man has in his personal safety + personal liberty, is violated." Madison

g to the most
t are familiar.
hts therefore
diminished or

e community
ers to life and
whether the
ut at the same
as remarked,
individuals is
, with govern-
:nment and to
)lerated before

the law for controls ......

this century...Now hundreds of thousands of Americans live entire lives without any real prospect of the dignity and autonomy that ownership of real property could confer. Protection of the human dignity of such citizens requires a *much modified view of the proper relationship of individual and state*."[6]

Brennan's critique of the right to property is at least as old as Jean Jacques Rousseau's *Discourse on the Origin of Inequality* (1755), and is best known to us today through the writings of Marx and his epigones. It almost goes without saying that this view of the right to property is wholly at odds with the view of the Framers of the Constitution. James Madison, for example, saw no inherent tension between the right to property and the rights to life and liberty. In Madison's view—a view that was almost universal in 1787—the security of the right to property was the great vehicle for securing life and liberty. Madison wrote in 1791, "That is not a just government, nor is property secure under it, where the property which a man has in his personal safety and personal liberty, is violated."[7] Madison, as did John Locke before him, viewed the right to property as the comprehensive right which, because of its comprehensiveness, assumed priority in the political community.

II. The Framers' View of Property Rights

In the Summer of 1787, the delegates to the Constitutional Convention met in Philadelphia to hammer out a constitution that was intended to put into motion those principles of constitutional government that had been enunciated in the Declaration of Independence. As Madison later wrote in the *Federalist*, the principles of the proposed Constitution were derived from "the transcendent law of nature and of nature's God, which declares that the safety and happiness of society are the objects at which all political institutions aim and to which all such institutions must be sacrificed."[8] Madison went on to note that the principles of the Declaration required "strictly republican" government:

> It is evident that no other form would be reconcilable with the genius of the people of America; with the fundamental principles of the Revolution; or with that honorable determination which animates every votary of freedom to rest all our political experiments on the capacity of mankind for self-government.[9]

A prominent contemporary historian, Leonard Levy, concurs, writing that the Constitution was the product of "the political philosophy of social compact, natural rights, and limited government that generated the Declaration of Independence."[10]

Many years later, Jefferson reflected on the purpose of the Declaration. "The object of the Declaration of Independence," he wrote, was:

> not to find out new principles, or new arguments, never before thought of, not merely to say things which had never been said before; but to place before mankind the common sense of the subject, in terms so plain and firm as to command their assent... Neither aiming at originality of principle or sentiment, nor yet copied from any particular and previous writing, it was intended to be an expression of the American mind... All its authority rests then on the harmonizing sentiments of the day, whether expressed in conversation, in letters, printed essays, or the elementary books of public right, as Aristotle, Cicero, Locke, Sidney, &c.[11]

Indeed the people were well acquainted with "the elementary books of public right," if not directly, then through conversation, a multitude of public documents, and—although not mentioned by Jefferson—above all through sermons.

A most remarkable example of a sermon extolling the social contract and natural law basis of civil society is John Tucker's "Election Sermon" delivered in 1771. In addition to Scriptural texts, Tucker quoted at length from John Locke. "Civil government," he declared, "is the dictate of nature:—It is the voice of reason, which may be said to be the voice of God." Tucker continued with an account of the origins of legitimate government that was drawn directly from Locke's *Second Treatise*, no doubt with some side (although not necessarily furtive) glances at Locke's *Reasonableness of Christianity* (1695).

> All men are naturally in a state of freedom, and have an equal claim to liberty. No one, by nature, nor by any special grant from the great Lord of all, has any authority over another. All right therefore in any to rule over others, must originate from those they rule over, and be granted by them. Hence, all government, consistent with that natural freedom, to which all have an equal claim, is founded in compact, or agreement between the parties,—between Rulers and their Subjects, and can be no otherwise. Because Rulers, receiving

their authority originally and solely from the people, can be rightfully possessed of no more, than these have consented to, and conveyed to them.[12]

The influence of such sermons on the sentiments and opinions of the people cannot be overestimated. As the constitutional historian Andrew McLaughlin wrote, "During the Revolution and in the process of setting up new governments, the preachers played a conspicuous role. The philosophy of the seventeenth century was repeated over and over again by New England divines, who preached about a law of reason and a law of God, the sacredness of covenant and the divine character of government."[13] Hyneman and Lutz note that "to men in the 1770s there seemed to be no essential conflict between what Locke and the Bible were telling them, [although] their synthesis of the two was in fact an American accomplishment, not a logical necessity."[14]

The Declaration of Independence is undoubtedly the most succinct account that has ever been written of the social contract as the legitimate foundation of civil society. Its central principle is the "self-evident truth" derived from the "laws of nature and nature's God" that "all men are created equal." This truth, immediately evident through experience, is the ground of the political morality of the Declaration and of the American Founding. The evident truth of human equality is apparent because, unlike every other species, the human species has no natural rulers. The God of nature distinguished man—not by instinct—but by reason. In this regard, the human species is unique. Every other species has its form of rule imposed upon it by nature, i.e., instinct.

Human beings seemingly have no such instinct for social life. The human mind is not determined in the same way that instinct determines all other beings. Human beings are capable of individual self-consciousness and, although members of a species, can see themselves as individuals within the species. It is this possibility of self-consciousness or reason, the proof that the human mind is not determined, that is the ground of human liberty. Without equality, i.e., without the absence of natural rulers, there would be no human liberty; liberty is the inexpugnable concomitant of equality. Human beings seem to have been left to their own devices, having reason and the potential to choose their form of government, but having no guides immediately from nature to inform the choice. As Locke explains it:

> there being nothing more evident, than that Creatures of the same species and rank promiscuously born to all the same advantages of Nature, and the use of the same faculties, should also be equal one amongst another without Subordination or Subjection, unless the Lord and Master of them all, should by any manifest Declaration of his Will set one above another, and confer on him by an evident and clear appointment an undoubted Right to Dominion and Sovereignty.[15]

But Locke had abundantly demonstrated in the *First Treatise* that no such manifest declaration of will could reasonably be said to exist. And in the very last letter of his life, Jefferson echoed Locke's analysis when he wrote, employing one of the most frequently used republican metaphors, that the Declaration embodied the "palpable truth, that the mass of mankind has not been born with saddles on their backs, nor a favored few booted and spurred, ready to ride them legitimately, by the grace of God."[16] If some men were born with saddles and others with boots then nature's intention (and the will of God) would be manifest.

The necessary inference from the absence of natural rulers is that by nature, i.e., in a state of nature, every human being is naturally his own ruler, having sole proprietorship over his own life, liberty, and property. Since the individual right to life, liberty, and property is derivative from natural human equality, these rights were known to the social contract philosophers as "natural rights"—the dictates of the "laws of nature and nature's God." It was the change from historical prescription to natural rights that represents the radical core of the American Revolution and the American Founding. It was not the rights of Englishmen, as we are so often told,[17] that was the subject of the Declaration, but the rights of man derived, not indeed from any particular constitution or positve law, but from nature. Historical prescription is ultimately traceable to accident; the existence of natural rights can be demonstrated as a "self-evident truth" from the laws of nature and nature's God, the first principle of which is the natural equality of all human beings. Jefferson, comparing the American Revolution to the Glorious Revolution, remarked that "Our Revolution commenced on more favorable ground. It presented us an album on which we were free to write what we pleased. We had no occasion to search into musty records, to hunt up royal parchments, or to investigate the laws and institutions of a semi-barbarous ancestry. We appealed to those of nature, and found them engraved on our hearts."[18] It was thus the laws of nature and nature's God that set the standards and bounds of civil society, and made possible not only a government derived from the principles of human nature, but a form of government that could honor human nature.[19] Governments founded on historical prescription are the products of "accident and force," not of "reflection and choice."[20]

III. The Completion of the Founding

Justice Brennan, in the speech quoted above, noted that the "progenitor" of the Fourteenth Amendment was not, as we might have expected, the principles of the Declaration, but Magna Charta.[21] Yet the debates surrounding the framing and adoption of the Fourteenth Amendment make it abundantly clear that the express purpose of its framers was to complete the regime of the Founding by extending civil rights to the newly freed slaves. The regime of the Founding had been incomplete because the Constitution tolerated the continued existence of slavery. It is true that the Framers resorted to political expedience in the matter of slavery; but without that expediency the Constitution would never have come into existence. The more thoughtful of the Framers knew that without a Constitution based on the Declaration's principles, the likelihood that slavery could ever be extirpated from the polity was remote.

But no matter how much the Framers may have looked forward to the eventual demise of slavery, its countenancing in the Constitution stood in opposition to the Declaration's principle that all legitimate government must be derived from the consent of the governed.* After all, no slave ever—or could have ever—consented to become a slave. The completion of the regime of the Founding awaited the Civil War and the passage of the Reconstruction Amendments (Thirteenth through Fifteenth). And it was clearly the self-conscious purpose of the framers of the Thirteenth and Fourteenth Amendments to bring the Constitution into harmony with the principles of the Declaration. Speaking of the original Constitution's acquiescence to the maintenance of slavery, Thaddeus Stevens, the leader of the Radical Republicans in the House of Representatives and one of the principal architects of the Fourteenth Amendment, remarked in May 1866 that: "Our fathers had been compelled to postpone the principles of their great Declaration, and wait for their full establishment till a more propitious time. That time ought to be now."[22] References to the Declaration of Independence

---

*The Constitution adverts to slavery in three places: (1) Article I, Section 3:

> Representatives and direct Taxes shall be apportioned among the several states which may be included within the Union, according to their respective Numbers, which shall be determined by adding to the whole Number of free Persons, including those bound for Service for a Term of Years, and excluding Indians not taxed, three fifths of all other Persons.

(2) Article I, Section 9, clause 1:

> The Migration or Importation of Such Persons as any of the States now existing shall think proper to admit, shall not be prohibited by the Congress prior to the Year one thousand eight hundred and eight, but a tax or duty may be imposed on such importation, not exceeding ten dollars for each Person.

and (3) Article IV, Section 2, Clause 3:

> No person held to Service or Labour in one State, under the Laws thereof, escaping into another, shall in Consequence of any Law or Regulation therein, be discharged from such Service or Labour, but shall be delivered up on Claim of the Party to whom such Service or Labour may be due.

as "organic law" were so frequent throughout the Reconstruction debates that it can hardly be doubted that the framers of the Civil War Amendments were attempting to complete the regime of the Founding by restoring the Declaration of Independence to its rightful place as the authoritative source of our political morality.[23]

Magna Charta, of course, was the product of unique British history, and consequently was not a natural right document. We must wonder, therefore, about its applicability to America. The language of Magna Charta is not the language of natural law; it is couched in the terms of a particular struggle between King and nobles, not the universal rights of man. A.E. Dick Howard has recently written that:

> The charter to which John agreed is an intensely practical document. Rather than being a philosophical tract redolent with lofty generalities, the charter was drafted to provide concrete remedies for specific abuses. Moreover, although the barons were rebelling against the abuse of royal power they were not seeking to remake the fabric of feudal society. They sought instead to restore *customary* limits on the power of the Crown.[24]

It is true that many commentators have traced the Fourteenth Amendment's "due process" clause back to Article 39 of Magna Charta, which accords to every "free man" a guarantee of judgments made according to "the law of the land." But this derivation is only a partial explanation. Since Magna Charta clearly does not rest on natural law grounds, it bears only a superficial resemblance to the Declaration of Independence, and therefore, by extension, to the Fourteenth Amendment. The preface to Magna Charta contains this expression: "We have also granted to all the free men of Our kingdom, for Us and Our heirs forever, all the liberties underwritten..." The Declaration of Independence, in contrast, views the *natural rights* of "all men" as derivative— not indeed from the will of a king ("We have...granted")—but from the "laws of nature and nature's God." To say nothing of other consideration which are not less important, this difference is decisive.[25]

Is it credible to say that the American people in 1776 were merely asking for their rights as Englishmen at the same time that they were declaring themselves no longer Englishmen? Or that the Fourteenth Amendment, designed to extend citizenship and civil rights to blacks was derived from their original rights as Englishmen?[26] The assertion that the Fourteenth Amendment finds its roots in Magna Charta stretches credulity beyond all possible limits. Yet Justice Brennan somehow realizes that it is necessary for his ideological stance—and the prospect of constitutional reform—to pretend that the Fourteenth Amendment (and the Bill of Rights) represents a radical break from the original Constitution and the principles that animated it.

In Brennan's analysis, the original Constitution is principally concerned with the arrangement of governmental power, while the Bill of Rights and the Civil War amendments deal with personal liberties. The simplistic view that

p. 51 Leo Strauss – Connection
between "property" + pursuit of
happiness

.eart of
litarian
.tion of
r of the
l of this
;—that
ution is
welfare
tions of
.mits to
led that
:state, a
.ards or

bounds to the human political condition.[28]

IV. Locke in the American Founding

In the Declaration, Jefferson did not speak of the right to life, liberty, and property (Locke's trinity), but of "life, liberty, and the pursuit of happiness." This change has occasioned much speculation as to Jefferson's intention in this choice of words. It is possible to argue that the change of phraseology indicates that the Declaration is not simply Lockean, but it would be absurd to maintain, as some have, that the change indicates that Jefferson was rejecting Locke's "bourgeois" philosophy.[29] The phrase "pursuit of happiness" does occur in Locke, but nowhere in the political *Treatises*. In *An Essay Concerning Human Understanding* (1690) Locke stated that:

> As therefore the highest perfection of intellectual nature lies in a careful and constant pursuit of true and solid happiness; so the care of ourselves, that we mistake not imaginary for real happiness, is the necessary foundation of our liberty. The stronger ties we have to an unalterable pursuit of happiness in general, which is our greatest good...the more are we free from any necessary determination of our will to any particular action."[30]

In *The Reasonableness of Christianity*, Locke argues that "Mankind" "must be allowed to pursue their happiness—nay, cannot be hindered" from doing so. He also calls the pursuit of happiness "the chief end" of mankind and more than intimates that it consists of the "enjoyments of this life."[31] It is clear that, for Locke, the "pursuit of happiness" is intimately connected with the right to property. This is indicated by the fact the Locke included "Lives, Liberties and Estates" under the general term "property." (II* 123)*

---

*All citations in the text in this form refer to Locke's *Second Treatise*, e.g., II*23 means paragraph number 123. Likewise, I*23 refers to paragraph 23 of the *First Treatise*.

Leo Strauss highlighted the connection between 'property' and 'pursuit of happiness' when he described "the relation of the right of self-preservation to the right to the pursuit of happiness":

> The former is the right to 'subsist' and implies the right to what is necessary to man's being; the second is the right to 'enjoy the conveniences of life' or to 'comfortable preservation' and implies, therefore, also the right to what is useful to man's being without being necessary for it."[32]

Being derivative from the right to life, both the right to property and the right to the pursuit of happiness must be accorded the status of natural rights. For Locke, the 'pursuit of happiness,' because it implies a right to possess beyond what is necessary for mere life, is the ground of individual liberty—it is also the ground of political liberty. The desire to pursue "true and solid happiness" as the "greatest good," is proof for Locke that the human mind is not determined and that human beings are free to choose the means—reason—of securing their happiness.[33]

In the political context, this natural freedom means that "consent of the governed" is the necessary requisite for legitimate government. The "pursuit of happiness"—the manifest expression of human freedom—thus becomes the object of civil society and the public good. This means that civil society must, above all, provide the security for the external goods—in Lockean terms "properties"—necessary for the "pursuit of happiness." I believe this is the precise sense in which Americans understood the matter in 1776. It was certainly the way James Wilson understood it when, in 1774, he wrote:

> All men are, by nature, equal and free: no one has a right to any authority over another without his consent: all lawful government is grounded on the consent of those who are subject to it: such consent was given with a view to ensure and to increase the happiness of the governed, above what they could enjoy in an independent and unconnected state of nature. The consequence is, that the happiness of the society is the *first* law of every government.[34]

Similar statements can be found in the Virginia Bill of Rights (1776) and the Massachusetts Bill of Right (1780). The latter document gives a perfectly Lockean account in Article I:

> All men are born free and equal, and have certain natural, essential and unalienable rights; among which may be reckoned the right of enjoying and defending their lives and liberties; that of acquiring, possessing, and protecting property; in fine, that of seeking and obtaining their safety and happiness.[35]

Thus, we see that the phrase "safety and happiness" is another phrase ("in fine") for the protection of life, liberty, and property. This, I believe, is the way in which Americans generally understood the phrase 'pursuit of happiness.'

In the *Second Treatise* Locke was under considerable pains to find a justification for the right of private property and to insure that property would always be in the service of political ends, i.e., would serve as a "fence" to liberty and thereby as a "fence" to life (II* 17).[36] As one prominent scholar has stated it, "Lockean economics served Lockean politics...Locke's political philosophy is the foundation, not the scaffolding or superstructure, of political economy."[37] The principal problem Locke faced in establishing the political character of property was how to overcome the variety of religious proscriptions against many of the measures he deemed essential in securing the right to property and in making that right a strong fence to political liberty. For Locke, it is the "rational and industrious" accumulators of property who are the benefactors of mankind, not those who adhere to the Christian virtues of brotherly love, faith, and charity. As Locke—and the other founders of modern liberalism—surely knew, the claims of religion would have to be attenuated in order to establish what came to be known as capitalism. In addition to a number of other considerations (not the least of them the religious proscription against usury), the emancipation of the desire to accumulate property would be looked upon as covetousness or greed. As one acute observer has noted, Locke attempted "to exorcise the still lingering phantom of theology in economic matters and in particular...the prejudice against the taking of interest."[38] Locke's ultimate purpose, however, can be summarized in this manner: "civil society must provide for the institutionalization of the right to property in such a way as to make *nature*, not theological teachings, the guide to action."[39] In other words, the political must take precedence over the theological. But as Locke well knew, the religious question is the political question *par excellence*. Accordingly, he notes that the "law of morality Jesus Christ hath given us in the New Testament... by revelation" is "a full and sufficient rule for our direction, and conformable to that of reason."[40] This statement is made intelligible by the fact that "[t]he greatest part cannot *know*, and therefore they must *believe*."[41]

V. Locke's Account of the Right to Property

Locke begins his account of the origin of the right to property in the *Second Treatise* by remarking that both natural reason and revelation agree that God has given the earth to mankind in common. How, then, can anyone acquire an exclusive right to any part of it? Locke solves this problem handily.

> Though the Earth, and all inferior Creatures be common to all Men, yet every Man has a *Property* in his own *Person*. This no Body has any Right to but himself. The *Labour* of his Body, and the *Work* of his Hands, we may say, are properly his. Whatsoever then he removes out of the State that Nature hath provided, and left it in, he hath mixed his *Labour* with, and joyned to it something that is his own, and thereby makes it his *Property*.... For this *Labour* being the

unquestionable Property of the Labourer, no man but he can have a right to what that is once joyned to, at least where there is enough, and as good left in common for others. (II* 27)

Everything of value derives from man's labor, that is, his transformation of nature. The right to property is ultimately grounded in each individual's original "*Property* in his own person" (II* 27,* 44). Labor is merely an extension of that original property.

The assertion that men have a property in their own person would seem to contradict an earlier statement of Locke's that "Men being all the Workmanship of one Omnipotent, and infinitely wise Maker... they are his Property, whose Workmanship they are." (II* 6) This statement is more in accordance with the orthodox religious view. If men are the property of God, then, of course, there would seem to be no right to property in the sense just described by Locke. But God (who might plausibly be described as "No body"), in creating man, endowed him both with the instinct for self-preservation and with rationality. Accordingly, one could conclude that the use of reason in the service of self-preservation is the fulfillment of the will of the "infinitely wise Maker," (II* 6) In the *First Treatise* Locke gives this remarkable explanation.

> God, I say, having made Man and the World thus, spoke to him, (that is) directed him by his Senses and Reason, as he did the inferior Animals by their Sense, and Instinct, which he had placed in them to that purpose, to the use of those things, which were serviceable for his Subsistence, and given him as means of his *Preservation*.... For the desire, strong desire of Preserving his Life and Being having been Planted in him, as a Principle of Action by God himself, Reason, *which was the Voice of God in him*, could not but teach him and assure him, that pursuing that natural Inclination he had to preserve his Being, he followed the Will of his Maker....(I* 86)

If God made men for their own preservation (and the preservation of the image of God [I* 30 and II* 11]), then they are perfectly pious in regarding themselves as their own property, and the creation of property through labor becomes a sacred obligation.[42] As Locke notes, "God gave the World to Men in Common; but since he gave it them for their benefit, and the greatest Conveniencies of Life they were capable to draw from it, it cannot be supposed he meant it should always remain common and uncultivated. He gave it to the use of the Industrious and Rational" (II* 34).

The greatest part of all value is created by labor. God may have given the earth in common to all mankind, but "Nature and the Earth furnished only the almost worthless Materials, as in themselves." (II* 43) "I think," Locke remarks:

> it will be but a very modest Computation to say, that of the *Products* of the Earth useful to the Life of Man 9/10 are the *effects of labour*; nay, if we will rightly estimate things as they come to our use, and cast up the several Expenses

about them, what in them is purely owing to *Nature*, and what to *labour*, we shall find, that in most of them 99/100 are wholly to be put on the account of *labour*. (II* 40)

Locke does not argue in terms of an absolute right to property. Rather, private appropriation is justified in terms of the common good. Private appropriation "does not lessen but increase the common stock of mankind." (II* 37) In Locke's calculation, the appropriation of one acre for private cultivation would return 999 acres back to mankind because the return or usefulness of that acre has been increased almost a thousand fold. Uncultivated nature is, as we have seen, "almost worthless." It is labor and therefore the establishment of private property that makes the things of nature useful to men. Private appropriation, although a completely self-regarding activity,[43] is thus in the service of mankind, and private property is the foundation of the common good and public happiness.

There is, however, a natural limit to the amount of property that can be accumulated. The state of nature, as we are told, "has a Law of Nature to govern it." Locke describes the Law of Nature as "reason" (II* 6), the "common Equity, which is that measure God has set to the actions of Men." (II* 8) Since the state of nature is ultimately a state of "penury," there are natural limits to how much a man may acquire. The law of nature creates a kind of utilitarian limit to property. An individual may appropriate only as much from the common stock of mankind as he can make use of, either for his own needs or in trade for other goods. Thus, the natural law limitations are directed, not against the covetous, but against the "waster," i.e., those who are not "Industrious and Rational." Appropriation beyond that is a robbery committed against mankind. (II* 46) If the state of nature were a state of plenty there would be no necessity of limits. Civil society is instituted not so much to preserve property as to facilitate its acquisition and to produce plenty—the necessary preconditions of peace and prosperity.

"The unquestionable right of the Labourer" to accumulate private property is also limited by the requirement that "there is enough, and as good left in common for others." (II* 28) This prohibition, however, seems to have no practical effect. If the state of nature is one of plenty, then there will always be "good enough left in common for others." If the state of nature is one of "penury," then the right to preservation—which takes precedence over the right to property—would dictate that one appropriate the necessary property without regard to the preservation of mankind.[44] Indeed, under conditions of dire necessity one would be justified in appropriating property by force (i.e., by means other than labor) to ensure survival. It would seem that under conditions of extreme penury, labor is not the only legitimate title to property since the right to property is obviously subordinate to the right to life.

In any case, what nature limits is emancipated by the "Fancy or Agreement" which created money as the medium of exchange. Now, accumulation could be limitless because money, having no intrinsic use value itself, could be accumulated limitlessly without decreasing the common stock of the goods necessary to the preservation and convenience of life. As Locke explains, an individual "might heap up as much of these durable things as he pleases; the *exceeding of the bounds of his just Property* not lying in the largeness of his Possession, but the perishing of any thing uselessly in it." (II* 46) And in a statement that was echoed by Madison in the *Federalist* No. 10, Locke notes that "as different degrees of Industry were apt to give Men Possessions in different Proportions, so this *Invention of Money* gave them the opportunity to continue to enlarge them." (II* 48) The right to property antedates civil society; civil society exists to protect those rights that it does not create. It is true that society creates new kinds of property, and provides a completely new ground for its protection in positive law, but the measure of any society is the extent to which it protects the natural right to property. The "emancipation of acquisitiveness" which is made possible by the advent of civil society, with its protections for property, will replace the scarcity of nature with the plenty of civilization. Thus the private right to property, nurtured and protected by civil society, will be the foundation of the common good, as every act of private accumulation becomes simultaneously an act of public-spirited devotion to the public interest. As Leo Strauss remarked, "Far from being straitened by the emancipation of acquisitiveness, the poor are enriched by it. For the emancipation of acquisitiveness is not merely compatible with general plenty but is the cause of it. Unlimited appropriation without concern for the need of others is true charity."[45]

C.B. Macpherson has written that "Locke's astonishing achievement was to base the property right on natural right and natural law, and then remove all the natural law limits from the property right,"[46] Nature, as we have seen, sets a utilitarian limit to the amount of property one can appropriate in the state of nature. It is the convention of money (which antedates civil society, as does the right to property) that allows unlimited accumulation without regard to its consequences for others. But Locke insists that "The Obligations of the Law of Nature, cease not in Society but only in many Cases are drawn closer, and have by Humane Laws known Penalties annexed to them, to inforce their observation." (II* 135) That there is a natural law that governs the state of nature, Locke declares "is certain." And that law is "as intelligible and plain to a rational Creature, and a Studier of that Law, as the positive Laws of Commonwealths, nay possibly plainer." (II* 12) But in the course of the argument, we learn that "in the state of Nature there are many things wanting," among them:

> an *establish'd*, settled, known *Law*, received and allowed by common consent to be the Standard of Right and Wrong, and the common measure to decide all Controversies between them. For though the Law of Nature be plain and intelligible to all rational Creatures; yet Men being biassed by their Interest, as

[handwritten note:] "the primary object of civil society are the security of property + public safety." p. 57 Madison see footnote # 49 Locke Madison

[handwritten:] All have an equal right to possess property but not everyone has the same talents

[handwritten:] The individual Component

ling

Only
ate of
hings.
, civil
ature,
ess of
great
er and
draw

The inequality among the "studiers" and non-studiers does not establish a claim to rule on the part of the "studiers." Rather, it gives to them only an inequality of possessions. And the way in which civil society protects property will be the litmus test of its adherence to natural law principles. The civil protection for unequal accumulation of property is a reflection of the natural human condition on the level of civil society—it is thus a reflection of natural law in a way that makes natural law effective in civil society. For Locke is clear that it is natural law principles—the natural rights to life, liberty, and property which are the irrefragable dictates of individual human equality—that set the bounds and limits to civil society. The right to property serves as the litmus test because it is the right which is derivative from life and liberty. As Harvery Mansfield explains:

> this does not mean that property (in the narrow sense) is more valuable than life or liberty; it means that property is the convention that best protects them. For when life and liberty are at stake, they are already in jeopardy. Locke's reasoning, one may assume, is that it is better to elevate a lesser good, and to pay the price of an increased love of gain and a somewhat arbitrary status for property and the propertied than to endanger the greater goods by endeavoring to protect them directly.[47]

In a sense, the right to property serves as a kind of "early warning system" to invasions of life and liberty. As M. Seliger rightly notes, "Locke's emphasis on the right of property seems to stem from his awareness that life and liberty may mainly be jeopardized through the violation of property rights—because men clash with each other on this ground most often and most violently, and because the government's demands on the citizens bear most immediately and visibly on their property."[48] It is prudent to make property the test because property can be regained while liberty, once lost, is rarely regained. Thus, Locke considered the private right to property to be in the ultimate service of political ends:

the increase of lands and the right imploying of them is the great art of government. And that Prince who shall be so wise and godlike as by established laws of liberty to secure protection and encouragement to the honest industry of Mankind against the oppression of power and narrowness of Party will quickly be too hard for his neighbours. (II* 42)

VI. Property and Consent

Madison undoubtedly expressed the settled sense of the Constitutional Convention when, early in the proceedings, he made the perfectly Lockean assertion that "the primary objects of civil society are the security of property and public safety."[49] Madison was to write later in his defense of the Constitution that "the first object of government" is the protection of "the diversity in the faculties of men from which the rights of property originate." Madison continued that:

[f]rom the protection of different and unequal faculties of acquiring property, the possession of different degrees and kinds of property immediately results; and from the influence of these on the sentiments and views of the respective proprietors, ensues a division of the society into different interests and parties."[50]

As a practical matter, the different and unequal individual abilities that exist in civil society are expressed most dramatically in terms of the right to property.

Everyone has an equal right to possess property, but all have different—even unique—faculties for its acquisition. In fact, without this diversity of faculties, property would be homogeneous and the right to property as an *exclusive* appropriation would be nonexistent. It is the individual diversity of faculties that makes property itself individual, that is, private. All property carries the mark of the unique ability or labor of the one who creates the property. If the faculties for acquiring property were homogeneous, everyone would be entitled to equal property, but no one would have an exclusive or private right to any particular property since no property would bear the stamp of creativity that was the exclusive possession of any single individual. Without human individuality, the natural right to property which is shared equally by all because of their participation in the human species could not be translated into a civil right. And without civil protection for the right to property, the right to property would be a nullity, for in the state of nature there would be no occasion for an individual to distinguish himself by labor or otherwise. The natural right to property, understood in this manner, provides both the principle of identity and difference. And this is true of the natural right to life and liberty as well. It is not so much one's equal participation in the species—or one's "species beingness" as it has been called—but one's individuation within the species that is uniquely human.

In Madison, as in Locke, the protection of natural talents—most manifest in the differing faculties for acquiring property—is the most practical manner of implementing natural law standards in civil society. The protection of the natural diversity for acquiring property is at one and the same time an affirmation of the equality of the right to property and a legitimation of the possession of different kinds and amounts of property. Strictly speaking, equality is incompatible with civil society. Without distinction ("different degrees and kinds") there would be no private rights. But also, the equal and undifferentiated possession of property would hinder the "pursuit of happiness" by removing the impetus for acquiring property beyond the barest necessities. "Theoretic politicians," Madison wrote, "have erroneously supposed that by reducing mankind to a perfect equality in their political rights, they would at the same time be perfectly equalized and assimilated in their possessions, their opinions, and their passions."[51]

Madison, of course, understood the right to property in its full political sense—as a fence to life and liberty. And, in its political meaning, property was understood as the comprehensive right: "as a man is said to have a right to his property, he may be equally said to have a property in his rights."[52] Madison did not, any more than Locke, posit an absolute right to property; the right to property was justified in purely political terms, i.e., in terms of the common good. As he remarked in *The Federalist*, "the regulation of the various and interfering interests form the principal task of modern legislation."[53] This means that property can be regulated from the point of view of maintaining a free economy as a fence to liberty.

The connection between property rights and human rights is often contemptuously dismissed. But Locke and the American Founders saw the connection in a clear and precise light. Locke notes that one of the "Bounds" put on the legislative power "by the Society, and the Law of God and Nature" was that the legislature "must *not raise taxes* on the Property of the People, *without the Consent of the People*, given by themselves, or their Deputies." (II* 142) This idea was repeated in unequivocal terms in the Declaration of Independence. As many have pointed out, the taxes imposed upon the Colonies by the British Parliament were not particularly onerous or burdensome. In a time of relative economic prosperity they could hardly have been judged tyrannical. But they were taken as evidence of a "design to reduce [the Colonies] under absolute despotism." Under these circumstances, the Declaration continues, it is the right of the people, "it is their duty to throw off such government and to provide new guards for their future security." If property can be taken (or taxes imposed) without the consent of the people, then the requirement of the consent of the governed is in jeopardy because "the right to property [is] the visible, formal protection of the right to consent."[54] This is the indefeasible connection between the right to property, understood as the comprehensive political right, and human rights. The right to property is the great fence to liberty, because it is the fence to consent.

Notes

1. *Property*, published anonymously in the National Gazette, March 29, 1792, in 14 THE PAPERS OF JAMES MADISON 268 (R. Rutland, *et al.*, eds. 1978-).

2. Brennan, *The Fourteenth Amendment*, Address to the Section on Individual Rights and Responsibilities, American Bar Association, New York University Law School, August 8, 1986 (quoting B. Schwartz, *The Amendment in Operation: A Historial Overview*, in THE FOURTEENTH AMENDMENT: CENTENNIAL VOLUME 29 (B. Schwartz ed. 1970).

3. Brennan, *id.*

4. *Id.* (emphasis in original).

5. Justice Brennan expressed his attachment to the most progressive opinions on the subject of distributive justice when he remarked that "the demands of human dignity will never cease to evolve." *The Constitution of the United States: Contemporary Ratification*, Text and Teaching Symposium, Georgetown University, Washington, D.C., October 12, 1985.

6. *Id.* (emphasis added).

7. 14 Rutland, *supra* note 1, at 267.

8. THE FEDERALIST No. 43, at 279 (C. Rossiter ed. 1961).

9. *Id.* No. 39, at 240. *See also* M. Meyers, *Revolution and Founding: On Publius-Madison and the American Genesis*, 37 QUARTERLY JOURNAL OF THE LIBRARY OF CONGRESS 197 (1980): "[T]he revolutionary language of the Declaration returned to justify another act of necessity. The Higher Law from which all human rights and obligations flow defines the ends of political institutions and sets limits to their special binding rules." And *see* H. JAFFA, HOW TO THINK ABOUT THE AMERICAN REVOLUTION 76 (1978): "...the innermost meaning of the American Revolution, and of the American political tradition which it established" depends upon an understanding of the "inner relationship" between the Declaration and the Constitution; and *see* at 110*ff.*

10. L. Levy, *Constitutional History, 1776-1789*, in THE ENCYCLOPEDIA OF THE AMERICAN CONSTITUTION 376 (L. Levy, K. Karst, D. Mahoney eds. 1986). The importance of a literal understanding of social contract theory for the founding generation can be clearly seen in Madison's speech to the House of Representatives on May 22, 1789, in Rutland, *supra* note 1, at 178-182.

11. Letter to Henry Lee, May 8, 1825, in JEFFERSON: WRITINGS 1501 (M. Peterson ed. 1984).

12. 1 Tucker, *An Election Sermon*, in AMERICAN POLITICAL WRITING DURING THE FOUNDING ERA, 1760-1805 161-162 (C. Hyneman & D. Lutz eds. 1983).

13. A. MCLAUGHLIN, FOUNDATIONS OF AMERICAN CONSTITUTIONALISM 71 (1st ed. 1932, 1961); *see also* 72, 74-76.

14. Tucker, *supra* note 12, at 158. Most contemporary commentators, however, do not understand the primacy of "the theological-political question" as clearly as Locke and the colonial divines. Walter Berns, for example, has written that "the very idea of natural right is incompatible with Christian doctrine and, by its formulators, was understood to be incompatible"; Berns, *Comment* [A reply to Norman, *Christians, Politics and the Modern State*], 7 THIS WORLD 98 (1983).

15. J. LOCKE, TWO TREATISES OF GOVERNMENT II* 4 (P. Laslett ed. 1963).

16. Letter to Roger Weightman, June 24, 1826, in Peterson, *supra* note 11, at 1517.

17. *See infra*, note 28; *compare* D. BOORSTEIN, THE GENIUS OF AMERICAN POLITICS 82*ff*. (1953), with H. JAFFA, EQUALITY AND LIBERTY 120*ff*. (1965).

18. Letter to John Cartwright, June 5, 1824, in Peterson, *supra* note 11, at 1491. In 1775, Alexander Hamilton used a similar image: "The sacred rights of mankind are not to be rummaged for, among old parchments, or musty records. They are written, as with a sun beam, in the whole *volume* of human nature, by the hand of the divinity itself; and can never be erased or obscured by mortal power." *Farmer Refuted*, in 1 THE PAPERS OF ALEXANDER HAMILTON 122 (H. Syrett ed. 1961-).

19. *See* THE FEDERALIST No. 36, at 217, 224.

20. *Id.* No. 1, at 33.

21. Brennan, *supra* note 2.

22. CONGRESSIONAL GLOBE, 39th Cong., 1st Sess., 2459 (1866).

23. *See* D. Farber & J. Muench, *The Ideological Origins of the Fourteenth Amendment*, 1 CONSTITUTIONAL COMMENTARY 235-237, 239, 241, 245, 246, 249, 259, 272 (1984); and Erler, *Natural Right in the American Founding*, in THE AMERICAN FOUNDING 195 (L. Levy, J. Barlow, & K. Masugi eds. 1988).

24. Howard, *Magna Carta*, in 3 THE ENCYCLOPEDIA OF THE AMERICAN CONSTITUTION, *supra* note 10, at 1195 (emphasis added); *see also* Erler, *The Constitution and the Separation of Powers*, in THE CONSTITUTION: A HISTORY OF ITS FRAMING AND RATIFICATION 156-157 (L. Levy & D. Mahoney eds. 1987).

25. G. M. Trevelyan wrote that Magna Charta was "a document so technical [and]. . .so deficient in the generalizations with which the Declaration of Independence abounds" that it was "totally ignorant of the 'rights of man'." 1 HISTORY OF ENGLAND 230 (1st ed. 1926, 1953).

26. *See* Lincoln's "Springfield Speech," June 26, 1857, in 2 THE COLLECTED WORKS OF ABRAHAM LINCOLN 406-407 (R. Basler ed. 1953).

27. *See especially* Brennan, *supra* note 5.

28. A rather unconvincing attempt to deny the natural right origins of the founding is John Philip Reid's *The Irrelevance of the Declaration*, in LAW AND THE AMERICAN REVOLUTION AND THE REVOLUTION IN THE LAW 46-49 (H. Hartog ed. 1981). Reid argues that despite the many statements contained in public documents, newspaper editorials, sermons, and innumerable speeches, the idea of natural law or natural rights played only a minor role in the pre-Revolutionary period, including the Declaration. Reid—a lawyer—insists that historians have romanticized the Declaration and the Revolution, surrounding them with a myth born more of the historians' imagination than of reality. "Far from being a statement of abstract, natural principles, the Declaration is a document of peculiarly English constitutional dogmas" (at 88). "The Declaration was not, and was never intended to be, either a statement of philosophy or political theory. It was, pure and simple, a legal document, claiming and executing a constitutional right." (at 82) When the Americans exercised the right to revolution (a right they thought derived from the "laws of nature and nature's God"), they were in reality merely exercising a constitutional right created by the English common law or English constitutionalism. That is, English constitutionalism, as a matter of positive law contains the right of revolution—the means of its own dissolution! Whatever this may say about Reid's acuity, it certainly is not the self-understanding of those who participated in the American Revolution nor, I dare say, a fair reading of the historical materials. Reid and others may dislike talk about natural rights, but this is

hardly a warrant to reconstruct history. Joseph Priestley stated the matter succinctly when, in an essay published in 1768 and widely read in America, he wrote "Lawyers, who are governed by rules and precedents, are very apt to fall into mistakes, in determining what is right and lawful." AN ESSAY ON THE FIRST PRINCIPLES OF GOVERN-MENT AND ON THE NATURE OF POLITICAL, CIVIL, AND RELIGIOUS LIBERTY 26 (1768). What Priestley understood—something that was also well understood by Jefferson and the American Revolutionaries—was that the identification of the legal and the just (the argument from fact to right) is the ground of political tyranny because at bottom it rests on the assertion that "justice is the interest of the stronger."

29. *See, e.g.,* G. WILLS, INVENTING AMERICA: JEFFERSON'S DECLARA-TION OF INDEPENDENCE 250-251, 255 (1978), and *infra* note 32. *See also* 1 PARRINGTON, MAIN CURRENTS IN AMERICAN THOUGHT 350 (1st ed. 1927, 1954):

> The substitution of 'pursuit of happiness' for 'property' marks a *complete break* with the Whiggish doctrine of property rights that Locke had bequeathed to the English middle class, and the substitution of a broader sociological conception; and it was this substitution that gave to the document the note of idealism which was to make its appeal so perennially human and vital. (emphasis added)

30. 2 J. LOCKE, AN ESSAY CONCERNING HUMAN UNDERSTANDING, Ch. XXI, 52 (A. Frasner ed. 1959).

31. J. LOCKE, THE REASONABLENESS OF CHRISTIANITY,* 245.

32. L. STRAUSS, NATURAL RIGHT AND HISTORY 228 n.92 (1953).

33. Lest we too quickly conclude that the quoted passage bears the distinct imprint of Aristotle, Locke adds within a few paragraphs that:

> I think that the philosophers of old did in vain inquire, whether *summum bonum* consisted in riches, or bodily delights, or virtue, or contemplation: and they might have as reasonably disputed, whether the best relish were to be found in apples, plums, or nuts, and have divided themselves into sects upon it. (Locke, *supra* note 30, at 56.)

The reference is clearly to Aristotle. *See* ARISTOTLE, ETHICS 1095b15*ff.*, 1173a13*ff.* In Locke, the pursuit of happiness remains essentially a private activity. In the SECOND TREATISE, the public good consists in securing the "peace and safety" necessary to the private pursuit of happiness.

34. *Considerations On the Nature and Extent of the Legislative Authority of the British Parliament,* in 2 THE WORKS OF JAMES WILSON 723 (R. McCloskey ed. 1967). Garry Wills, in his INVENTING AMERICA (*supra* note 29, at 240*ff*), unsuccessfully attempts to use this passage to prove the *non-Lockean* origins of Wilson's thought. The use of the word "happiness" here, Wills asserts, was derived from Hutcheson's "moral sense" philosophy rather than from Locke. In Wills' account, Hutcheson was the proponent of "communitarianism," whereas Lockeanism rests on an individualistic natural rights philosophy that is destructive of community. Since Wills' ideological liberalism rests upon the priority of the community to the individual, he

attempts to reinterpret the American Founding in terms of the moral sense philosophers who are, at least on the surface, more amenable to this interpretation. Needless to say, Wills' attempt utterly fails. For a devastating critique of Wills, *see* Jaffa, *Inventing the Past: Garry Wills's Inventing America and the Pathology of Ideological Scholarship*, in AMERICAN CONSERVATISM AND THE AMERICAN FOUNDING 76-109, especially 101-108 (1984).

35. 1 DOCUMENTS OF AMERICAN HISTORY 107 (H. Commager ed. 1968). The Virginia Bill of Rights states that "all men are by nature equally free and independent, and have certain inherent rights of which, when they enter into a state of society, they cannot by any compact deprive or divest their posterity; namely, the enjoyment of life and liberty, with the means of acquiring and possessing property, and pursuing and obtaining happiness and safety." *Id.* at 103.

36. Locke employs the metaphor of a "fence" throughout the SECOND TREATISE: *see*⁕ 17 (freedom as fence to preservation);⁕ 93 ("what Security, what Fence");⁕ 136 ("determine the Rights, and fence the Properties";⁕ 222 ("The Reason why Men enter into Society, is the preservation of their Property; and the end why they chuse and authorize a Legislative, is, that there may be Laws made, and Rules set as Guards and Fences to the Properties of all the Members of the Society");⁕ 222 ("For the People having reserved to themselves the Choice of their *Representatives*, as the Fence to their Properties");⁕ 226 ("*the best fence against Rebellion*"). Nathan Tarcov (*Locke's Second Treatise and 'The Best Fence Against Rebellion'*, 43 THE REVIEW OF POLITICS 198-217 [1981]), notes that the radical character of Locke's right of resistance is that the people may act in *anticipation* of the dissolution of the legislative. The sense of "anticipation" seems to be conveyed by Locke in the "fence" metaphor. Tarcov further argues that "Locke's concern for fences against the worst, rather than for paths to the best or for a balance of good and bad, is not only the basis of the right of resistance and of the principle of anticipation, but the fundamental principle of Locke's liberal politics."

37. Mansfield, *On the Political Character of Property in Locke*, in POWERS, POSSESSIONS, AND FREEDOM 24 (A. Kontos ed. 1979). *See also* M. SELIGER, THE LIBERAL POLITICS OF JOHN LOCKE 171-172 (1969).

38. Parson, *Locke's Doctrine of Property*, 36 SOCIAL RESEARCH 389 (1969).

39. *Id.* at 398.

40. LOCKE, *supra* note 31, at 243.

41. *Id.* (emphasis in original)

42. See J. TULLY, A DISCOURSE ON PROPERTY: JOHN LOCKE AND HIS ADVERSARIES 95, 108-111 (1980).

43. *See* FIRST TREATISE⁕ 92. "Property. . .is for the benefit and sole Advantage of the Proprietor."

44. *Id.*⁕ 6: "Everyone as he is *bound to preserve himself*, and not to quit his Station willfully; so by the like reason when his Preservaton comes not in competition ought he, as much as he can, *to preserve the rest of Mankind*."

45. STRAUSS, *supra* note 32, at 242-243.

46. C. MACPHERSON, THE POLITICAL THEORY OF POSSESSIVE INDI-VIDUALISM: HOBBES TO LOCKE 199 (1962).

47. Mansfield, *supra* note 37, at 37.

48. Seliger, *supra* note 37, at 166.

49. 1 THE RECORDS OF THE FEDERAL CONVENTION OF 1787 147 (M. Farrand ed. 1966). Madison's statement was echoed throughout the Convention: *see*

Hamilton's remarks on June 18 (*id.* at 302): "One great objt of Govt is personal protection and the security of Property"; Gouverneur Morris on July 5 (*id.* at 553): "property was the main object of society"; Rufus King on July 6 (*id.* at 541): "property was the primary object of Society"; James Wilson seems to have been a notable exception, remarking on July 13 (*id.* at 605) that "he could not agree that property was the sole or the primary object of Governt. & Society. The cultivation & improvement of human mind was the most noble object." It almost goes without saying, however, that this is not a non-Lockean statement.

50. THE FEDERALIST No. 10, at 78.

51. *Id.* at 81.

52. *Property*, 14 Peterson, *supra* note 11, at 26.

53. THE FEDERALIST No. 10, at 79.

54. Mansfield, *The Forms of Liberty*, in DEMOCRATIC CAPITALISM? ESSAYS IN SEARCH OF A CONCEPT 19 (F. Baumann ed. 1986).

Jefferson and Property Rights
JEAN YARBROUGH

The starting point for any discussion of Jefferson's view of property rights must be his failure to include property among the inalienable rights enumerated in the Declaration of Independence. Although some scholars have minimized the importance of this substitution, arguing that the pursuit of happiness does not differ significantly from the Lockean focus on property, others have found the omission to be crucial.[1] According to Garry Wills, Jefferson's failure to enshrine property is another proof that the Declaration is not merely non-Lockean, but positively anti-Lockean in its political principles. Moreover, Wills argues, this interpretation of the Declaration's principles accords with Jefferson's own political philosophy, which was fundamentally shaped by Scottish communitarianism, rather than Lockean individualism.[2]

In what follows I will first explore what Jefferson means by property, how property rights arise, and what kind of right he understands property to be. Here I will argue that the single greatest influence on Jefferson's understanding of property was the eighteenth century Scottish moral philosopher, Lord Kames.[3] But far from supporting Wills's communitarian interpretation, Kames's view of property was essentially liberal, i.e., individualistic, and so was Jefferson's. I shall then consider the relationship of property rights to republicanism, examining first whether Jefferson considered the protection of property to be a legitimate object of republican society, and what, if any, measures he took to secure this end. In this connection, I shall consider what dangers Jefferson believed property might pose for the preservation of republican institutions. I shall then examine the connection between property and republican character. Here I will explore the connection between one kind of property, land, and one occupation, agriculture, to republican virtue.

Throughout I shall argue that although Jefferson's view of property was essentially liberal, his liberalism was qualified by his understanding of the requirements of republican government and his view of human nature. Just as important, and all too often overlooked by the Scottish and republican revisionists, however, Jefferson's republicanism was tempered by his commitment to the principles of liberal democracy.[4] It is this blend of liberal, republican, and Scottish moral sense theory which gives Jefferson's understanding of property its distinctive character.

I. Why Property Is not an Inalienable Right

If we begin by examining the meaning of inalienable, Jefferson's failure to include property in his revolutionary trilogy is not so remarkable. For inalienable rights are not simply synonymous with natural rights. Inalienable rights refer to that category of natural rights which we cannot *transfer* to another either because it is not possible for others to exercise these rights for us (e.g., the right of conscience), or because such a transfer would run contrary to our own self-preservation. Although all inalienable rights are natural rights, deriving their inalienability from man's "inherent" nature, and, therefore, do not depend upon the consent of others, not all natural rights are inalienable.[5] Indeed some natural rights, like the right of judging in our own cause, *must* be alienated if civil society is to exist at all.[6]

If property had been declared an inalienable, i.e., non-transferable right, Jefferson would have found it more difficult to attack semi-feudal aristocratic property laws then in force in Virginia.[7] But these laws had to be overturned if republican government was to be established. It was precisely because the people have the right to alter or abolish their governments that existing property laws could not be held to rest upon an inalienable right.

Thus, in the same year that Jefferson declared the colonies "free and independent states," he introduced into the Virginia legislature bills for the abolition of entail and primogeniture.[8] Speaking of the "Bill to Abolish Entails" in his *Autobiography*, Jefferson wrote:

> the transmission of this property from generation to generation in the same name raised up a distinct set of families who, being privileged by law in the perpetuation of their wealth, were thus formed into a Patrician order....[9]

In his Draft for the Virginia Constitution of 1776, Jefferson proposed several additional provisions affecting the existing property relations. These included altering the inheritance laws so that women could inherit equally with men. Other provisions, particularly the abolition of slavery and the equal partition of land among male citizens, will be considered later.

Nine years later, while serving as Minister to France, and observing the "wretchedness" occasioned by the "enormous" inequality of property under the Old Regime, Jefferson condemned aristocratic privilege in even stronger language. Writing to James Madison from the royal estate at Fountainbleau, he left no doubt that justice required a fundamental revolution in the existing property laws.

> I am conscious that an equal division of property is impracticable. But the consequences of this enormous inequality producing so much misery to the bulk of mankind, legislators cannot invent too many devices for subdividing property, only taking care to let their subdivisions go hand in hand with the natural affections of the human mind.[10]

Seen in the light of existing property relations, and their fundamental incompatibility with republican principles of justice, we can now better appreciate why Jefferson did not regard property as an inalienable right.

How then did Jefferson understand property rights? Before proceeding to this question, it is necessary to point out two methodological difficulties. First, Jefferson never systematically examined the nature of property rights; consequently, his theory of property must be constructed from suggestions in his public writings and fragments of his letters. Moreover, Jefferson's writings span nearly fifty years, raising the distinct possibility that his views may have changed over time. Indeed, as we shall see, Jefferson did change his mind somewhat on the *kind* of property compatible with republican government. But in his few theoretical pronouncements on the origin of property and the status of property rights, Jefferson's views remain essentially unchanged.

II. The Origin, Meaning, and Status of Property

In 1816, Jefferson, responding to a query whether there exists a natural right to the "exclusive property" of our ideas or inventions, delivered his most complete thoughts on the origin of property. Significantly, these opinions closely follow the argument set forth by Lord Kames in his "History of Property," which Jefferson had entered into his *Commonplace Book* while a student, nearly a half century earlier. If, as Gilbert Chinard has persuasively argued,[11] Jefferson recorded only those theories with which he was already in agreement, Kames's views on property would appear to have had a lifelong influence on his own ideas. That Kames was the only philosopher whose views on property Jefferson cited in his notebook only reinforces this point.

In his letter of response Jefferson disposes of the immediate question at issue: there is no natural right to inventions or ideas. Indeed, nature's intention seems to be the opposite. "Ideas should freely spread from one to another over the globe, for the moral and mutual instruction of man, and improvement of his condition..."[12] This is why nature made ideas, "like fire, expansible over all space...and like air...incapable of confinement or exclusive appropriation." Societies may choose to protect the property of ideas in order to encourage useful inventions. Elsewhere, Jefferson indicates that he approves of such protection,[13] but there is no *natural* right to the protection of this form of property.

In the course of his response, Jefferson reflects upon the origin of property rights in general, observing that it is "a moot question whether the origin of any kind of property is derived from nature at all." This passage has frequently been interpreted to mean that Jefferson did *not* regard any aspect of property as grounded in natural right, but, as we shall see, the issue is more complicated. To understand more fully what Jefferson intended, we must first consider what precisely Jefferson meant by property, and why private property arises in the first place.

When we speak of property it is important to be clear about what we mean. Do we mean the acquisition of property through labor, momentary possession based on physical occupation, or the secure ownership of property?[14] From Jefferson's comments in this letter, as well as their conformity to the fuller treatment of this issue by Kames, it would appear that Jefferson understands property to mean "stable ownership," especially of land. It is in this sense, then, that Jefferson examines whether we have a natural right to property, and concludes that we do not. According to Jefferson, no one who has seriously studied the subject (and this of course includes Kames) believes that there is a natural right to a separate "acre of land." This is because this right to land presupposes "stable ownership," and "stable ownership is the gift of social law, and is given late in the progress of society."

Before "stable ownership" was introduced, fixed and movable property was grounded in the right of the first occupier, and lasted only as long as the occupier "possessed" it—that is, was physically able to defend it. Here, Jefferson's argument becomes clearer if we recur to Kames. In the section from the "History of Property" which Jefferson had entered in his *Commonplace Book*, Kames had explained that the right of the first occupier corresponds to hunting and grazing societies, which have no need for settled ownership. It is only with the emergence of agricultural societies that the question of stable ownership arises, for men would not undertake the arduous task of cultivating the earth if they were not guaranteed the enjoyment of the fruits of their labor. But this guarantee is grounded in social agreement rather than nature.

Jefferson does not here consider why men consent to the appropriation of private property in the first place, but in a letter to James Madison, written nearly a quarter of a century earlier, we have evidence that Jefferson had already considered this question.[15] Again, following Kames, Jefferson believed that we allow property to be appropriated out of the common stock "for the encouragement of greater industry." The vast estates in France, "kept idle mostly for the sake of game," encourage indolence, not industry. Following Kames' argument, Jefferson seemed here to be suggesting that if men wish simply to hunt, they have no right to the stable ownership of private property. In a hunting society, property is based on the right of the first occupier, and "belongs" to an individual only as long as he physically remains there. When he leaves, he relinquishes his claim. Stable ownership of property, which comes about with agriculture, and is rooted in labor,[16] can only be justified if it promotes greater industry. When it does not, as in the enclosure of royal estates for mere pleasure, the property laws are unjust. "Whenever there is in any country uncultivated lands and unemployed poor, it is clear that the laws of property have been so far extended as to violate natural right." When this occurs, society has a responsibility to those who, through no fault of their own, have been excluded from the appropriation. For they agreed to stable ownership only on condition that it would benefit society as a whole. Society must then furnish them with "other employment" so they can survive. If it does not, "the fundamental right to labor returns to the unemployed."

Jefferson's argument has sometimes been interpreted to mean that he thought property rights were simply conventional, but this is a mistake. Although stable ownership is the result of human agreement, it must conform to other more "fundamental," i.e., natural, principles. The right to labor is more fundamental than property, understood essentially as stable ownership, because it is more closely bound up with each individual's right to life.

There is, moreover, another way in which property rights, though based on consent, have a certain natural foundation. As Jefferson observed to DuPont de Nemours, the right to property is rooted in certain natural needs and faculties:

> the right to property is founded on certain natural wants, in the means by which we are given to satisfy these wants, and the right to what we acquire by these means, without violating the similar rights of other sensible beings.[17]

The implications of this statement will become clearer if we compare it with Madison's famous argument in *Federalist* No. 10. Whereas Madison saw the rights of property originating in men's unequal faculties alone, and believed that society's first task was to protect these unequal faculties, Jefferson believed that property was grounded in *two* conflicting natural principles: men's equal wants and their unequal talents for satisfying these needs. It is this need to strike a balance between these two contradictory aspects of human nature, rather than the mistaken belief that property is merely conventional, which gives Jefferson's understanding of property its distinctive character.

Nevertheless, Jefferson, no less than Madison, believed that men entered into society to secure their property as well as their persons, and that the protection of property was a legitimate concern of society. There is no warrant for concluding that Jefferson rejected these essentially liberal principles in favor of a more radical redistribution of wealth. Indeed, if Kames' thought is any guide, Jefferson agreed that such a system was "unnatural and uncomfortable." As Jefferson noted in his *Commonplace Book*:

> the bounds of society may be too lax, but they may also be overstrained. A society where every man shall be bound to dedicate the whole of his industry to the common interest, would be of the strictest kind, but it would be unnatural and uncomfortable, because destruction (sic) of liberty and independency; so would be the enjoyment of the goods of fortune in common. Besides there subsists in man a remarkable propensity for appropriation, which makes us averse to a communion of goods. Property gives life to industry, and enables us to gratify the most dignified natural affections.[18]

Turning from theory to practice, it is noteworthy that, even in France, where the plight of the unemployed poor was desperate, Jefferson's recommendations were surprisingly mild. Jefferson's observation that "legislators cannot invent too many devices for subdividing property" is substantially qualified by his next phrase which reads "only taking care to let their subdivisions go hand in hand with the natural affections of the human mind." What Jefferson principally has in mind is the abolition of entail and primogeniture, so that all the children of the same family inherit equally. Although he adds a second "device," progressive taxation, Jefferson's understanding of this measure is far more limited than the contemporary view. Though he does not take up the question here, elsewhere Jefferson makes it clear that he opposed all direct taxation. By "progressive taxation" he apparently meant no more than a tax on imported luxuries. Such a tax would penalize anti-republican ostentation, but was never intended to eliminate the disparity of wealth among families. For this inequality was rooted in men's unequal faculties for acquiring property, and was one ineradicable aspect of human nature.

III. Property and Republican Government

On the eve of his departure from France in 1789, Jefferson gave voice to his famous thought experiment, "the earth belongs in usufruct to the living."[19] Reflecting upon this principle, Jefferson concluded that it was:

> of very extensive application and consequences, in every country, and most especially in France. It enters into the resolution of the question Whether the nation may change the descent of the lands holden in tail? Whether they may change the appropriation of lands given antiently to the church, to hospitals, colleges, orders of chivalry, and otherwise in perpetuity? Whether they may abolish the charges and privileges attached on lands, including the whole catalogue ecclesiastical and feudal? It goes to hereditary offices, authorities and jurisdictions; to hereditary orders, distinctions and appelations; to perpetual monopolies in commerce, the arts and sciences; with a long train of et ceteras; and it renders the question of reimbursement a question of generosity and not of right.[20]

It is this passage, more than any other, which has led some scholars to argue that Jefferson was an economic and political radical.[21] But, significantly, Jefferson never carried this principle to its extreme. For example, although the principle would have allowed Virginia to claim lands granted in perpetuity by the Crown to the Anglican Church, Jefferson's draft of a bill disestablishing the Church of England permitted the Church to retain its ancient holdings.[22] Moreover, in his "Report on the Peace Treaty" (December 16, 1783), Jefferson urged Congress to recommend to the state legislatures the restitution of all estates, rights, and properties belonging to British subjects, which had been confiscated provided they had not borne arms against the United States. This discrimination between "those who took side against us before the Declaration of Independence" and those "who remained among us and strove to injure us by their treacheries" was founded on both "justice and generosity." It was not, as Jefferson in his thought experiment proposed, merely a question of generosity. Justice, understood as the protection of men's inalienable rights, was also involved because the "right to take the side which every man's conscience approves in a civil contest, is too precious a right, and too favorable to the preservation of liberty not to be protected by all its well informed friends."[23] As Stanley Katz has rightly observed, we fundamentally misunderstand Jefferson's radicalism if we do not "see how consistently he defended private property rights."[24]

To be sure, Jefferson sought to encourage a wide distribution of property throughout society. Acting on the principle that "small landholders are the most precious part of the State,"[25] Jefferson's draft constitution for Virginia in 1776 would have granted "every person of full age neither owning nor having owned [50] acres of land... an appropriation of [50] acres or so much as shall make up what he owns or has owned [50] acres in full and absolute dominion" out of unappropriated or forfeited public lands. But however desirable Jefferson considered a republic of small landholders to be, it was not his intention to involve government in any radical scheme of redistribution, for this would have violated Jefferson's principle of limited government, and run contrary to the purposes for which civil society was instituted. As long as property was rightly used,[26] that is, that it promoted industry, government must protect its unequal distribution. Jefferson made this point explicitly in his "Prospectus" recommending the liberal political economist, DeStutt de Tracy,

> To take from one, because it is thought that his own industry and that of his father's has acquired too much, in order to spare to others, who, or whose fathers have not exercised equal industry and skill, is to violate arbitrarily the first principle of association—the *guarantee* to every one of his industry and the fruits acquired by it.[27]

Just as we are cautioned against reading too much into Jefferson's observation that "the earth belongs in usufruct to the living," so should we be careful in interpreting his endorsement of progressive taxation. All he apparently intended for America was a tax by the general government on imported luxuries, which tax he supported because it fell "exclusively on the rich."[28] Significantly, when Jefferson, in a fit of enthusiasm, looked forward to America's becoming "a paradise on the contribution of the rich alone," the tax on imported luxuries was the only levy he mentioned. The limitations of Jefferson's principle of progressive taxation could hardly be made clearer than in his "Prospectus":

> If the overgrown wealth of an individual be deemed dangerous to the state, the best corrective is the law of equal inheritance to all in equal degree; and the better as this enforces a law of nature, while extra-taxation violates it.[29]

In keeping with this general principle, Jefferson consistently maintained that "the equal partition of intestate estates" together with a tax on imported luxuries constituted "the best agrarian law."[30]

As these remarks suggest, Jefferson was not seriously troubled by the inequality of wealth in republican America. The only time he doubted the economic future of the United States was while he was outside the country serving as Minister to France (1784-1789). Surrounded daily by aristocratic decadence and luxury, Jefferson gave full play to his worst fears. It was during this period that he wondered whether at some point in the future the unemployed of America might be forced to reclaim their fundamental right to labor for a livelihood by cultivating someone else's idle lands merely to survive. Even in France, however, this was not a persistent theme with Jefferson,[31] and it vanished altogether upon his return. Observing American society again at first hand, he wrote approvingly to Jean Nicholas Demeunier in 1795 that "there is no such thing in this country as what would be called wealth in Europe."[32] Twenty years later, as America moved gradually to develop its own manufactures, Jefferson still found no reason to doubt his original assessment. The rich, "who can live without labour, either manual or professional," are "few and of moderate wealth."[33] Nor was there the grinding poverty Jefferson had feared might develop. In contrast to the "starved and rickety paupers and dwarfs of English workshops,"[34] America had "no paupers, the old and crippled among us, who possess nothing and have no families to take care of them, being too few to merit notice as a separate section of society, or to affect a general estimate."[35] Instead, America had developed into the rarest of social phenomena: a middle class republic.

> The great mass of our population is of laborers. . . .Most of the laboring class possess property, cultivate their own lands, have families, and from the demand for their labor are enabled to exact from the rich and the competent such prices as enable them to be fed abundantly, clothed above mere decency, to labor moderately and raise their families.[36]

On this point, it is instructive to compare Jefferson's position with Madison's. Jefferson's view of property as a positive right allowed society to alter property laws which conflicted with men's inalienable rights, but his analysis of post-Revolutionary America made any such action unnecessary. By contrast, Madison feared that in the future, American society would be divided between the few rich and the many poor. The task of republican institutions would then be to protect property rights from majority faction. What, if any, responsibility republican governments might have to the many poor, Madison did not adequately consider. Yet in view of his predictions, Madison's failure to confront this issue is significant.[37]

Unlike Madison, Jefferson did not see the danger to republican government coming from the majority. In France, the poor were simply the victims of unjust property laws; in America, the people posed no danger to property rights at all. "I am not one of those who fear the people. They and not the rich, are our dependence for continued freedom."[38] Having observed fifteen to twenty legislatures in his native Virginia, Jefferson confidently declared that he "had no fears of an equalization of property" from the majority of the people.[39] Thus, Jefferson's observation that "persons and property make the sum of the objects of government"[40] posed no special problems for him as it did for so many of the Framers. Unlike Madison, he saw no tension between these two principles; unlike Adams, he saw no need for separate institutions to protect these competing claims. In this latter connection, he emphatically rejected Adams's suggestion that the wealthy and ambitious be given their own legislative chamber, "where they may be hindered from doing mischief by their coordinate branches, and where, also, they may be a protection to wealth against the agrarian and plundering enterprises of the majority of the people." As Jefferson put it, somewhat acerbically,

> I think that to give them power in order to prevent them from doing mischief is arming them for it, and increasing instead of remedying the evil....Nor do I believe them necessary to protect the wealthy; because enough of these will find their way into every branch to protect themselves.[41]

Since Jefferson saw no tension between the rights of persons and the rights of property, he had no difficulty equating republican government with rule by the majority. Over the years, Jefferson's definition of majority rule would become more exacting, but the starting point was always representation based strictly on population in both houses of the legislature, or what he called "a representation permanently equal."[42] Accordingly, Jefferson's draft constitution of 1776 as well as his draft of the revised constitution of 1783 made no provision for the representation of property. Speaking of the Virginia Constitution in the *Notes*, Jefferson commented favorably:

> in some of the American States, the delegates and Senators are so chosen as that the first represent the persons, and the second the property of the State. But with us, wealth and wisdom have equal chance for admission to both houses.[43]

Finally, in both these drafts, Jefferson sought to abolish slavery. Unlike many southern slaveholders, Jefferson did not regard slaves as property.[44]

But we may ask, why, given the weight traditionally accorded class conflict, was Jefferson *not* concerned with protecting property rights? Jefferson has already partly answered this question: America will be a middle class society in which class conflict is muted. In addition, Jefferson believed in the power of institutions and the environment to shape human character. Republican institutions, affording each individual the equal opportunity to pursue his own happiness, would unleash new opportunities for self-development. And, as we shall see, an agrarian society would promote those virtues necessary to the preservation of republican institutions.

Jefferson did not, however, rely simply upon these external influences. Ultimately, his optimism was rooted in his view of human nature. Again, following Kames and others of the Scottish school, Jefferson held that man was by nature a social animal. Since nature intended men for society, she equipped them with a moral sense which enabled them to live together in peace and justice. According to Jefferson, all men were endowed with a moral sense which enabled them to distinguish right from wrong. Although this sense depends to some extent upon the reasoning faculty, "it is a small stock which is required for this, even a less one than what we call common sense." Continuing with this democratic epistemology, Jefferson insisted that ordinary men could more easily discern principles of justice than the educated, who could be "led astray by artificial rules."[45]

The opposite side of Jefferson's faith in the common people, endowed with a benevolent nature and nurtured by benign institutions, was his distrust of the rich and powerful. If there was a danger of class conflict, it would come from the few and not the many. In any such confrontation, Jefferson's sympathies would be, as in 1789, on the side of the many.

Although Jefferson saw no danger of the many unjustly infringing upon the property rights of the few, he did believe that the people posed their own threat to republican institutions, through the decline of civic virtue. Here too, property, and the desire for property, figure prominently in Jefferson's analysis.

As Jefferson reflected upon the problem of how to preserve America's republican institutions, he concluded that the core of the problem lay in keeping alive the civic spirit which the Revolution had unleashed. Jefferson's solution, in part, was to broaden the suffrage, and to include the citizens as participants in those public affairs within their competence.

> Where every man is a sharer in the direction of his ward republic, or of some of the higher ones, and feels that he is a participator in the government of affairs, not merely at an election one day in the year, but every day; when there shall not be a man in the State who will not be a member of some of its councils, great or small, he will let the heart be torn out of his body sooner than his power be wrested from him by a Caesar or a Bonaparte.[46]

Initially, Jefferson linked suffrage to property ownership.His draft constitution of 1776 for Virginia provided that "all male persons of full age and sane mind having a freehold estate in [one fourth of an acre] of land in any town, or in [25] acres of land in the country" would be eligible to vote and hold office. But at the same time, the constitution granted to every "person" not owning fifty acres of land an absolute appropriation in that amount, or double what was necessary to vote. On the theory that small freeholders make the best citizens, Jefferson would have made every eligible male a freeholder.

When this proposal failed to win acceptance, Jefferson chose to extend the rights of persons at the expense of property. In his draft constitution of 1783 for

Virginia, Jefferson would have extended the suffrage to those who "have enrolled in the militia," as well as those who possessed a certain amount of property. Later Jefferson would have extended the right to vote still further, including "every man who fights or pays" taxes.[47] As of 1816, however, the Virginia legislature had failed to act on Jefferson's proposals. Writing to John Taylor, Jefferson condemned the exclusion of those "who fight and pay taxes" as a blatant violation of republican principles, "as if society were instituted for the soil, and not for the men inhabiting it, or one half of these could dispose of the rights and will of the other half without their consent."[48] Jefferson's first goal was to unite the rights of persons and property, but failing in this attempt, he chose to extend the rights of persons. For Jefferson, political participation and civic spirit were too important to be sacrificed to the rights of property.[49] Conversely, Jefferson's generous view of the common man vitiated any danger from the many to the few.

There is, moreover, another connection between property, or to be more precise, the desire for property or acquisitiveness, and republicanism. We have already seen how, while in France, Jefferson occasionally indulged his worst fears about the economic future of the poor in America. At the same time, and far more frequently, however, he repeated the traditional republican concern that his countrymen would be corrupted, not by poverty, but by post-war prosperity. Frugality was by no means an altogether new theme with Jefferson. Already in the *Notes on Virginia*, composed in 1780-1781, and published in 1785 in France, Jefferson had sounded the alarm. "From the conclusion of this war we shall be going downhill....[The people] will forget themselves, but in the sole faculty of making money and will never think of uniting to effect a due respect for their rights."[50] But while in France, the need to return to republican frugality and simplicity assumed a new urgency. "Every thing I hear from my own country fills me with despair as to their recovery from their vassalage to Great Britain. Fashion and folly is plunging them deeper and deeper into distress..."[51] Jefferson's letters from France are full of nostalgia for the enforced deprivation brought on by the war. "How happy a people we were during the War from the single circumstance that we could not run into debt."[52] Now that the war is over, a fatal "disposition to luxury" threatens to undermine "those manners which alone can preserve republican government."[53] So essential are these manners that:

> would a missionary appear who would make frugality the basis of his religious system, and go through the land preaching it up as the only road to salvation, I would join his school...[54]

Unlike Jefferson's fear that America might produce a class of unemployed poor, his concern with republican frugality and simplicity did not disappear upon his return to America. Rather it found a concrete expression in his opposition to Hamilton's economic policies, and it is to this issue that we now turn.

IV. Agrarian Virtue and Republican Government

However important the formal structures of government were to Jefferson's understanding of republicanism, the essence of republicanism was to be found in the manners and spirit of the people.[55] In this regard, Jefferson saw a powerful connection between one kind of property, land, one way of life, farming, and the perpetuation of republican virtue. Jefferson first set forth this argument in the *Notes on Virginia*, where he declared farmers "the chosen people of God, if ever he had a chosen people, whose breasts he has made his peculiar deposit for substantial and genuine virtue."[56]

Without here exploring the dubious proposition that any occupation can by itself promote "genuine virtue" we turn to a consideration of those qualities Jefferson believed agriculture was uniquely qualified to promote. These include industry, independence, and moderation.[57] Because the farmer works for himself, he labors assiduously; because he answers neither to bosses nor customers, he keeps his self-respect and independence. Then, too, although the farmer works hard, he is not compelled to labor incessantly, as European laborers are, merely to survive. Cultivating one's own plot of land gives each man the time and incentive to participate in public affairs. For Jefferson, the autonomy engendered by a nation of agrarian freeholders provides the foundation for moral and political autonomy. Finally, and closely connected with this last point, Jefferson expects agriculture to encourage moderation. "The moderate and sure income of husbandry begets permanent improvement, quiet life, and orderly conduct both public and private."[58]

At the same time, Jefferson recognized that agricultural abundance would eventually force Americans to seek employment outside the farm. But he rejected out of hand any turn to domestic manufacturing. "I consider the class of artificers as the panders of vice and the instruments by which the liberties of a country are generally overturned."[59] Here Jefferson rings a change on the traditional republican argument that commerce undermines civic virtue, substituting for commerce broadly understood a more narrow focus on manufacturing as the source of those luxuries which corrupt republican manners. It is not, however, only the taste for "superfluities" to which Jefferson objects, it is also the kind of wealth a manufacturing society creates. "The wealth acquired by speculation and plunder is fugacious in its nature and fills society with the spirit of gambling."[60] For Jefferson, the moderate wealth created by industrious farmers is honorable, while the unlimited riches created by avarice and speculation are not.[61] Accordingly, Jefferson opposed all economic policies which would have encouraged the growth of manufactures, such as the national bank or a national bankruptcy law, as well as federal support for public improvements.

Instead of manufacturing, Jefferson recommends that the surplus population of America seek employment in navigation, "because comparing the characters of the two classes, I find the. . .[sailors] the most valuable citizens."[62]

This suggestion is astonishing because it flies in the face of the entire republican tradition, which from the time of Plato and Aristotle, had viewed the life of the sailor as destructive of sound character and virtue.[63] Indeed, James Madison, reflecting on "A Republican Distribution of Citizens" only a few years later (1792), regarded the sailor as the least eligible occupation for republican governments. "His virtue, at no time aided, is occasionally exposed to every scene that can poison it."[64]

Why then did Jefferson break with the tradition and defend navigation on moral grounds? Jefferson does not answer this question directly, but it would seem to have something to do with the relationship of these two occupations to agriculture. Unlike manufacturing, which threatens to supplant the economic primacy of agriculture, navigation, properly confined, is an essential component of Jefferson's agricultural policy.

Jefferson's view of agriculture has sometimes been understood as a romantic return to the pastoral ideal of the self-sufficient farmer, living in virtuous isolation from the rest of the world.[65] Indeed, Jefferson did occasionally express such a wish.

> Were I to indulge my own theory, I should wish them [the states] to practice neither commerce nor navigation but to stand with respect to Europe precisely on the footing of China. We should then avoid wars, and all our citizens would be husbandmen.[66]

But even Jefferson recognized that this was fantasy. Instead, he sought to encourage the production of an agricultural surplus, especially in flour and wheat. These cash crops would then be carried on American ships to Europe, and traded in the open market, with the profits used to purchase manufactured "necessaries" and wants.

Jefferson's agricultural policy envisioned the farmer participating in the international market, exporting his surplus, and importing European manufactures. Despite his occasional nostalgia for the self-sufficient farmer, Jefferson's agricultural policy was, as Joyce Appleby has made abundantly clear, essentially commercial and scientific. Wherever possible, Jefferson sought to apply modern technological advances to agricultural production; Jefferson himself invented a threshing machine, improved the plow, introduced new seeds and plants to America, and advocated soil conservation.[67] Nevertheless, Appleby goes too far in discounting altogether the influences of the republican tradition on Jefferson's thought. Jefferson's commitment to agriculture, even scientific and commercial agriculture, is best understood not as a "struggle between two different elaborations of capitalistic development in America," but as a moral struggle for the soul of the American republic.[68] This interpretation need not rule out economic arguments, but Jefferson's economic theories are best understood as corollaries to his republicanism, to be disposed of as political developments dictated. Early on, for example, Jefferson's economic theories followed closely the views of the French Physiocrats, especially Francois Quesney. Criticizing the mercantile policy initiated by Louis XIV, which artificially promoted manufacturing at the expense of agriculture, the Physiocrats insisted that only agriculture was productive of national wealth. In their view, it was principally nature, and not labor, which supplied the materials for human prosperity. For obvious reasons, Jefferson was sympathetic to this argument, though his early writings give no more than a hint of it. Prior to the abortive Embargo Act of 1807, in which the Republicans sought to retaliate against British aggressions by keeping American ships and goods at home, while barring English imports, Jefferson's defense of the agrarian republic was couched chiefly in moral terms. These early pronouncements, while not ruling out economic issues, tended to emphasize the moral advantages of an agricultural republic.

It was only after he was forced by the failure of his unilateral boycott to accept the necessity of domestic manufacturing that Jefferson shifted the ground of his argument from morals to economics, and in the process, repudiated Physiocratic theory.

> I was once a doubter whether the labor of the cultivator, aided by the creative powers of the earth itself, would not produce more value than that of the manufacturer, alone and unassisted by the dead hand of the subject on which he acted.[69]

Jefferson then proceeded to the heart of the Physiocratic argument:

> to the labor of the husbandman a vast addition is made by the spontaneous energies of the earth on which it is employed: for one grain of wheat committed to the earth, she renders twenty, thirty, and even fifty fold, whereas to the labor of the manufacturer, nothing is added. Pounds of flax in his hands, yield, on the contrary, but penny weights of lace.[70]

Now, however, "labor saving machines do as much for the manufacturer, as the earth for the cultivator." Although Jefferson continued to doubt that manufacturing is as productive of wealth as agriculture, he conceded that it is more productive than he once thought. But even this is not the point: in the face of European hostilities, the question of national wealth "assumes a new form." It must now be measured not in dollars and cents, but in political independence. The question becomes:

> shall we make our own comforts, or go without them, at the will of a foreign nation? He, therefore, who is now against domestic manufacture, must be for reducing us either to dependence on that foreign nation, or to be clothed in skins, and live like wild beasts in dens and caverns. I am not one of these: experience has taught me that manufactures are now as necessary to our independence as to our comfort.[71]

In these letters Jefferson focuses on the economic and political advantages of domestic manufactures; he discreetly passes over the moral implications of this shift. To his trusted friend, William Short, however, Jefferson made it clear that his thoughts on the subject had not changed.

> Our enemy has indeed the consolation of Satan on removing our first parents from Paradise: from a peaceable and agricultural nation, he makes us a military and manufacturing one.[72]

Jefferson never ceased to regard manufacturing as the principal source of corruption in republican governments, observing that:

> in proportion as commercial avarice and corruption descend on us from the north and the east, the principles of free government are to retire to the agricultural States of the south and west, as their last asylum and bulwark.[73]

Ironically, for Jefferson the commercial and manufacturing North posed a greater threat to republican institutions than did the slaveholding South.[74]

Accordingly, Jefferson accepted manufacturing only reluctantly as a political necessity, and hoped to confine it to a small scale. Unlike some of the younger Jeffersonians, who were forced to rethink their program after the War of 1812, Jefferson never accepted the development of large-scale manufactures in America, and steadfastly refused to believe they could compete against the "charms" of agrarian life.[75] In practice, Jefferson's idea of an "equilibrium" meant:

> manufactures, sufficient for our own consumption, of what we raise the raw material (and no more). Commerce sufficient to carry the surplus of agriculture, beyond our own consumption, to a market for exchanging it for articles we cannot raise (and no more). These are the limits of manufacturing and commerce.[76]

And severe limits they were, for the Hamiltonian encouragement of these interests meant the endangerment of the very soul of Jefferson's republic.

Conclusion

Whatever the weaknesses of Jefferson's argument, and we have seen several of them, Jefferson's defense of one kind of property, land, and one way of life, agriculture, is essentially moral. Unlike many of the other Founders, Jefferson believed that the preservation of republican government depends primarily upon the character of the people. Agriculture was important because it helped to mold that character. To be sure, agriculture could also be defended on economic grounds, and the morality Jefferson expects husbandry to promote is not incompatible with trade and profit, or scientific progress. In these respects, it is worlds away from the classical republican ideal, but that ideal had been in retreat since Machiavelli, and Jefferson is by no means alone in his flawed attempt to make republican virtue safe for liberal democracy.

Notes

1. L. HARTZ, THE LIBERAL TRADITION IN AMERICA (1955); C. BECKER, THE DECLARATION OF INDEPENDENCE (1942); and more recently, Diamond, *Ethics and Politics: The American Way*, in THE MORAL FOUNDATIONS OF THE AMERICAN REPUBLIC 39-72 (1979); Berns, *The New Pursuit of Happiness*, THE PUBLIC INTEREST No. 86, 65-76 (1987). Those scholars who emphasize the difference between property and the pursuit of happiness include V. PARRINGTON, MAIN CURRENTS IN AMERICAN POLITICAL THOUGHT: THE COLONIAL MIND, 1620-1800 (1927); and R. MATTHEWS, THE RADICAL POLITICS OF THOMAS JEFFERSON (1984).

2. G. WILLS, INVENTING AMERICA (1978), especially Ch. 16.

3. Henry Home, Lord Kames (1696-1782), moral philosopher and jurist, was one of the leading figures in the Scottish Enlightenment.

4. By 'liberal,' I mean an individualistic view of man, in which the purpose of government is to protect men's individual natural rights. By 'republican,' I mean the belief that citizens should share in the responsibilities and privileges of self-government, and that such participation requires some degree of civic virtue. Although it would be difficult if not impossible to reconcile a strict definition of these terms, since one points in the direction of personal freedom and the other in the direction of public virtue, a looser understanding of the requirements of republicanism, i.e., civic spirit, is compatible with, and indeed essential to, modern liberal democracy.

5. T. HOBBES, THE LEVIATHAN Ch. 14 (Dutton ed. 1950). *See also* the discussion in M. WHITE, THE PHILOSOPHY OF THE AMERICAN REVOLUTION (1980), especially Ch. 5.

6. Indeed, for Jefferson, "all. . .natural rights may be abridged or modified. . .[by the people, either] by their own consent, or by the law of those who depute them, if they meet in the right of others. . . ." Opinion on the Residence Bill, July 15, 1790, in 5 THE WRITINGS OF THOMAS JEFFERSON 206 (P. Ford ed. 1895).

7. More difficult, though not impossible, for he could have argued that aristocratic property laws violated the inalienable right to the property of one's labor. But owing to the particular way in which he understood property, to be discussed below, he did not take this tack.

8. Primogeniture means the right of the eldest son to inherit the whole of his father's estate.

Entail means the restriction of the line of inheritance, so as to keep property within the family and prevent its being legally transferred.

9. In THE LIFE AND SELECTED WRITINGS OF THOMAS JEFFERSON 38 (A. Kock & W. Peden eds. 1944).

10. Jefferson to James Madison, October 28, 1785, in 8 THE PAPERS OF THOMAS JEFFERSON 682 (J. Boyd ed. 1950).

11. THE COMMONPLACE BOOK OF THOMAS JEFFERSON 5 (G. Chinard ed. 1926).

12. Jefferson to Isaac McPherson, August 13, 1813 in THOMAS JEFFERSON: WRITINGS 1291 (M. Peterson ed. 1984). Unless otherwise noted, all quotes in this section are from this letter.

13. Jefferson to Madison, September 6, 1789, in 15 Boyd, *supra* note 10, at 392-398.

14. Here I am drawing on distinctions elaborated by Jennifer R. Nedelsky in the opening chapter of "Property and the Framers of the United States Constitution" (dissertation, University of Chicago, 1979). Nedelsky does not deal with Jefferson except in passing, but I have found her comments on Madison and James Wilson to be helpful in understanding Jefferson's position.

15. Jefferson to Madison, Oct. 28, 1785, in 8 Boyd, *supra* note 10, at 681-683.

16. *See especially* Jefferson's argument in *A Summary View of the Rights of British America*, where he argues that the colonists' claim to American lands is absolute, and is based on labor. "America was conquered, and her settlements made, and firmly established, at the expense of individuals, and not of the British public. Their own blood was spilt in acquiring land for their settlement, their own fortunes expended in making that settlement effectual; for themselves they fought, for themselves they conquered, and for themselves alone they have the right to hold." Peterson, *supra* note 12, at 106.

17. Jefferson to DuPont de Nemours, April 24, 1816, in CORRESPONDENCE BETWEEN THOMAS JEFFERSON AND PIERRE SAMUEL DUPONT DE NE-MOURS, 1798-1817 (D. Malone ed. 1970).

18. Chinard, *supra* note 11, at 107-108.

19. Jefferson to James Madison, September 6, 1798, in 15 Boyd, *supra* note 10, at 396.

20. *Id.*

21. *See* C. WILTSE, THE JEFFERSONIAN TRADITION IN AMERICAN DEMOCRACY (1935); S. LYND, INTELLECTUAL ORIGINS OF AMERICAN RADICALISM (1968); and MATTHEWS, *supra* note 1.

22. Katz, *Jefferson and the Right to Property*, J. OF L. & ECON. 467 (1976).

23. Jefferson to Katherine Sprowle Douglas, July 5, 1785, in 8 Boyd, *supra* note 10, at 260.

24. Katz, *supra* note 22, at 469.

25. Jefferson to Madison, October 28, 1785, in 8 Boyd, *supra* note 10, at 682.

26. *Cf.* J. LOCKE, SECOND TREATISE OF GOVERNMENT Ch. 5. But whereas Locke regarded property as a natural right, Jefferson's view combined elements of both the natural rights and utilitarian arguments.

27. Jefferson sent a copy of the *Prospectus* to Joseph Milligan, April 6, 1816, 14 THE WRITINGS OF THOMAS JEFFERSON 456 (A. Lipscomb & A. Bergh eds. 1903). (emphasis in original)

28. Jefferson to DuPont de Nemours, April 15, 1811, in Malone, *supra* note 17, at 133. Jefferson's position here does not differ significantly from Hamilton's. In his "Report on Credit" (1790), Hamilton too recommended a tax on foreign luxuries.

29. *Id.*, Jefferson to Milligan, at 466. Although society has the right to fix the laws of inheritance, Jefferson believes these laws, like the laws of property in general, should conform to certain natural principles. He understands these natural principles to include both the equal affection that parents naturally feel for all their children as well as the equality of the children with respect to their "powers and wants." This is the

natural justification for equal inheritance.

It will be noticed that Jefferson's discussion of inheritance laws differs somewhat from his discussion of property rights in general. Whereas property rights must balance men's equal wants and their unequal faculties for acquiring property, no such inequality of faculty enters into the matter of *inherited* property or wealth. On the contrary, the inequality of natural talents, which plays an important role in the *acquisition* of property, is replaced by the equal affection of the parent for all his children.

30. *Id.* Also, Jefferson to John Adams, October 28, 1813, in Bergh, *supra* note 27, at 399.

31. At the same time he expressed the opposite opinion to John Jay, "we now have lands enough to employ an infinite number of people in their cultivation," Jefferson to John Jay, August 23, 1785, in 8 Boyd, *supra* note 10 at 426.

32. Jefferson to M. Jean Nicholas Demeunier, April 29, 1795, in Peterson, *supra* note 12, at 1027-1028.

33. Jefferson to Thomas Cooper, September 10, 1814, in 14 Bergh, *supra* note 27, at 183.

34. Jefferson to DuPont de Nemours, December 31, 1815, in Malone, *supra* note 17, at 173.

35. Jefferson to Thomas Cooper, September 10, 1814, in 14 Bergh, *supra* note 27, at 182.

36. *Id.*

37. *See* the important discussion of Madison's position in Nedelsky, *supra* note 14.

38. Jefferson to Samuel Kercheval, July 12, 1816, in 15 Bergh, *supra* note 27, at 39.

39. Jefferson to John Adams, October 28, 1813, 13 *id.* at 397.

40. Jefferson to Madison, September 6, 1789, *id.* at 396.

41. Jefferson to John Adams, October 28, 1813, *id.* at 397.

42. Jefferson to Samuel Kercheval, *id.*; Jefferson to John Taylor, May 28, 1816, in Peterson, *supra* note 12, at 1391-1395.

43. NOTES ON THE STATE OF VIRGINIA 119-120 (W. Peden ed. 1955).

44. Jefferson to John Holmes, April 22, 1820, in Peterson, *supra* note 12, at 1433-1435. Nevertheless, when Jefferson's efforts failed, he accepted the prevailing view. Jefferson to Jared Sparks, February 4, 1824, *id.* at 1484-1487.

45. Jefferson to Peter Carr, August 10, 1787; Jefferson to Thomas Law, June 13, 1814, in Peterson, *supra* note 12, at 902.

46. Jefferson to Joseph Cabell, February 2, 1816, in Peterson, *supra* note 12, at 1380.

47. Jefferson to Samuel Kercheval, July 12, 1816, in 15 Bergh, *supra* note 27, at 36.

48. Jefferson to John Taylor, May 28, 1816, in Peterson, *supra* note 12, at 1393.

49. *See* the discussion of James Wilson in Nedelsky, *supra* note 14.

50. NOTES, *supra* note 43, at 161.

51. Jefferson to Thomas Pleasants, May 8, 1786, in 9 Boyd, *supra* note 10, at 472-473.

52. Jefferson to James Currie, August 4, 1787, 11 *id.* at 682.

53. Jefferson to Archibald Stuart, January 25, 1786, in 9 *id.* at 218.

54. Jefferson to John Page, May 4, 1786, in Peterson, *supra* note 12, at 854.

55. Jefferson to Samuel Kercheval, July 12, 1816 in Peterson, *supra* note 12, at 1395-1403; Jefferson to John Taylor, May 28, 1816, *id.* at 1391-1395.

56. NOTES, *supra* note 43, at 164-165.

57. Compare these "virtues" with the qualities Hamilton expects commerce to promote, *e.g.*, in FEDERALIST No. 12 and the *Report of Manufactures*, SELECTED WRITINGS & SPEECHES OF ALEXANDER HAMILTON 277-318 (M. Frisch ed. 1985).

58. Jefferson to George Washington, August 14, 1787, in 7 Boyd, *supra* note 10, at 38.

59. Jefferson to John Jay, August 23, 1785, 8 *id.* at 426.

60. Jefferson to George Washington, August 14, 1787, 7 *id.* at 38.

61. D. MCCOY, THE ELUSIVE REPUBLIC: POLITICAL ECONOMY IN JEFFERSONIAN AMERICA 173*ff.* (1980); for the persistence of this theme through the Jacksonian era, *see* M. MEYERS, THE JACKSONIAN PERSUASION: POLITICS AND BELIEF (1957).

62. Jefferson to John Jay, August 23, 1785, in 8 Boyd, *supra* note 10, at 426.

63. PLATO, LAWS BK. II 704b (Cambridge ed. 1961); ARISTOTLE, THE POLITICS BK. VII, Ch. 6 (C. Lord trans. 1985); CICERO, ON THE COMMON-WEALTH BK. II (1929). *See also* the discussion of sailing and its relationship to republican virtue among the Greeks and Romans in MONTESQUIEU, THE SPIRIT OF THE LAWS BK. XXI, Ch. 13 (T. Nugent trans., 1949).

64. 14 PAPERS OF JAMES MADISON 244-246 (R. Rutland *et al.* eds. 1983).

65. MATTHEWS, *supra* note 1, at 43, 48. *See also* R. HOFSTADTER, THE AGE OF REFORM: FROM BRYAN TO F.D.R. (1955); and J. POCOCK, THE MACHIAVELLIAN MOMENT: FLORENTINE POLITICAL HISTORY AND THE ATLANTIC REPUBLICAN TRADITION Ch. 9 (1975).

66. Jefferson to G.K. van Hogendorp. October 13, 1785, in 8 Boyd, *supra* note 10, at 633.

67. Appleby, *Commercial Farming and the 'Agrarian Myth' in the Early Republic*, 68 JOURNAL OF AMERICAN HISTORY 833 (1982).

68. *Id.* at 836. So intent is Appleby on rooting out every vestige of republicanism from Jefferson's thought that she overlooks Jefferson's innovative synthesis of liberal and republican principles.

69. Jefferson to William Sampson, 1817, in 10 Ford, *supra* note 6, at 73.

70. Jefferson to Benjamin Austin, January 9, 1816, in 14 Bergh, *supra* note 27, at 390. In this respect, Jefferson does depart from Locke: *see* LOCKE, *supra* note 26, Ch. 5.

71. Bergh, *id.*

72. Jefferson to William Short, November 28, 1814, in 14 Bergh, *id.* at 214.

73. Jefferson to Henry Middleton, January 8, 1813, in 13 Bergh, *id.* at 203.

74. MCCOY, *supra* note 61, at Ch. 10; *see also* H. JAFFA, *The Virtue of a Nation of Cities*, in THE CONDITIONS OF FREEDOM 99 (1975).

75. Jefferson to DuPont de Nemours, April 15, 1811 in Malone, *supra* note 17, at 132; *but cf.* Jefferson to David Williams, November 14, 1803, in 10 Bergh, *supra* note 27, at 420. *Also see* the discussion in MCCOY, *id.* at 209*ff.*

76. Jefferson to Governor James Jay, April 7, 1809, in 12 Bergh, *id.* at 271. Also, to Thomas Leiper, January 21, 1809, *id.* at 236-271.

Republicanism, Commerce, and Private Rights: James Madison's Path to the Constitutional Convention of 1787

CHARLES F. HOBSON

From his debut in public life in 1776 to his death in 1836, James Madison was committed to establishing a republican political order in the United States. In his eyes the achievement of this goal was nothing less than the fulfillment of the purpose of the American Revolution. This commitment to republicanism forms the unifying theme of his statesmanship and his political writings. How this commitment led Madison to advocate a radical plan of constitutional reform in 1787 is the subject to be explored in this essay.

What did republicanism mean to Madison? In the ordinary sense it signified attachment to "popular" (a term he used synonymously with "republican") government. "We may define a republic to be...a government which derives all its powers directly or indirectly from the great body of the people; and is administered by persons holding their offices during pleasure, for a limited period, or during good behaviour," he wrote in *Federalist* No. 39, adding: "It is *essential* to such a government, that it be derived from the great body of the society, not from an inconsiderable proportion, or a favored class of it."[1]

Although his preoccupation with the dangers of majority factions is well documented, Madison always fully accepted the legitimacy of majority rule—"the fundamental principle of republican Government."[2] His reflections about that principle prompted him to search for means consistent with popular government to prevent its injurious consequences—to discover, in short, "a republican remedy for the diseases most incident to republican government."[3] A government that excluded the majority from power, he always insisted, was an aristocracy, not a republic. Thus, despite a tenacious belief in the necessity of property qualifications for voting, Madison was willing to sacrifice this preference to the larger ideal. He favored extending the suffrage so far as necessary to keep the government resting on the majority of the society—at least the white male portion of it.[4]

To the American revolutionaries, republicanism implied more than adherence to popular government. It was an all-encompassing ideology, a cluster of ideals, beliefs, assumptions, aspirations, and anxieties that shaped their understanding of human behavior and social development. In broadest terms, republican ideology explained the interrelationships among seemingly discrete phenomena; it linked the present with the past and the future. American republicans assumed in particular that there was a close relationship between government, economy, and society. Republican government was believed to require a republican social order and a system of political economy conducive to such an order.[5]

The unsettling dilemma that confronted Madison and his generation was the impermanence of republics, a condition that was abundantly confirmed by history. Everywhere they had been established, republics had followed a disturbingly familiar cycle, inexorably degenerating into corrupt oligarchies or into licentiousness and anarchy, followed by despotism.[6] Despite variations in the circumstances of the death of particular republics, the perceived cause of their mortality was the same in every case: the loss of "virtue" among the citizenry. Virtue meant above all unselfish devotion to the public good and included such related attributes as temperance, frugality, and industry. In the tradition of classical republicanism, virtue was regarded as the vital principle of republics, without which they ceased to exist. Virtue in turn could flourish only in a society of autonomous citizens, rendered independent through the possession of property, particularly landed property. The opposite of virtue was "corruption," a state characterized by dependence, either of citizens upon each other or upon the government. The prevalence of corruption signaled the destruction of the republic.[7]

Madison was most truly a republican revolutionary in acting on the belief that the United States might avoid the fate of past republics. At the same time, he repudiated the shallow optimism prevalent among many of his countrymen, who naively assumed that America was immune from the political and social evils of the Old World. While he fully recognized the peculiar advantages enjoyed by the new nation, and the unique opportunity it afforded to establish a republican order on a lasting foundation, no one understood better than he that America's experiment in republicanism was fraught with peril.

The danger was never more ominous than in the years immediately preceding the Convention of 1787, when the noble experiment seemed suddenly to have gone awry. The evidence was to be seen in the increasingly unrepublican behavior of the people since the end of the war. There is no more revealing illustration of Madison's fundamental assumptions than his attributing the decline of republican morality in large measure to faulty institutional arrangements. His faith in the efficacy of constitutional reform as a means of restoring and reinforcing republican habits in the people was the animating motive behind his statesmanship at the Philadelphia Convention in 1787.

Madison embraced the cause of constitutional reform in order to save the republican revolution. The failure of the Articles of Confederation in this regard first became evident in the inability of the government to solve the problems besetting American trade. In consequence of a growing perception that the decline of republican morality could be traced to commercial ills— severely restricted markets for agricultural exports, an excessive importation of manufactured goods from abroad, and an unfavorable balance of trade— Madison came to advocate placing the power to regulate commerce in the hands of the general government. The brief interval between the treaty of peace (1783) and the meeting of the Federal Convention also brought into view a more serious danger to republicanism: the alarming frequency with which the state governments violated the private rights of individuals and minorities, most commonly be enacting laws that made paper currency a legal tender in payment of debts, that allowed debtors to pay debts in specific property (at a valuation higher than the market price), and that postponed the payment of debts. This in turn exposed what Madison regarded as the radical defect of the Articles—the absence of any negative restraints upon the state governments.

I. Republicanism and Commercial Policy

Reforming the general government and promoting the republican revolution first became linked in Madison's mind in his reflections upon the problem of commerce. As Drew McCoy has demonstrated, Madison's ideas about commercial policy were designed to achieve the goals of a republican political economy, that is, to foster and preserve a social order based on agriculture and household manufactures. Only a society in which the mass of the citizens were owners and cultivators of the soil, and whose "essential consumption" could be supplied by themselves, Madison believed, would possess the virtue necessary to sustain republican government. "The class of citizens who provide at once their own food and their own raiment," he wrote, "may be viewed as the most truly independent and happy. They are more; they are the best basis of public liberty and the strongest bulwark of public safety."[8]

Madison and other votaries of republican government, however, had to contend with a disturbing predicament: that the inexorable process of social evolution seemed destined to destroy a republican social order. Eighteenth-century social science, notably the writings of such Scottish-school thinkers as Adam Ferguson, Lord Kames, John Millar, and Adam Smith, taught that society evolved through successive stages of development, from rude simplicity to civilized complexity. Agriculture represented a high stage of development, but it was only a prelude to the most advanced stage, the commercial society exemplified by modern Europe.[9] Advanced commercial civilization was characterized by increasing complexity of social organization, by extremes of wealth and indigence, by the prevalence of luxury, venality, and corruption, and by the erosion of virtue. Thus, progress in civilization would appear to threaten the very values embraced by enthusiasts of republican government.

In seeking to escape this dire prospect, Americans were forced to reject or modify many of the assumptions of classical republicanism. In particular, they discarded as patently unrealistic the ideal of a rude and simple republic of austere, selfless citizens devoted to the common good. Unlike classical republicanism, which regarded commerce as antithetical to public and private virtue, the American brand of republicanism accepted the civilizing function of commerce and its potential to promote rather than to destroy virtue. American republicans redefined virtue, departing from the classical notion that stressed self-denial and disinterested devotion to the public good, toward a more modern meaning that emphasized productive industry. If virtue meant only that citizens should be industrious and avoid idle dissipation, then commerce would become "the lifeblood of a republican system."[10]

Madison's political economy attempted to solve the problem inherent in accommodating commerce to republicanism, of how to give play to commercial forces yet ensure that America would remain predominantly agricultural. Somehow Madison hoped to prevent, or at least forestall, America's economic and social development into a more dangerous stage of large manufacturing establishments and the evils it brought in its train. America, Madison foresaw, had one great advantage over Europe in avoiding this unhappy fate, and that was its large vacant territory to the westward which could keep an ever expanding population profitably employed in agriculture for the indefinite future. Expansion through space could suspend America's development through time, though in the long run, Madison pessimistically concluded, the nation must inevitably turn to manufacturing. At the very least, however, wise policies could prevent America from reaching this stage prematurely.

Unless the settlers had a vent for their produce, there could be no incentive to westward migration. Implementing a republican political economy was thus directly tied to foreign trade policies that would expand the market for America's agricultural surpluses. While agreeing that free trade was the best means to encourage agriculture, Madison recognized that such a policy was unrealistic until the American states freed themselves from the British commercial monopoly. With the return of peace, Great Britain regained the market in its former colonies for imported manufactured goods and resumed control of America's export trade as well. At first reluctant to concede new powers to Congress to throw off British commercial shackles, he was soon forced by events to conclude that the advantages of a general authority over trade outweighed the disadvantages. No sooner had peace been declared than Great Britain, carrying out a threat to make the United States pay the price of political independence, closed its West Indies possessions to American shipping and restricted the market for American products in these islands. The need to counteract this British policy was uppermost in Madison's mind in persuading him that the power of regulating trade should be vested in Congress. Beginning in 1785 he actively worked to add this power to the Confederation.[11]

Madison expected Congress to exercise its power over trade by means of discriminatory tariff and tonnage duties aimed chiefly at Great Britain. Most

American produce was carried in British bottoms to British ports and then reexported to the continent. By cutting into the British reexport trade and by promoting direct trade between America and Europe, notably France, discrimination would serve to restore international commerce to its "natural" channels. It would also induce Britain to enter into recipocal arrangements and, most importantly, open its West Indies ports to American ships. The prospect of commercial warfare with Great Britain did not worry Madison, for he was persuaded that the former mother country was dependent on American produce, and that British manufactured goods, on the other hand, were either not essential or detrimental to American well-being—"either superfluities or poisons."[12] This conviction of British weakness and nascent American strength formed the core of a republican foreign policy that Madison pursued throughout his career.

Madison's commercial policy was one of temporary mercantilism, designed in the short run to build up American maritime strength and achieve commercial independence. This was a necessary prelude, he believed, to a system of free trade, to which he always professed adherence. "I own myself the friend to a very free system of commerce, and hold it as a truth," he remarked in a speech to the House of Representatives in 1789, "that if industry and labour are left to take their own course, they will generally be directed to those objects which are most productive, and this in a more certain and direct manner than the wisdom of the most enlightened legislature could point out." Commercial retaliation was an expedient to secure a desirable republican end. By opening up foreign markets for America's agricultural surpluses, this policy sought to preserve the nation's social youth, to postpone as long as possible the day when America must turn to large-scale manufacturing to employ its surplus population.[13]

II. The Insecurity of Private Rights

The more he grasped the importance of uniform commercial policies to achieve the goals of a republican political economy, the more willingly Madison accepted the need to reform the general government. If commerce pushed him in a nationalist direction, however, it was his increasing preoccupation with another problem—as disturbing as it was unexpected—that drove him to the point of scrapping the Articles of Confederation altogether in favor of reconstituting the government on an entirely new basis.

The problem in this instance arose not from the manifest impotence of the Confederation government, but from the excess of power, and its actual and potential abuse, in the hands of the several state governments. As the decade of the 1780s unfolded, Madison became progressively more alarmed by popular government as practiced in the states. Public laws, he unhappily observed, too often violated private rights, especially the rights of property, and in general promoted instability and injustice rather than the public good. Reflecting upon this problem, he perceived another advantage of a reformed general government. In addition to enhancing the external security of the union and creating the conditions for greater commercial prosperity, a strengthened central government might also promote internal tranquility within the several states. Both of these objectives, he now understood, were essential to the survival of republican government in the United States.

Before 1787 Madison betrayed few hints of his deep anxiety about the internal administration of the state governments. From that time, however, this concern was a recurring theme of his correspondence, speeches, and essays. A letter to George Washington in February 1787 contains his earliest recorded opinion that a plan for "a thorough reform of the existing system" must also "redress the ills experienced from our present establishments." By this time, if not earlier, he had begun to draft his memorandum, "Vices of the Political System of the United States," in which he devoted as much space to the instability of the state governments as he did to the weaknesses of the Confederation.[14]

At the Constitutional Convention Madison repeatedly urged the importance of attending to the problems emanating from the states. When early in the proceedings a fellow deputy remarked that the objects of the general government were limited to defense, foreign affairs, commerce, and revenue, the Virginian quickly added another: the need to provide "more effectually for the security of private rights, and the steady dispensation of Justice." He insisted that, "Interferences by the states with these, were evils which had more perhaps than any thing else produced this convention." He made the same point even more forcefully in a private letter to Jefferson soon after the convention:

> I am persuaded I do not err in saying that the evils issuing from these sources contributed more to that uneasiness which produced the Convention, and prepared the public mind for a general reform, than those which accrued to our national character and interest from the inadequacy of the confederation to its immediate objects.

To Madison, then, the Convention was called into being as much to reform the state governments as to amend the general government of the union.[15]

Madison reached this conclusion after three years of close observation of state politics. A seat in the Virginia House of Delegates, which he entered soon after leaving Congress in 1783, provided an excellent vantage point for this purpose. With the aid of a wide circle of well-placed correspondents, moreover, he was able to extend his observations beyond Virginia to embrace the whole continent. The information he collected, which he supplemented by his extensive reading in the field of politics and government, in time provided him with a diagnosis and a cure for the ills of the American political system.

In "Vices of the Political System," Madison defined the internal malady in terms of the "multiplicity," "mutability," and "injustice" of the laws of the states. In every state, he found that the number of laws far exceeded what was necessary for orderly government, and to that extent they were "a nuisance of the most pestilent kind." The multiplicity of the laws went hand in hand with their mutability, for much of the profusion of unnecessary legislation consisted of repealing or overturning previous acts. "We daily see laws repealed or superseded," he complained, "before any trial can have been made of their merits; and even before a knowledge of them can have reached the remoter districts within which they were to operate."[16]

Multiplying and changing laws had pernicious effects upon commerce. No plans could be made in consequence of a law for fear that it might be removed from the books at the next session. Uncertainty of the laws laying duties upon trade, or otherwise regulating it, was the bane of the merchant. The vicissitudes of the Virginia port bill were no doubt much on Madison's mind in his comments upon the mutability of the laws. First enacted in 1784, this law restricted Virginia's foreign trade to certain enumerated ports. The operation of the law was suspended for two years, so the necessary preparations for receiving this trade could be made at the designated ports. Madison doubted that such preparation would take place, for "so little ground is there for confidence in the stability of the Legislature that no preparations will ever be made in consequence of a preceding law." At succeeding sessions the bill was repeatedly threatened with repeal and finally underwent so many amendments as to lose much of its original force.[17]

Another evil effect of public instability, Madison repeatedly emphasized, was the creation of opportunities for sharpers and speculators to exploit. The mass of conflicting and inconsistent legislation, he wrote, became "jobs in the hands of enterprizing and influential speculators, and snares to the more industrious and less informed part of the community.... Every new regulation concerning commerce or revenue, or in any manner affecting the value of the different species of property presents a new harvest to those who watch the change and can trace its consequences; a harvest reared not by themselves but by the toils and cares of the great body of their fellow citizens." The "vicissitude of laws" allowed "sagacious men" to take advantage of "industrious farmers and tradesmen, who are ignorant of the means of making such advantages."[18]

More alarming than the multiplicity and mutability of the state laws, Madison believed, was their injustice, for this defect brought "into question the fundamental principle of republican Government, that the majority who rule in such Governments, are the safest Guardians both of public Good and of private rights." In discussing this point in "Vices of the Political System," Madison first advanced the proposition (later incorporated in his speeches and in the *Federalist*) that "all civilized societies are divided into different interests and factions, as they happen to be creditors or debtors—Rich or poor— husbandmen, merchants or manufacturers—members of different religious sects—followers of different political leaders—inhabitants of different districts—owners of different kinds of property &c &c." At the same time, he announced his proposed cure for the mischiefs of faction, namely, extending the sphere so that "the Society becomes broken into a greater variety of interests, of pursuits, of passions, which check each other, whilst those who may feel a common sentiment have less opportunity of communication and concert."[19]

The sobering lesson Madison learned from his experience as a Virginia legislator was that the acts of a republican government often reflected not the general good but the selfish interests of a majority faction. Unhappily, successful candidates for the legislature frequently had some private interest to pursue. Madison focused upon land speculators as the class from whom most of the unjust state laws originated. "It had often happened," he remarked at the Convention, "that men who had acquired landed property on credit, got into the Legislatures with a view of promoting an unjust protection agst. their Creditors." Unjust laws resulted not only when selfish legislators acted contrary to the wishes of their constituents, but also when they faithfully carried out the will of the majority. Legislation, indeed, had the aspect of a litigant being "a judge in his own cause" in cases involving private rights. "What are many of the most important acts of legislation," asked "Publius" in *Federalist* No. 10, "but so many judicial determinations, not indeed concerning the rights of single persons, but concerning the rights of large bodies of citizens; and what are the different classes of legislators, but advocates and parties to the causes they determine?" Justice or concern for the public good could never "hold the balance" when, for example, a majority faction of creditors or debtors passed a law concerning private debts.[20]

Such observations persuaded Madison that a mere patching up of the existing Confederation would not attack the fundamental "vices" of the system. A constitutional reform that failed to "make provision for private rights must be materially defective," he wrote.[21] The private rights he wished to safeguard were preeminently the rights of property, though not exclusively. The one episode that probably had more to do with provoking his reflections on majority rule concerned a threat to the rights of conscience, although even here economic interests were intertwined. While he was serving in the state legislature, a bill to levy a tax for the support of "Teachers of the Christian Religion" came perilously close to adoption. This incident deeply impressed upon him the precariousness of so-called unalienable rights in a society operating under the rule of the majority.[22]

Far more common in the 1780s were encroachments upon property rights effected through laws that authorized the government to issue paper money and make it a legal tender for public and private debts, that permitted citizens to offer specific property instead of money in payment of debts, that provided for the payment of debts in installments, and that postponed executions for debts. Madison's passionate denunciation of these laws, while congenial to the interests of creditors and holders of property, sprang from a much wider concern. What truly disturbed him was that the law-making process itself seemed to have degenerated into a scramble among competing factions seeking to promote their selfish interests. In his view, the legislation interfering with private contracts was not drawn with the larger public good in mind, that is, for the purpose of providing long-term relief of economic distress. Such laws, on the contrary, represented the successful efforts of a faction to exploit general economic unrest in order to escape the consequences of its own folly. While factionalism in Virginia, as in the other states, most commonly pitted debtors against creditors, Madison did not perceive this conflict as one between "poor" and "rich." His "debtors" typically were land speculators and consumers of foreign luxuries who overextended themselves.

It was this class of debtors, not the great body of the honest and industrious citizens, who stood to benefit from the laws Madison regarded as so obnoxious. His solicitude for the rights of property must be understood, then, as deriving from his larger interest in preserving the republican character of the people, and in making republican government serve the needs of justice and the public good. It was not simply that paper money and tender laws subverted property rights, but that they subverted republican virtue and morality.

This broader republican concern comes through most clearly in Madison's attitude toward paper money. Of all the state laws he condemned, none were as wicked, in his opinion, as those that authorized the government to issue paper currency and make it a lawful tender in payment of debts. The most common form of paper money in this period consisted of "bills of credit" that were redeemable in coin (specie) at some future date—in effect, they were governmental promissory notes. Since bills of credit were not redeemable on demand, their value almost invariably sank below that of specie—the degree of depreciation being the measure of the public's faith in the ability of the government to redeem the bills. During the war, Congress and the states had issued vast quantities of bills of credit, which eventually became worthless through depreciation. The war had scarcely ended, however, when the states turned once again to a paper medium. By 1786, there was "a general rage for paper money," seven states having adopted the expedient and others about to. Virginia managed to resist the contagion, but knowing the fickleness of the public good, Madison never ceased to worry about a recurrence of the fever. Within a few months of the Virginia legislature's overwhelming rejection of a paper emission, the forces in favor of it seemed to be gaining renewed support.[23]

Madison understood perfectly well that the agitation for paper arose from a general absence of circulating coin in America, which in turn was caused by an unfavorable balance of trade. "Another unhappy effect of a continuance of the present anarchy of our commerce," he wrote in March 1786, "will be a continuance of the unfavorable balance on it, which by draining us of our metals furnishes pretexts for the pernicious substitution of paper money, for indulgences to debtors, for postponements of taxes. In fact most of our political evils may be traced up to our commercial ones, as most of our moral may to our political."[24] Among the moral evils that had surfaced since the end of the war was an excessive consumption of foreign goods, particularly luxury items. In Virginia "a general ardor" for British goods particularly distressed Madison, for it threatened to perpetuate the prewar pattern of extensive indebtedness to British merchants. Chronic indebtedness, as he well knew, was incompatible with a healthy republican society. Diligence, industry, and frugality were required to prevent a "return to the Indolence & extravagance that was Our Character formerly." The "crowds of people" at the stores operated by Scotch merchants, however, gave "an unfavourable prospect" of Virginians' willingness to practice republican virtue. British merchants, Madison unhappily observed, would continue to extend credit to the limit, and this would be "far enough to perpetuate our difficulties unless the luxurious propensity of our people can be otherwise checked."[25]

Madison's aversion to paper money can only be properly understood in the broader context of his views on the relationship between the commercial crisis and the republican character of the people. His objections to paper were not merely that it was a panacea for the commercial and economic ills of the country. That it exacerbated rather than alleviated economic distress was clear enough. Although in the short run it supplied the want of circulating coin, paper currency ultimately increased the scarcity of specie. Money-lenders either refused to lend specie out for paper, or, if they did, the coin soon disappeared in payment for imported goods. But the real evil of this "fictitious money," Madison emphasized, was its corrupting effect on the morals of the people. It fed rather than cured "the spirit of extravagance" that caused the unfavorable balance of trade. Its fluctuating value made it a ripe instrument for speculation, diverting attention away from productive enterprise. It fostered luxury, destroyed confidence among individuals, enriched speculators, vitiated morals, punished good and rewarded evil, and in general served "to disgrace Republican Govts. in the eyes of mankind." While Madison was attending the Convention in Philadelphia, the paper currency of Pennsylvania suddenly ceased to circulate, apparently in consequence of refusals (or rumors of refuals) by local merchants to accept it. Some blamed this incident on a conspiracy by brokers to buy the paper at a much depreciated rate and then sell it to citizens who needed it for payment of taxes. "Nothing but evil springs from this imaginary money wherever it is tried," he commented, "and yet the appetite for it where it has not been tried, continues to be felt."[26]

III. Toward the Constitution

The erratic policies of the state governments, their increasing predispositon to trample upon private rights, portended, so it seemed to Madison, the imminent collapse of the republican experiment in America. On the eve of the

Convention he was particularly concerned that the widespread political and social malaise would make other solutions—monarchy or partition into separate confederacies—more attractive than republicanism.[27] Hence the sense of impending crisis that pervades his correspondence in the winter and spring of 1787. However, the fundamental conclusion he drew from the depressing spectacle of state politics was one of optimism rather than despair. It was not that the people had lost their virtue and thus their capacity to sustain republican government, rather, their governments were not properly constructed to bring forth virtuous behavior. Madison's remedy for the defects of the existing system reflected his abiding conviction that there was an essential relation between the structure of a government and the character of the people.

The key insight that Madison derived from his reflections on the behavior of the state legislatures was that factions were endemic to republics, and that the danger of a faction becoming a majority and carrying out its interested designs was greater in smaller rather than larger jurisdictions. Extending the sphere of the republic brought "in a greater variety of parties and interests," making "it less probable that a majority of the whole will have a common motive to invade the rights of other citizens."[28] This startling observation led Madison to overturn the conventional wisdom (put forward by Montesquieu and other writers) that republics were suitable only for small territories. The instability that had always plagued republics was now seen to be directly related to their narrow extent. Did this insight suddenly crystallize from a reading of David Hume? Or did the Scotsman's writings merely confirm what the Virginian discovered independently through his direct experience with post-Revolutionary state politics?[29] Whatever its source, Madison's theory did provide a persuasive explanation for the instability of the state legislatures and for their disposition to sacrifice the private rights of individuals and minorities.

In this regard, the *relative* stability of Virginia, the largest and most populous of the American states, may have suggested to Madison the moderating effects of an enlarged jurisdiction. Virginia, to be sure, was by no means immune from factionalism, yet its legislature did avoid committing the worst evils. At Madison's final session as a member of the House of Delegates in the fall of 1786, that body held firm on paper money and rejected various other expedients favoring the interests of debtors.[30] The previous year it had struck a blow for religious liberty by defeating a bill to levy a tax for the support of Christian ministers, and then enacting Thomas Jefferson's celebrated statute for religious freedom, which brought about the separation of church and state in Virginia. This episode taught Madison that religious liberty arose from "that multiplicity of sects, which pervades America." In Virginia there was a healthy competition for adherents among Episcopalians, Methodists, Presbyterians, and Baptists. Where such diversity existed, there could not "be a majority of any one sect to oppress and persecute the rest."[31] These observations also applied to the problem of political factions.

If Virginia seemed to demonstrate a connection between moderation and largeness of extent, Rhode Island, the smallest state, was the scene of the most virulent factional politics of the 1780s. The triumph of a paper-money faction in that state in 1786 was accompanied by political and economic upheaval as a result of the government's attempt to coerce merchants and creditors to accept its paper currency. The next year it refused to send deputies to the Convention. "Nothing can exceed the wickedness and folly which continue to reign there," wrote Madison. "All sense of Character as well as of Right is obliterated." Writing as "Publius," Madison used Rhode Island to illustrate his theory of factions: "It can be little doubted, that if the state of Rhode-Island was separated from the confederacy, and left to itself, the insecurity of rights under the popular form of government within such narrow limits, would be displayed by such reiterated oppressions of factious majorities, that some power altogether independent of the people would soon be called for by the voice of the very factions whose misrule had proved the necessity of it."[32]

Madison's "republican remedy for the diseases most incident to republican government" was an extended national republic superimposed on the existing system of state republics. Vested with new positive powers of taxation and the regulation of trade, the national government could deal more effectively and economically with such problems as public credit and the unfavorable balance of trade. A clearer division of responsibility between the two levels of government would promote internal tranquility. As Madison remarked, "When general powers will be vested in the general government, there will be less of the mutability which is seen in the legislation of the states. The consequence will be a great saving of expence and time."[33]

The truly radical nature of Madison's reform lay in his means of controlling the "centrifugal tendency of the States," which otherwise must "continually fly out of their proper orbits and destroy the order & harmony of the political System." No other idea Madison put forward at the Convention so nearly captures the essence of his constitutional thinking as his proposal to give the national government a power to "negative," or veto, state laws "in all cases whatsoever."[34] The negative was intended to effect a radical restructuring of the relationship between the state and national governments. Instead of states forming the constituent elements of the national government, as under the Articles of Confederation and to a partial degree under the present Constitution, the national government armed with this veto power would become an integral part of the state governments. As Madison explained, the national legislature would be "an essential branch of the State Legislatures," which, accordingly, could pass no operative act without the former's approval.[35]

In no other way does Madison appear more in the guise of a nationalist, even a consolidating one, than in his advocacy of the negative on state laws. Yet he indignantly objected to suggestions or insinuations that consolidation was his object.[36] Writing to Jefferson shortly after the Convention adjourned, Madison identified five shades of opinion on the question of the division of power between the general and state governments, listing them in descending order of degrees of consolidationist sentiment: "A few contended for an entire abolition of the states; some for indefinite power of Legislation in the Congress, with a negative on the laws of the States: some for such a power without a negative: some for a limited power of legislation, with such a negative: the majority finally for a limited power without the negative."[37] He himself belonged to the fourth group, those that favored limited legislative power and the negative.

Far from being a consolidating device—a means of reducing the states to counties of one great republic—the negative on state laws was an attempt to find a "middle ground" between "an individual independence of the States" and "a consolidation of the States into one simple republic." Madison perceived that the crucial task of the Convention was to find a way to keep the state governments within proper bounds, that is, to turn them into truly limited governments. Left to themselves they were virtually unlimited in the extent of their powers; their constitutions and bills of rights, experience had shown, were ineffectual barriers to the designs of interested majorities. The negative, which he invariably described as a "defensive" expedient, "the least possible abridgement of the State Sovereignties," presupposed that the states would continue to play an important role as political societies, retaining the great mass of the ordinary powers of government.[38] Through its operation, the state governments, no less than the national government, would feel the moderating effects of the extended republic.

Conclusion

Madison's perception of the crisis of the 1780s led him to seek a nationalist solution at Philadelphia in 1787. Only in a qualified sense, however, can he be called a nationalist. He is more accurately described as a "structural" nationalist, that is, he endorsed the idea of a government that was "national" (operating directly on the people) rather than "federal" (operating on states). It was never his intention to effect a substantial transfer of governing powers from the states to the nation.[39] The positive powers of the new national government, as he conceived them, would not significantly differ in scope from those of the Confederation government. Aside from such traditional and legitimate national concerns as defense and foreign affairs, the one area in which Madison foresaw an active and positive role for the national government was in the adoption of an economic policy to ensure that America would remain a nation of industrious and productive cultivators of the soil. Such a policy was to be effected not by direct intervention, but indirectly, by means of a judicious use of the power to regulate trade.

If a unified commercial policy had been his only goal in 1787, Madison may well have been content with amending the Articles by adding the regulation of trade to the powers of Congress. By then, however, he had concluded that the existing constitutional framework was not merely inadequate but positively injurious to the republican cause in America. Patchwork reform would not address the fundamental vice of the existing system, the one that posed the greatest danger to the survival of republicanism, that is, the rampant factionalism of the state governments, their constant interferences with contracts, and their encroachments on private rights. The novelty and originality of Madison's plan lay in its vision of a reconstituted national government, republican in form, as the cure for the chronic instability of state politics, and as a bulwark for the protection of private rights. To be sure, a reorganized and restructured national government, acting directly on individual citizens rather than through the states, would be able to exercise its positive powers more effectively. But for Madison the chief advantage of a reformed national government was its negative capacity to prevent the abuse of power in the states, "to break and control the violence of faction." It would stand as a steadying counterweight to the state republics, an "anchor against the fluctuations which threaten the shipwreck to our liberty."[40] In both its positive and negative aspects, national power was a means to an end, subservient to the larger aim of establishing a durable republican regime in the United States.

Notes

1. THE FEDERALIST No. 39, in 10 THE PAPERS OF JAMES MADISON 377 (W. Hutchinson, R. Rutland et al. eds. 1962-   ). Hereafter cited as MADISON PAPERS.

2. Vices of the Political System of the United States, in 9 id. at 354.

3. THE FEDERALIST No. 10, 10 id. at 269-270.

4. For Madison's views on suffrage and property qualifications, see Madison to Caleb Wallace, Aug. 23, 1785; speech, Aug. 7, 1787; Observations on Jefferson's Draft of a Constitution for Virginia [Oct. 15, 1788], in 8 MADISON PAPERS at 353-354; 10 id. at 138-140; 11 id. at 287-288. And, Note on Speech of Aug. 7, 1787 [ca. 1821]; Note during Convention of 1829, in THE MIND OF THE FOUNDER: SOURCES OF THE POLITICAL THOUGHT OF JAMES MADISON 502-509, 512-516 (M. Meyers ed. 1973). And, Adair, ed., James Madison's Autobiography, 3rd ser., 2 WILLIAM AND MARY QUARTERLY 208-209 (1945).

5. D. MCCOY, THE ELUSIVE REPUBLIC: POLITICAL ECONOMY IN JEFFERSONIAN AMERICA 5-8 (1980).

6. For a useful summary of the concept of cyclical decay in republican thought, see F. MCDONALD, NOVUS ORDO SECLORUM: THE INTELLECTUAL ORIGINS OF THE CONSTITUTION 70-71 (1985).

7. POCOCK, Civic Humanism and Its Role in Anglo-American Thought, in POLITICS, LANGUAGE, AND TIME: ESSAYS ON POLITICAL THOUGHT AND HISTORY 80-103 (1973).

8. McCoy, Republicanism and American Foreign Policy, 3rd ser., 31 WILLIAM AND MARY QUARTERLY 633-646 (1974); Madison, Republican Distribution of Citizens, in MEYERS, supra note 4, at 242.

9. MCCOY, *supra* note 5, at 18-20; MCDONALD, *supra* note 6, at 132-135.

10. MCCOY, *supra* note 5 at 77. Much of what follows is drawn from his work.

11. Madison to Edmund Randolph, May 20, 1783; Madison to James Monroe, Aug. 7, 1785; Draft of Resolutions on Foreign Trade, *ca.* Nov. 12, 1785; Notes for Debate on Commercial Regulations by Congress, Nov. 30-Dec. 1, 1785, in 7 MADISON PAPERS at 59-61; 8 *id.* at 333-336, 409-410, 431-432.

12. Madison to Jefferson, June 30, 1789, 12 *id.* at 268-270.

13. Speech, April 9, 1789, *id.* at 71; MCCOY, *supra* note 5, at 143-145.

14. 9 MADISON PAPERS, at 286, 348-357.

15. Speech, June 6, 1787; Madison to Jefferson, Oct. 24, 1787, 10 *id.* at 32, 212.

16. 9 *id.* at 353-354.

17. McCoy, *The Virginia Port Bill of 1784,* 83 VIRGINIA MAGAZINE OF HISTORY AND BIOGRAPHY 288-303 (1975); Madison to Monroe, May 13, 1786, 9 MADISON PAPERS, at 55.

18. THE FEDERALIST Nos. 44, 62; Speech, June 11, 1788, in 10 MADISON PAPERS, at 421-422, 539-540; 11 *id.* at 118.

19. *Vices of the Political System,* 9 *id.* at 354-357.

20. Speech, July 26, 1787; THE FEDERALIST No. 10, 10 *id.* at 117, 266.

21. Madison to Jefferson, Oct. 24, 1787, 10 *id.* at 212.

22. Madison to Jefferson, Jan. 9, 1785; *Memorial and Remonstrance,* June 20, 1785, 8 *id.* at 229, 299.

23. Madison to Jefferson, Aug. 12, 1786; Madison to Edmund Pendleton, Apr. 22, 1787, 9 *id.* at 94-95, 396.

24. Madison to Jefferson, Mar. 18, 1786, 8 *id.* at 502.

25. Randolph to Madison, May 24, 1783; Pendleton to Madison, May 26 and June 16, 1783; Madison to Jefferson, Mar. 18, 1786, 7 *id.* at 73, 81, 150; 8 *id.* at 502.

26. Madison to Jefferson, Aug. 12, 1786; Notes for Speech Opposing Paper Money, *ca.* Nov. 1, 1786; Madison to Jefferson, July 18, 1787, 9 *id.* at 94-95, 158-159; 10 *id.* at 105-106.

27. Madison to Washington, Feb. 21, 1787; Notes on Debates, Feb. 21, 1787; Madison to Randolph, Feb. 25, 1787, 9 *id.* at 286, 291-292, 299.

28. THE FEDERALIST No. 10, 10 *id.* at 269.

29. *See* Adair, *'That Politics May be Reduced to a Science': David Hume, James Madison, and the Tenth Federalist,* in FAME AND THE FOUNDING FATHERS 93-106 (T. Colbourn ed. 1974); Draper, *Hume and Madison,* 58 ENCOUNTER 34-47 (1982); Coniff, *The Enlightenment in American Political Thought: A Study of the Origins of Madison's Federalist No. 10,* 8 POLITICAL THEORY 381-402 (1980).

30. Madison to Jefferson, Dec. 4, 1786; Madison to Washington, Dec. 7, 1786; Madison to James Madison, Sr., Dec. 12, 1786; Madison to Washington, Dec. 24, 1786, in 9 MADISON PAPERS at 189, 200, 205, 224-225.

31. Speech, June 12, 1788, 11 *id.* at 130.

32. Madison to Jefferson, Aug. 12, 1786; Madison to Randolph, Apr. 2, 1787; THE FEDERALIST No. 51, 9 *id.* at 95, 362; 10 *id.* at 479.

33. Speech, June 11, 1788, 11 *id.* at 118.

34. Speech, June 8, 1787, 10 *id.* at 41. On the negative, *see* Hobson, *The Negative on State Laws: James Madison, the Constitution, and the Crisis of Republican Government,* 36 WILLIAM AND MARY QUARTERLY 215-235 (1979).

35. Speech, June 28, 1787, 10 MADISON PAPERS at 80.

36. See his exchange with George Mason at the Virginia ratifying convention in 3 THE DEBATES IN THE SEVERAL STATE CONVENTIONS ON THE ADOPTION OF THE FEDERAL CONSTITUTION 522 (J. Elliot ed. 1863).

37. Madison to Jefferson, Oct. 24, 1787, 10 MADISON PAPERS at 209.

38. Madison to Edmund Randolph, Apr. 8, 1787, 9 *id.* at 369-370.

39. Banning, *The Practicable Sphere of a Republic: James Madison, the Constitution, and the Emergence of Revolutionary Federalism,* in BEYOND CONFEDERATION: ORIGINS OF THE CONSTITUTION AND AMERICAN NATIONAL IDENTITY 169-170 (R. Beeman, S. Botein, E. Carter II eds. 1987).

40. THE FEDERALIST No. 10; Madison to Washington, Dec. 14, 1787; 10 *id.* at 263-264, 327.

One People As to Commercial Objects
BERNARD H. SIEGAN

Capitalism is the economic system in which the investment in and ownership of the means of production, distribution, and exchange of materials is made and maintained chiefly by private individuals or corporations.[1] To survive, this system must function mainly on its own, separated and insulated from the government. Certain liberties must be protected: first, the freedom of the person from molestation by government; second, the freedom to acquire, use, and dispose of property; third, the freedom to produce and distribute goods and services; and fourth, the freedom to enjoy a stable currency. The United States Constitution together with the first ten amendments, I shall argue, substantially provide this kind of protective environment for capitalism.

Capitalism has firm roots in the original Constitution. The Framers sought to create a common market within the confines of the thirteen states, "to make us, in a great measure, one people as to commercial objects."[2] "If there was any one object riding over every other in the adoption of the Constitution, it was to keep the commercial intercouse among the States free from all invidious and partial restraints."[3] Thus, the document specifically bars the states from levying "Imposts or Duties on Imports or Exports, except what may be absolutely necessary for executing its inspection laws."[4]

More generally, the fundamental law protects the commercial market from all but essential regulation or subsidy either at the state or federal levels, for such laws would also be adverse to the pursuit of commerce. In this paper, I discuss the relevant constitutional provisions safeguarding investment, ownership, and exchange, beginning with those relating to the states and concluding with those concerning the federal government.[5]

To understand these provisions, it is important to recognize that they were drafted by individuals who were committed to protecting the right of private property, which comprehended both tangible interests and contracts. The right to property—the freedom to acquire, use and dispose of it—was a major concern of the time. Thus, Gouverneur Morris of Pennsylvania, one of the more influential Framers, encountered little controversy at the Constitutional Convention in describing his concern for private ownership in Lockean terms:

Life and liberty are generally said to be of more value, than property. An
accurate view of the matter would nevertheless prove that property was the
main object of Society. The savage state was more favorable to liberty than the
Civilized; and sufficiently so to life. It was preferred by all men who had not
acquired a taste for property; it was only renounced for the sake of property
which could be secured by the restraints of regulated government.[6]

James Madison was of similar mind. During the Convention, he said that in
civilized communities the preservation of property, as well as of personal rights,
was an essential object of the law. Later, he wrote that the protection of the
"faculties of men, from which the rights of property originate," is the first
object of government.[7] Madison voiced apprehensions about what would occur
in the absence of such protections:

An increase of population will of necessity increase the proportion of those who
will labour under all the hardships of life and secretly sigh for a more equal
distribution of its blessings. These may in time outnumber those who are placed
above the feelings of indigence. According to the equal laws of suffrage, the
power will slide into the hands of the former. No agrarian attempts have yet
been made in this Country but symptoms of a leveling spirit. . .have sufficiently
appeared in certain quarters to give notice of a future danger.[8]

Securing property was not only important in preserving personal freedom, but
also for its benefit to society as a whole:

I own myself the friend to a very free system of commerce, and hold it as a truth
that if industry and labour are left to their own course, they will generally be
directed to those objects which are the most productive, and this in a more
certain and direct manner than the wisdom of the most enlightened legislature
could point out.[9]

At the Convention, other delegates emphasized property rights. Rufus
King of Massachusetts and John Rutledge of South Carolina agreed with Morris
and Madison that the protection of property was the primary or principal
object of society. Pierce Butler of South Carolina contended that "property was
the only just measure of representation." William R. Doyle of North Carolina,
Abraham Baldwin of Georgia, and Charles Pinckney of South Carolina thought
the Senate should represent property or wealth. George Mason of Virginia
stated that an important objective in constituting a Senate was to secure the
right of property. John Dickinson of Delaware considered freeholders as the
best guarantors of society.[10]

Consistent with such thinking, the Framers confined the economic
powers of the states, and provided the newly created central government with
only limited economic authority. Unlike the states, which continued to
maintain those powers not restrained, the Constitution accorded the national

government only those powers expressly enumerated or clearly implied. On this basis, the national and state governments together possessed a relatively small amount of control over the economy.

I. Limitations on State Economic Powers

There is little question that the Framers of the original Constitution sought to curtail the economic powers of the states. The economic barriers the states erected against each other were a major source of discontent with the existing Confederation. Although they are not as well documented, the regulatory abuses of the state legislatures probably contributed at least as much to the movement for a new plan of government.

Following the revolutionary period, the economies in some states deteriorated markedly, leading to "an ignoble array of legislative schemes for the defeat of creditors and invasion of contractual relations."[11] Some states passed "stay laws," extending the due date of notes, and "installments laws," allowing debtors to pay their obligations in installments after they had fallen due. Some states were reluctant to pass legislation allowing the British to collect debts owed by Americans, payment of which had been suspended during the Revolutionary War. According to Alexander Hamilton, "creditors had been ruined, or in a very extensive degree, much injured, confidence in pecuniary transactions had been destroyed, and the springs of industry had been proportionately relaxed" because of the failure of the states to safeguard commercial rights.[12]

The experience of South Carolina exemplifies the problems creditors faced. In 1782, the state passed a stay law, and in 1785, a law terminating suits for debts. When the latter act expired, another act was passed allowing debts to be paid in installments. The state also issued public obligations that effectively increased the money supply.[13]

Those interested in preserving and expanding a national commercial market viewed events in Rhode Island and Massachusetts as ominous. The Rhode Island Assembly provided that if a creditor refused to accept state paper currency—which it furnished abundantly—at par, the debtor could discharge his debts simply by depositing the scrip with a local judge. As a result, some creditors were pursued by debtors eager to tender depreciated paper for use for full value of their debts. "Rather than sell for worthless paper, merchants shut up shop, hid their stock, or loaded it on a vessel and escaped to New York or the West Indies."[14]

Massachusetts was the site of a relatively bloodless and unsuccessful insurrection by poor farmers under the leadership of Captain Daniel Shays. They protested both their high taxes and debts. The objective of Shays's Rebellion was to prevent courts from sitting, and thereby to stop the collection of unpaid debts. Due to a poor economy, judgments for overdue taxes or other debts could in most cases be satisfied only by taking a farmer's land, cattle, and personal property. The rebellion was put down by the state's armed forces without help from the Confederation.[15]

These experiences alarmed many about the economic viability and stability of the states, if they remained largely autonomous. According to Madison, laws infringing contractual obligations "contributed more to that uneasiness which produced the convention...than those [frustrations] which accrued...from the inadequacy of the Confederation to its immediate objects."[16] To the same effect, John Marshall observed during the ratification debates that the Confederation took away "the incitements to industry by rendering property insecure and unprotected." The Constitution, on the contrary, Marshall explained, "will promote and encourage industry."[17]

During the Convention, Madison said that the Union "must provide more effectively for the security of private rights, and the steady dispensation of justice." He asked: "Was it to be supposed that republican liberty could long exist under the abuses of it, practised in [some of] the states?"[18] Edmund Randolph, who later became the first attorney general, proposed the Virginia plan—a plan that would give Congress power to overrule the state legislatures. He contended that the Virginia plan would overcome the "turbulence and follies of democracy" prevalent in the states. Gouverneur Morris likewise found in every state legislative department "excesses against personal liberty, private property, and personal safety."[19]

Whoever was in financial distress, it seemed (whether the small farmer, large planter, or merchant), sought and frequently obtained political aid to overcome his problems. Some used the process to acquire greater riches. Such a political climate was not conducive to investment or other financial undertakings. Understandably, as Albert Beveridge, John Marshall's biographer, concluded, the "determination of commercial and financial interests to get some plan adopted under which business could be transacted, was the most effective force that brought about [the Philadelphia Convention]."[20]

To overcome such obstructions to economic enterprise, Article I, Section 10, Subsection 1 of the Constitution contains substantial protection for owners and entrepreneurs. It reads:

> No State shall enter into any Treaty, Alliance, or Confederation; grant Letters of Marque and Reprisal; coin Money; emit Bills of Credit; make any Thing but gold and silver Coin a Tender in Payment of Debts; pass any Bill of Attainder, ex post facto law, or Law impairing the Obligation of Contracts, or grant any Title of Nobility.

Let us consider separately the meaning and impact of these provisions.

Prohibition of Bills of Attainder and Ex Post Facto Laws

Subsection 1 thus limits the discretionary powers of state authorities to either harm or favor certain owners or entrepreneurs. For commercial enterprise to function effectively, state legislatures must not have the power to penalize certain people by passing bills of attainder or ex post facto laws.* (The Constitution also forbids Congress from passing bills of attainder and ex post facto laws.) Such laws enable lawmakers to deprive people of the constitutional protections generally afforded those charged with a crime. Legislatures which have the power to pass these laws have enormous discretion over the lives and liberty of their constituents. They can harm people whom they dislike or whose practices they disfavor. How many of us are courageous enough to pursue activites or policies that may lead to the loss of life, liberty or property? Subsection 1 also prohibits a state from bestowing favors by granting any person a Letter of Marque and Reprisal or a Title of Nobility.[21]

In my view, besides protecting individuals from unjust punishment, the prohibiton of the passage of ex post facto laws also protects them from the deprivation of property and other economic interests. At the time the Constitution was framed and ratified, the term ex post facto was applied both to retroactive penal and civil laws. Many newspapers and courts of the period considered stay and installment statutes as ex post facto laws;[22] similarly, some congressmen (perhaps most) used the term ex post facto to include civil laws that retroactively deprived people of economic interests.[23] This broad definition of the term is supported in later years by the commentaries of three leading constitutional authorities: Justice Joseph Story, Chancellor James Kent, and Justice Thomas Cooley among others.[24] However, in 1798, in *Calder v. Bull*[25] the Supreme Court refused to define the ex post facto clauses this broadly. The Court interpreted ex post facto as applicable only to penal laws. Although accounts of the Constitutional Convention do not disclose the exact meaning the Framers ascribed to the term, they do not negate the position that the ex post facto clauses applied to all retroactive laws, civil as well as criminal.

A law operates retroactively if it eliminates tangible interests or personal rights possessed or obtained under existing laws. Thus, if someone purchases a tract of land at a time when the law permits it to be developed for a particular use, and a subsequent statute prohibits this use, the later statute retroactively eliminates an interest or a right the owner had legitimately acquired. A recent opinion by the Court of Appeals for the District of Columbia observes:

> Retroactive impositions of civil liability are conceptually of a piece with *ex post facto* criminal laws. Instead of packing the actor off to jail, the legislature, with the judiciary's cooperation, more modestly requires the payment of sums of money and the reordering of affairs.[26]

---

*Briefly, a bill of attainder is a legislative act that inflicts punishment without a judicial trial. Originally the term was limited to capital punishment. An ex post facto law makes criminal an action done before the law was enacted. The Constitution forbids both Congress and the states from passing these types of laws.

After reviewing commentaries and decisions of the framing period, I have concluded that contemporary opinion viewed retroactive economic impositions as oppressive and contrary to the natural law, something from which all people should be immune.[27] The purchaser obviously would never have made the commitment had he been aware of the legislature's future action. Lawmakers act oppressively when they change the rules of the game after the play has commenced. It is probable that most Framers had this perspective.

Blackstone, among other early commentators, asserted that "[a]ll laws should be... made to commence in *futuro*, and [those affected] should be notified before their commencement."[28] About a century earlier, Lord Edward Coke wrote to the same effect, declaring that "no Act of Parliament should be construed in such a way as to do a man any damage when he was free from wrong." He maintained that one was effectively penalized if one was affected disadvantageously by the retroactive invocation of a law.[29]

Application of the Constitution's ex post facto provisions to property laws would strengthen personal rights by curtailing regulatory injustices. However, the ex post facto provision would not affect the powers of the government to invoke eminent domain and forbid uses of property injurious to public health and safety. These powers have long been regarded as inherent and necessary attributes of government, essential to its independent existence.[30]

The Contracts Clause and the Freedom of Contract

One of the strongest statements supporting the view that the Constitution was designed to establish a capitalist economy is proffered by Chief Justice John Marshall in his dissenting opinion in *Ogden v. Saunders*.[31] That case concerned the interpretation of the contracts clause. While he was not a member of the Constitutional Convention, Marshall was a delegate to the Virginia ratification convention, where he played an important role in explaining the meaning of the document. In *Ogden*, Marshall asserted that the clause prohibits states from regulating economic activity inasmuch as such regulation limits freedom of contract, which the provision guarantees. The clause, he explains, implements the natural law of contractual freedom: "individuals do not derive from government their right to contract, but bring that right with them into society; that obligation is not conferred on contracts by positive law, but is intrinsic, and is conferred by all of the parties."[32] He went on to say:

> This results from the right which every man retains, to acquire property, to dispose of that property according to his own judgment, and to pledge himself for a future act. These rights are not given by society, but are brought into it. The right of coercion is necessarily surrendered to government, and this surrender imposes on government the correlative duty of furnishing a remedy. The right to regulate contracts, to prescribe rules by which they shall be evidenced, to prohibit such as may be deemed mischievous, is unquestionable,

and has been universally exercised. So far as this power has restrained the original right of individuals to bind themselves by contract, it is restrained; but beyond these actual restraints, the original power remains unimpaired. This reasoning is, undoubtedly, much strengthened by the authority of those writers on natural and national law, whose opinions have been viewed with profound respect by the wisest men of the present, and of past ages.[33]

Thus, according to the chief justice, the contracts clause generally secures to private parties the liberty to contract freely without the state's interference. Marshall's analysis of the contracts clause was part of the only dissent he wrote on a constitutional issue during the thirty-four years that he served on the court. Justice Joseph Story, one of the nation's ablest jurists and legal commentators, concurred in Marshall's dissent (along with Justice Duval).[34]

The case in question involved a suit for payment of a note. The defendant pleaded that he had been discharged from his obligations as an insolvent debtor under the New York bankruptcy law. The question was whether the New York bankruptcy law, which had been in effect prior to the time that the note became legally binding, was unconstitutional. By a 4-3 vote, the Supreme Court replied in the negative, and held that application of the bankruptcy statute to discharge the debtor did not violate the contracts clause.

All of the justices agreed that a retroactive law limiting the obligation of the debtor would be a violation of the contracts clause, but this case concerned a law already in existence at the time the obligation became binding. Unfortunately, the bankruptcy question clouded the Court's interpretation of the provision. Commentators believe the majority's decision was brought about by a quarter of a century of failure to obtain a national bankruptcy law.[35] Marshall's opinion would have limited the availability of the bankruptcy option at the state level, and the majority rejected this outcome.

The chief justice believed that the contracts clause prohibited a state from changing the terms of a contract freely entered into by the parties. Accordingly, if a law limits the written understanding of the parties, it impairs their contractual obligation, whether the law is enacted before or after the contract is formed.

> If the enactment of the legislature becomes a condition of the contract, because it is an enactment, then it is a high prerogative, indeed, to decide, that one enactment shall enter the contract, while another, proceeding from the same authority, shall be excluded from it.[36]

Marshall contended that New York's bankruptcy law, although passed before the execution of the note, was not part of the contract and, therefore, changed the understanding of the parties, impairing their contractual obligation.

Had Marshall's opinion prevailed, the states would have had little authority to regulate economic activity. Laws that curtail the right to contract for the production and distribution of goods and services would have been unconstitutional. According to Marshall, our union was intended to create one commercial market; "so far as respects the intercommunication of individuals, the lines of separation between states are, in many respects, obliterated." He added:

> We cannot look back to the history of the times when the august spectacle was exhibited, of the assemblage of a whole people, by their representatives, in convention, in order to unite thirteen independent sovereignties under one government, so far as might be necessary for the purposes of union, without being sensible of the great importance which was at that time attached to the tenth section of the first article. The power of changing the relative situation of debtor and creditor, of interfering with contracts, a power which comes home to every man, touches the interest of all, and controls the conduct of every individual in those things which he supposes to be proper for his own exclusive management, had been used to such an excess by the state legislatures, as to break in upon the ordinary intercourse of society, and destroy all confidence between man and man. This mischief had become so great, so alarming, as not only to impair commercial intercourse, and threaten the existence of credit, but to sap the morals of the people, and destroy the sanctity of private faith. To guard against the continuance of the evil, was an object of deep interest with all the truly wise, as well as the virtuous, of this great community, and was one of the important benefits expected from a reform of the government. To impose restraints on state legislation, as respected this delicate and interesting subject, was thought necessary by all those patriots who could take an enlightened and comprehensive view of our situation; and the principle obtained an early admission into the various schemes of government which were submitted to the convention.[37]

Marshall contended that "those laws which had effected all that mischief the constitution intended to prevent, were prospective as well as retrospective, in their operation. They embraced future contracts, as well as those previously formed."[38]

Marshall's opinion suggests a reason for inserting both ex post facto and contracts clauses in the Constitution. The two partially complemented each other. The latter applied to retrospective and prospective civil laws, while the former affected only retrospective measures, criminal as well as civil.

Although Marshall did not present historical evidence for his postion, some subsequently became available. The contracts clause came into the Constitution as part of the report presented on September 12 by the Committee on Style. The clause, as the committee reported it, read: "No State shall. . .pass any. . .laws altering or impairing the obligation of contracts. . ."[39] George Mason of Virginia seems to have proposed the insertion of the word *previous* after the words *obligation of*—a change that would have limited the provision to contracts previously formed. In his record of the various proposals that he presented, Mason reported that this change was refused.[40] One may surmise, therefore, that the generality of the clause was considered and purposeful; it was to apply to both prospective and retrospective laws. (On 14 September the words *altering or* were removed.)[41] That the distinction between the two kinds of contracts was a consideration for legal draftsmen of that period is also evident from the use in the Northwest Ordinance of 1787 of language prohibiting impairment solely of private contracts "*bona fide* and without fraud previously formed."[42]

The opinions in *Ogden* raise the question of the extent to which the Framers sought to block state intervention into the economy. The irresponsibility of the states in this area persuaded the Framers to deny them a host of powers they (and other autonomous governments) had long exercised, as set forth in Section 10. Notwithstanding the *Ogden* majority opinion, the prohibitions are vast in scope. Marshall asserted that the Framers' objective was to eliminate legislation that effectively restricted economic activity ("mischief the constitution intended to prevent"). Indeed, it would have been foolhardy to banish certain evils only to have them arise in another form—as Marshall argued would be the situation if distinctions were drawn between pre- and post-contract laws. The Framers' purpose—to maintain economic viability and stability—would not be achieved unless regulatory powers of the states were curtailed.

I do not read Marshall's opinion as requiring the elimination of all state economic regulation. His test for validity appears to be related to the impact of the regulation on the market for goods and services: how "mischievous" the result could be. Applying current thinking, this test would require high judicial scrutiny to determine if the legislation was justified. Thus *state* bankruptcy laws—which few would find objectionable—do not have sufficient societal benefits to warrant limitations upon freedom of contract. On the other hand, Marshall considered usury laws as constitutional, largely for technical reasons. He asserted that usury laws make a contract void in the beginning, and therefore, no obligation exists that can be impaired. Marshall was also guided by contemporary interpretations of natural law which did not regard protected liberties as absolute. Accordingly, Marshall likely would have accepted as constitutional economic regulation when strongly justified.

The willingness of the Framers to limit state powers that threatened investment is further evident in the diversity of citizenship provision of Article III, defining federal court jurisdiction. This provision accords jurisdiction to federal courts in suits "between citizens of different states;" the purpose apparently was to assure out of state investors that their claims would be adjudicated in a neutral forum and not in state courts, which might favor their own residents.[43]

Prohibiting Government from Inflating the Currency

During the pre-Constitutional period, entrepreneurs and investors assumed the risk that a state might inflate the currency to favor debtor interests. Such actions were very harmful to commerce. Individuals or companies would be reluctant to lend money at other than high rates, when confronted with the serious possibility that the debt would be worth much less at maturity than at its inception. Some might even avoid making loans altogether because of such uncertainty, limiting the credit markets. In part, the Framers remedied the problem by denying the states (in Subsection 1 of Section 10) the power to coin money, emit paper money not backed by gold or silver, or give legal tender status to anything other than these precious metals.

They also sought to deal with the problem at the federal level. As a government of enumerated powers, the national government, unlike the states, can exercise only such powers as the Constitution specifically accords it. The Constitution nowhere grants the central government the power to issue unbacked paper money. At best, the federal government could issue such paper money only under its necessary and proper powers (about which more later).

The evidence is convincing that the delegates to the 1787 Convention intended to ensure that the national currency would be based on gold and silver. But they did not insert a specific provision into the Constitution to secure this purpose, and this omission enabled the Supreme Court to apply an entirely different interpretation. James Madison's notes on the convention's debates, the most informative we have on those proceedings, are not extensive on this point. These notes do reveal, however, that the speakers assumed that the authority to issue unbacked paper money did not have to be expressly forbidden for it to be denied to Congress.

The foregoing explanation is based on the understanding that Congress possessed only such powers as are set forth in the Constitution. The power to issue paper money not backed by specie might also be effected under Article I, Section 8, giving Congress the power to "make all laws which shall be necessary and proper for carrying into execution the foregoing powers." And in fact, the Supreme Court has so construed the necessary and proper clause.[44] In my view, this was incorrect. To the contrary, the Framers feared paper money and sought to prohibit it, except possibly in extraordinary situations (when application of the necessary and proper clause would be appropriate).

II. Limitation on Federal Economic Powers

As the prior discussion indicates, the Supreme Court has not always been an accurate interpreter of the Framers' meaning. The Court has strayed from original understanding with regard to the extent of both state and federal powers. The Framers sought to limit the powers of the states over both local and national commerce. Although the Framers' intentions regarding the protection of property and economic liberties from federal lawmakers are not as apparent, they did seek to confine the powers of the federal government in this regard. The contracts clause does not affect the federal government, but, as previously explained, the ex post facto clauses might well have prohibited federal impairment of existing agreements. (Interestingly, the Constitution authorized Congress to pass bankruptcy acts, suggesting that laws that might operate retroactively required specific authorization to be exempt from the ex post facto prohibitions.) The federal government is also barred from passing bills of attainder. Much additional protection for property and economic rights is provided in the Bill of Rights, to be discussed subsequently.

The assessment of the Framers' intentions regarding federal powers is complicated by the thinking of James Madison, Alexander Hamilton, and John Marshall. For them, lodging powers in the national government was a means for preserving liberty. They feared that the same powers in the hands of state authorities would result in far greater limitations on property and other rights. All viewed the wide diversity of interests comprising the national govern-ment—political, sectional, occupational, and pecuniary—as conducive to a free society because their conflicts would minimize the political power of any particular group. Madison presented this position in his famous *Federalist* No. 10. He asserted that a "rage for paper money, for an abolition of debts, for an equal division of property, or any other improper or wicked project, will be less apt to pervade the whole body of the Union than any particular member of it..."[45] The separation of powers at the national level would provide further checks and balances against arbitrary power.

In the ratification debates, the Federalists emphasized the confines under which the new government would have to operate. For example, in the *Federalist*, Hamilton and Madison minimized the scope of the necessary and proper clause against charges that it greatly expanded the domain of national authority. Both founders denied that it or any other clause significantly expanded the powers specifically granted to Congress.[46] The Constitution might never have been ratified had the Federalists' representation in this respect not been accepted by the public. During the ratification period, it should be recalled, great sentiment existed against the creation of a strong federal government.

Besides the power to regulate commerce (to be discussed subsequently), the Framers provided Congress with a limited amount of economic authority. Some of the powers would not have been needed if the commerce power were very broad. These other powers include the authority to impose only proportional and not progressive taxes; to spend for constitutional purposes; to borrow money; to establish uniform bankruptcy laws; to coin money and regulate its value; to fix standards of weights and measures; to establish post office and post roads; and to grant copyrights and patents. Professor William Grampp observes that the economic controls which the Constitution expressly authorizes are modest when compared with those France and England exercised or tried to exercise during their mercantilist period, which spanned the sixteenth through the mid-eighteenth century. Their governments, for instance, regulated the quality of goods, licensed labor, granted monopolies and other exclusive rights, protected domestic industries, and controlled foreign trade and finance. Grampp writes:

> Not even proposed [at the Philadelphia Convention] were the powers to
> control prices, wages, interest rates, the quality of goods, the conditions of their
> sale, and the allocation of labor. All of these powers were cherished by the
> *practitioners* (although not the theorists) of mercantilism, and could they have
> been asked for an opinion of the Constitution, they would have said it provided
> a feeble economic policy indeed. Those who today believe the Federal
> government has extensive economic authority to exercise, if it will, cannot
> support their belief by the records of the constitutional convention (nor the
> Constitution of course), because the delegates were not agreed upon the issue.[47]

Given that only an enumerated and limited central government was
established, the omission of these important powers is very persuasive evidence
for the proposition that they were not granted. Many of these controls appear
no less important or significant than those the Framers did authorize.

The commerce clause states that Congress shall have the power to
"regulate Commerce with foreign Nations, and among the several States, and
with the Indian Tribes."[48] The Supreme Court has invoked this provision often
since the late nineteenth century to advance and broaden federal powers over
the economy. In the *Federalist*, however, Madison minimized the scope of this
clause. It was one, he asserted, "which few opposed and from which no
apprehensions are entertained."[49] The clause was not an important issue in the
ratification debates and met with only scattered opposition; apparently, the
domestic portion was not considered as a grant of substantial authority to the
national government. Hamilton did not expound on the domestic power in the
Federalist—again indicating the lack of concern about it.

Madison explained that the power to regulate domestic commerce
supplemented the foreign powers of the national government; without it, the
foreign powers would have been incomplete and ineffectual. The domestic
component of the commerce clause, he wrote, was designed to relieve states
which import and export through other states from the burden of improper
contributions levied on them by the latter. Were the states at liberty to regulate
trade between themselves, some would contrive to impose duties on other
states even though the Constitution elsewhere barred them from doing so. In
1829 Madison stated that the power over domestic commerce was not intended
to be as extensive as the power over foreign commerce: it was intended as a
negative and preventive provision against injustice among the states themselves. The domestic power was not to be used for the positive purposes of the
federal government.[50]

The commerce clause was among those drafted by the Committee on
Detail in response to a direction to prepare provisions that the national
government was "to legislate in all cases for the general interests of the
union...and in those in which the states are separately incompetent."[51] As
previously reported, a major concern of the time was to remove direct state

impediments to the functioning of a common market, a problem remedied in part by the aforementioned ban on state imposts and duties, contained in Article I, Section 10. In all likelihood, lodging the commerce power in the Congress was intended to limit other state restraints on national commerce, or in Madison's words, to prevent trade injustices perpetrated by the states against each other. Pursuant to such thinking, the United States Supreme Court has long recognized that the clause limits the power of the states to erect barriers against interstate trade. Thus, the Court has ruled that a state statute affecting interstate commerce in invalid if it (1) discriminates against interstate commerce; (2) unreasonably burdens interstate commerce; or (3) regulates commerce which is essentially interstate in character.[52] Such state restraints might be as or more harmful to interstate commerce than imposts and duties on exports and imports.

The "negative" commerce clause is well established. Recent state laws which the United States Supreme Court has found to have improperly interfered with interstate commerce include a Wisconsin regulation forbidding operation of sixty-five foot-long trucks on its highways; a North Carolina law, passed at the behest of local growers, prohibiting the sale of apples from out-of-state in cartons labeled with information about their quality; a Florida statute barring out-of-state banks from owning Florida investment advisory businesses; a New Jersey ban on the importation of most solid or liquid fuel waste that was collected outside the territorial limits of the state; and an Oklahoma law that no person may ship minnows for sale to another state that were seined within the waters of the state.[53] However, the Court has also held that the limitation on state regulatory power imposed by the commerce clause is not absolute and that the states retain authority to regulate matters of "legitimate local concern" even though interstate commerce may be affected.[54]

Under existing judicial interpretation, Congress may at its will overrule the Court and validate any state restraints affecting interstate commerce.[55] As we have seen, from the perspective of the early nationalists, such federal power would not have been viewed as a threat to liberty; they believed economic liberties were quite secure under federal authority, clearly more so than under the states.

The application of the commerce clause in a negative manner—to remove state economic restriction—advances freedom. However, as previously stated, the national government has also interpreted the clause over the years as possessing a positive dimension. In this guise, it has been employed to uphold much federal regulation over the nation's economy. Under contemporary Supreme Court rulings, Congress is authorized to regulate virtually any commercial transaction in the nation, even though the transaction is confined entirely within a state.[56]

In my view, this interpretation of the commerce clause is incorrect. Supporters of this position frequently contend that the Framers originally meant to bestow large economic powers on the federal government. They argue that the reason the Constitution enumerates relatively few specific powers is that broader powers are generally implied in the commerce power. During the closing days of the Constitutional Convention, however, when the delegates were preoccupied with clarifying the document they had drafted, a debate occurred which casts grave doubts on this theory.

On September 14, 1787, three working days before final adjournment, and after the language relating to commerce and other major national powers had been settled, some prominent delegates apparently believed either that the Convention did not confer extensive enough economic powers on the federal government, or that the constitutional language on this point was not clear. On that day, Benjamin Franklin moved to add to Article I, Section 8, after the language giving Congress power to establish post offices and post roads, "a power to provide for cutting canals where deemed necessary." James Madison moved to enlarge the motion "to grant charters of incorporation when the interests of the U.S. might require and legislative provisions of individual states may be incompetent." James Wilson, who later became a Supreme Court justice, seconded Franklin's motion, and Edmund Randolph, who later became the first United States attorney general, seconded Madison's motion.

Either or both of the proposed powers would appear to be inherent in a government possessed of substantial economic authority. If the government had broad powers of commerce, there would be no need to specifically authorize such powers. Under these proposals, the federal government would have been able to establish public and private enterprises to engage in public works or other activities. Franklin's motion was rejected by a vote of eight to three, and Madison noted that the "other part fell of course, as included in the power rejected."[57]

We cannot be certain, of course, why these proposals were rejected. However, the episode does lend credence to the view that the Constitution did not grant extensive economic power to Congress. In opposing legislation to authorize a national bank before the House of Representatives in 1791, Madison, now a House member, argued that the measure was unconstitutional, citing among other things, the Convention's rejection of federal chartering of corporations.[58] Years later, Madison explained that Franklin's proposal on canals had been rejected as conveying a power either that should not be invested in Congress, or that would not likely be yielded by the states. Accordingly, Madison did not consider it as a power the federal government possessed under the Constitution. In 1817, President Madison vetoed a bill appropriating funds for the building of national roads and canals on the ground, among others, that the commerce power did not include the required power. President Monroe was of similar view, vetoing in 1822 a bill appropriating funds for the preservation and repair of the Cumberland Road. He urged that the Constitution be amended to authorize this action.[59]

The conclusion that the national government is bereft of significant economic authority is also buttressed in the Bill of Rights, framed by the First

Congress which was composed predominantly of Federalists, as was the 1787 Convention. Supporters of the Constitution had promised that if it were ratified, they would quickly introduce in Congress amendments to safeguard individual rights. The Federalists were true to their word, and in 1789 Congress passed and submitted to the states for adoption twelve amendments, ten of which were ratified by 1791.

A substantial portion of the Bill of Rights is directed to the protection of property and economic rights. In addition to the requirement of the Fifth Amendment that private property not be taken, except for public use, and only then with just compensation, the Bill contains six other material guarantees: the prohibition of infringing the people's right to keep and bear arms (Amendment II); the prohibition of quartering soldiers on private property (III); the prohibition of unreasonable searches and seizures (IV); the prohibition of depriving any person of life, liberty or property without due process of law (V); the right to trial by jury for controversies exceeding twenty dollars (VII); and the prohibition of excessive bails and fines (VIII). The guidelines shielded from federal intrusion those property interests of most concern in that period. In addition to those specified, owners and entrepreneurs could also obtain protection under the Ninth Amendment: "The enumeration...of certain rights shall not be construed to deny or disparage others retained by the people." Thus, as will be presently explained, the fact that freedom of contract is not mentioned, did not necessarily mean it is unprotected under the Bill of Rights.

Madison authored the original version of the Ninth Amendment as part of the amendments he proposed to the First Congress; it read as follows:

> The exceptions here or elsewhere in the Constitution, made in favor of particular rights, shall not be so construed as to diminish the just importance of other rights retained by the people; or as to enlarge the powers delegated by the Constitution; but either as actual limitations of such powers, or as inserted merely for greater caution.[60]

Under this language and the version finally adopted, rights may be secured that are not listed. Madison drafted this amendment to allay fears that a bill of enumerated rights could not be broad enough to cover all essential rights and that the mention of certain ones would be interpreted as a denial that others were secured. Thus, freedom of contract might well be construed as sufficently important—natural and fundamental—to merit Constitutional protection. John Marshall's *Ogden* opinion would seem to accord it this stature. The Supreme Court has not had occasion to consider this issue.

The due process clause is another nonspecific guarantee that might have been similarly construed in the late eighteenth century. The meaning of due process of law has been vigorously disputed over the years. It would take us considerably beyond the scope of this essay to resolve the conflict. However, if the Framers sought guidance on the issue from commentators then regarded as among the leading authorities on English law—Sir Edward Coke (1552-1634) and Sir William Blackstone (1723-1800)—they would have concluded that it constituted general protection for the individual against government oppression, whether through deprivation of procedural or substantive liberties. Due process of law was, in the constitutional period, regarded as identical to the law of the land (*per legem terrae*), which for these commentators seemed to embody law rights.

Consider Coke's view. In explaining disseisin of property (i.e., a deprivation of possession), he, in one of his influential decisions, cited two civil cases in which the denials of property interests without judicial process were adjudged "against the law of the land." On Magna Charta's (1215) protection for liberties, he wrote that "[g]enerally all monopolies are against this great charter, because they are against the liberty and freedom of the subject, and against the law of the land."[61] Coke appears to be identifying "law of the land" with common law rights.

Interestingly, in a dictum that may have been more persuasive than accurate, Coke asserted that when an act of Parliament "is against common right and reason, or repugnant, or impossible to be performed, the common law will controul it, and adjudge such Act to be void."[62] Although precedent for this conclusion is doubtful, the dictum was used both in the colonies to justify resistance to the British Parliament and by jurists after the Revolution as a basis for judicial review.

Blackstone, after summarizing the main provisions of the Magna Charta, emphasized the substantive protection provided by its Chapter 39 for every individual's life, liberty and property:

> And, lastly, (which alone would have merited the title that it bears, of the *great* charter) it protected every individual of the nation in the free enjoyment of his life, his liberty, and his property, unless declared to be forfeited by the judgment of his peers or the law of the land.[63]

Blackstone declared that the "law of the land" protected the absolute rights of personal security, personal liberty, and private property. He enumerated many rules, both legislative and judicial in origin, that have to be observed before a subject can be deprived of life, liberty, or property. Some substantially limited certain powers of government. For example, in his discussion of the protection afforded the right of property, he wrote that the legislature can acquire property "not by absolutely stripping the subject of his property in an arbitrary manner; but by giving him a full indemnification and equivalent for the injury thereby sustained." Blackstone asserted that this is but one instance "in which the law of the land has postponed even public necessity to the sacred and inviolate rights of the private property."[64]

The conclusion is warranted, given the high and fundamental status accorded to economic rights during the constitutional period, that the United States Supreme Court would have been on solid ground if it had expansively interpreted the Ninth Amendment to include these rights although they are not explicitly mentioned in the other Amendments.

The question arises why the Bill of Rights does not contain an explicit protection for freedom of contract from Congressional infringement. Three explanations come to mind. First, the Bill is applicable solely to the federal government, which because of its very diverse interests, would be most unlikely to pass stay, installment, or other comparable debtor relief measures, that prompted inclusion of the contracts clause against the states in the original constitution. Moreover, unlike the states, the central government had little authority to adopt oppressive economic measures, as previously explained.

Second, a contracts clause applicable to the national government might possibly impede free commerce by protecting undesirable private agreements executed under state laws subject to congressional veto. For example, Congress in the exercise of the negative commerce power may strike down state restraints on interstate commerce, and thereby nullify private agreements made pursuant thereto. Similarly, under the supremacy clause (Article VI), which makes federal laws supreme over state laws in certain areas, Congress may invalidate state statutes and the accompanying private agreements. A national contracts clause might operate to interfere with such process by possibly affording protection to the agreements entered into under the offending statutes.

Third, the congressional debates disclose that, as late as 1805, some congressmen believed that the ex post facto provision safeguarded against the impairment of contracts by the federal government. Five congressmen took this position in 1790 in debate contrary to Madison's rejection of it.[65] Since no vote was taken specifically on this issue, we do not know the extent of its acceptance in the Congress. Some who accepted this definition might have felt that a provision in the Bill of Rights protecting the obligation of contracts was unnecessary, or at least not very essential.

Conclusion

Strong evidence exists that the Framers of the Constitution sought to establish a commercial republic whose success depended upon the initiative, productivity and creativity of the people in their capacity as *individuals*, alone or in voluntary association with others. The Framers may not have sought to impose a system strictly in keeping with Adam Smith's writings, for as we know, Alexander Hamilton, as the first secretary of the treasury, and the Federalist-dominated First Congress favored some mercantilist policies. However, these were exceptions to the dominant view that strongly emphasized an individualist, not collectivist, economic system. Our American Founders clearly believed in personal freedom as the best source for prosperity and development.

118   BERNARD H. SIEGAN

Notes

1. THE RANDOM HOUSE DICTIONARY OF THE ENGLISH LANGUAGE (1967).

2. Ogden v. Saunders, 25 U.S. (12 Wheat.) 212, 232 (1827) (Marshall, C. J., dissenting).

3. Gibbons v. Ogden 22 U.S. (9 Wheat.) 1 (1824) (Johnson, J., concurring).

4. U.S. CONST. Art. 1, § 10, c1.2.

5. Much of the material herein presented is discussed more extensively in my book, ECONOMIC LIBERTIES AND THE CONSTITUTION (1980). Subsequent amendments reinforced the general economic design of the provisions adopted in the late eighteenth century.

6. 1 M. FARRAND, THE RECORDS OF THE FEDERAL CONVENTION OF 1787 533-34 (rev. ed. 1937, 1966).

7. Id. at 450; THE FEDERALIST No. 10 (J. Madison).

8. 1 FARRAND at 422-23.

9. 12 THE PAPERS OF JAMES MADISON 71 (W. Hutchinson, R. Rutland et al., eds. 1962).

10. 1 FARRAND, supra note 6 at 533, 534, 541-42, 528, 469-70, 542; 2 id. at 202; 3 id. at 110.

11. Chief Justice Hughes in Home Building and Loan Ass'n v. Blaisdell, 290 U.S. 398, 427 (1934).

12. 25 THE PAPERS OF ALEXANDER HAMILTON 479 (H. Syrett ed. 1977).

13. J. MAIN, THE ANTIFEDERALISTS: CRITICS OF THE CONSTITUTION, 1781-1788 26 (1961).

14. S. MORISON, THE OXFORD HISTORY OF THE AMERICAN PEOPLE 302 (1965).

15. Id. at 302-03.

16. 1 JAMES MADISON LETTERS 350 (1865).

17. 1 A. BEVERIDGE, THE LIFE OF JOHN MARSHALL 416-17 (1916).

18. 1 FARRAND, supra note 6, at 134.

19. Id. at 512.

20. 1 BEVERIDGE, supra note 17, at 242.

21. A letter of Marque and Reprisal is an authorization granted by government to a private citizen to capture and confiscate the ships of another nation.

22. SIEGAN, supra note 5, at 74-76.

23. Id. at 76-77, 79.

24. Dash v. Van Kleeck, 7 Johns (N.Y.) 477, 505 (1811); 3 J. STORY, COMMENTARIES ON THE CONSTITUTION OF THE UNITED STATES 212-13 (1970); T. COOLEY, A TREATISE ON THE CONSTITUTIONAL LIMITATIONS 264 (1972).

25. 3 U.S. (3 DALL) 386 (1798).

26. Ralis v. RFE/RL, Inc., 770 F.2d 1121, 1127 (D.C. Cir.) (1985).

27. SIEGAN, supra note 5, at 71-73.

28. 1 W. BLACKSTONE COMMENTARIES, *46.

29. Smead, The Rule Against Retroactive Legislation: A Basic Principle of Jurisprudence, 20 MINN. L. REV. 775, 777 (1936).

30. SIEGAN, supra note 5, at 80-81.

31. 25 U.S. (12 Wheat.) 213, 332 (1827) (Marshall, C.J., dissenting).

32. *Id.* at 346.

33. *Id.* at 346-47.

34. Among other things, Story is noted for his detailed treatise on the Constitution, titled COMMENTARIES ON THE CONSTITUTION OF THE UNITED STATES.

35. *E.g.*, 1 W. CROSSKEY, POLITICS AND THE CONSTITUTION 359 (1953); 4 BEVERIDGE, *supra* note 17, at 480-81.

36. 25 U.S. at 340.

37. *Id.* at 354-55.

38. *Id.* at 357.

39. 2 FARRAND, *supra* note 6, at 596-97.

40. *Id.* at 636; 4 *id.* at 59.

41. *Id.* at 619.

42. Ordinance of 1787, July 13, 1787, reprinted in THE MAKING OF THE AMERICAN REPUBLIC 47, 52 (C. Transill ed. 1972).

43. *See* 1 MOORE'S FEDERAL PRACTICE 701.22-23 and authorities cited (2d ed. 1964); CONST. Art. III, § 2.

44. Julliard v. Greeman, 110 U.S. 421 (1884).

45. THE FEDERALIST No. 10 (J. Madison).

46. THE FEDERALIST No. 33 (A. Hamilton) and No. 44 (J. Madison).

47. 1 W. GRAMPP, ECONOMIC LIBERALISM 109 (1965).

48. U.S. CONST. Art. 1, § 8.

49. THE FEDERALIST No. 45 and No. 42 (J. Madison).

50. 3 FARRAND, *supra* note 6, at 478.

51. *See* Sterns, *Which Concerns More States Than One*, 47 HARV. L. REV. 1335, 1337-48 (1947).

52. SIEGAN, *supra* note 5, at 243.

53. Raymond Motor Transportation, Inc. v. Rice, 434 U.S. 429 (1978); Hunt v. Washington State Apple Advertising Commission, 432 U.S. 333 (1977); Lewis v. BT Investment Managers, 447 U.S. 27 (1980); Philadelphia v. New Jersey 437 U.S. 617 (1978); Hughes v. Oklahoma, 99 S.Ct. 1727 (1979).

54. SIEGAN, *supra* note 5, at 243.

55. Gibbons v. Ogden, 22 U.S. (9 Wheat.) 1 (1824); Cooley v. Board of Wardens of the Port of Philadelphia, 53 U.S. (12 How.) 299 (1851).

56. L. TRIBE, AMERICAN CONSTITUTIONAL LAW 236-38 (1978).

57. 2 FARRAND, *supra* note 6, at 615-16.

58. 3 *id.* at 362.

59. 3 *id.* at 463, E. BARRETT, JR. & W. COHEN, CONSTITUTIONAL LAW— CASES AND MATERIALS 167-68 (7th ed. 1985). Interestingly, Chief Justice John Marshall in McCulloch v. Maryland, 17 U.S. (4 Wheat.) 316 (1819), ruled in a contrary view, that Congress had vast powers under the Constitution. *See:* B. SIEGAN, THE SUPREME COURT'S CONSTITUTION, Ch. 1 (1987).

60. 1 ANNALS OF CONGRESS 436 (1789-90).

61. 2 E. COKE, INSTITUTES OF THE LAWS OF ENGLAND 46, 47, 63 (1817).

62. Dr. Bonham's Case, 77 Eng. Rep. 646 (K.B. 1610).

63. 4 BLACKSTONE *417.

64. 1 BLACKSTONE *135.

65. 2 ANNALS OF CONGRESS at 1206, 1214, 1216-24, 1227, 1249 (1790).

The Economic Policy of the Constitution
WILLIAM LETWIN

What theory of economic policy is built into the Constitution? More specifically, did the Framers mean to lay the foundations of a capitalist society? Did they go even further: did they wish to establish a general regime of laissez faire?

These questions are strictly historical. They have no bearing at all on normative issues, on whether the Constitution should have fostered or should foster capitalism or socialism or any mixed form, a minimal state or one that dominates the economy. Neither do the historical questions, as posed, admit of answers based on how the Constitution has evolved since 1789. Instead, the pertinent evidence is to be found, first of all, in what the Framers, as well as their contemporaries, thought and did up through 1789, which includes the ratification of the Constitution and the approval by Congress of the Bill of Rights. Admissible also as evidence is what they thought and did in the remaining years of their lives, though this must be weighed more scrupulously, because people may change their minds about what should be done, and they may revise their recollections about what they did and why. Excluded entirely from consideration here are interpretations placed on the Constitution, since 1789, by justices, advocates, and learned commentators who were not themselves Framers or their contemporaries, and historians—for aside from the fact that none of them witnessed what went on up through 1789, some of them acted, knowingly or otherwise, to reshape the Constitution.

As a further preliminary, we should note that the questions as posed are anachronistic. Before 1789 the word 'capitalism' was unknown to speakers of English. If we can trust the *Oxford English Dictionary*, the word only entered our language at about the middle of the nineteenth century, and it only assumed its present connotation later in that century, when Marx's theory of socio-economic stages became known to the English-speaking world. In order therefore to uncover the attitude of the Framers toward what we now call 'capitalism,' we must translate that term into words that would have been used in 1789 to express the same concept. Let us stipulate that the essence of capitalism is private ownership of the means of production, ownership not merely in the sense of actual possession and legal title but also the right—broad, though within any system of law necessarily incomplete—to use those means of production as the owner sees fit.

121

'Laissez-faire,' according to the *Oxford English Dictionary*, also entered the language during the nineteenth century. Its governing idea had of course been explored in great depth in Adam Smith's *Wealth of Nations* (1776); that idea is that government, while maintaining a framework of law to prohibit force and fraud, should refrain from intervening in the operation of markets. Laissez-faire thus pre-supposes capitalism, yet it goes further, by prescribing that government should not aim to direct private enterprise toward ends designated by government, ends such as accumulation of foreign reserves, equality of income, puritanical styles of consumption, or territorial aggrandizement.

Thus, although the words 'capitalism' and 'laissez faire' do not appear in the Constitution itself or, so far as I have discovered, in any American writing before 1789, the ideas they represent should be readily identifiable if they occurred in the Constitution or in the surrounding literature.

I propose to arrange the evidence bearing on our historical questions in the following order: (I) evidence stemming from the text of the Constitution, including the Bill of Rights; (II) evidence from contemporary writings; and (III) evidence from the public policy of American governments.

I. Evidence from the Text of the Constitution

The Due Process Clause

It is well to begin by considering the due process clause of the Fifth Amendment, because so many subsequent commentators have interpreted it as compelling evidence that the Framers intended to create or perpetuate a capitalist economy. The clause ordains that "No person shall be...deprived of life, liberty, or property, without due process of law." Read casually, it seems to prohibit American governments, or at least the federal government, from taking anyone's property—and can thereby be interpreted as sanctifying private property and thus capitalism. Read carefully, however, it prohibits government from taking private property "without due process of law." In other words, the prohibition is conditional rather than absolute. This being so, the extent to which the due process clause can legitimately be interpreted as favorable to capitalism turns on the meaning that the Framers and their contemporaries attached to "due process of law."

Light is shed on that question by considering the historical antecedents of the due process clause.[1] Earliest of these was Chapter 39 of Magna Charta (1215), in which King John undertook not to arrest, imprison, outlaw, or dispossess any free man, "except by the lawful judgment of his peers and by the law of the land."[2] During the next century that provision was reformulated in a statute which enacted that "no man...shall be put out of land or tenement, nor taken nor imprisoned, nor disinherited nor put to death, without he be brought [to] answer by due process of the law."[3] Assuming that the draftsmen in both cases intended to express the same idea albeit in different words, then "due process of law" stood for the two elements, trial by jury, and proceedings according to the "law of the land." We can safely take it that "law of the land" meant law as distinct from fiat or order. "Law of the land" thus carried the connotation of published, general rules with prospective operation, in other words rules stemming from common law or statute.

Leaping centuries to the earliest American counterpart, we find in the Massachusetts Body of Liberties of 1641 the provision that "...no mans goods or estaite shall be taken away from him...under coulor of law or Countenance of Authoritie, unlesse it be by vertue...of some expresse law of [Massachusetts] warranting the same, established by [the legislature of Massachusetts] and sufficiently published, or in case of the defect of a law in any partecular case by the word of god."[4] Here "law of the land" is identified with statutes passed and published by legitimate authority—the colony's legislature—or where it has not yet spoken, by a theocracy's Ultimate Legislator. When other of the colonies promulgated their independent constitutions in 1776, they entrenched similar views about "the law of the land" as a prerequisite for the taking of private property.[5]

Drawing on these illustrations from a continuous tradition that stretched from Magna Charta to the Fifth Amendment's due process clause, we can infer that the Framers and their contemporaries meant "due process" to comprehend fair trial and authentic law. What they meant was that only if these two conditions were fulfilled could a person be deprived of property. But this entails, to put it in less optimistic terms, that (leaving aside the requirement of fair trial) the legislature is empowered to deprive any person of private property by passing laws to do so, provided those laws are procedurally valid. No limit is set by the due process clause on how far Congress may go in authorizing public taking of private property. In other words, the clause, as understood by the Framers and their contemporaries, was just as much a charter for wholesale nationalization of the means of production as for private ownership, as much a license for socialism as for capitalism.

The Takings Clause

One passage that does limit the property-taking power of government is in the immediately following section of the Fifth Amendment, namely the takings (or eminent domain) clause. It ordains that "private property [shall not] be taken for public use, without just compensation." Did the Framers and their contemporaries intend this as a substantive limitation? It seems rather to be a procedural one. It requires the government to pay for any property that it takes, but it does not debar the government from taking any property that it is prepared to pay for. In other words, the compensation requirement leaves the road open to thoroughgoing nationalization of property. To say this is not to suggest that the Framers and their contemporaries desired socialism or even imagined it as a possibility. But it does mean that the compensation principle of the takings clause would make socialism possible, unlike a hypothetical rule against any expropriation or forced exchange. In other words, by conferring on the federal government the power of eminent domain, the Framers authorized action that can threaten the security of private property and thus of a capitalist order. Since 1789, actions of the government have in fact diminished the scope of rights associated with private ownership, as Richard Epstein has shown.[6] Although it may be argued that such actions have violated the original intent of the takings clause, I find it impossible to believe that the Framers established a power to seize private property with the intent of fortifying the right to private property.

This conclusion is not in any way altered by the "public use" phrase in the takings clause. It dictates that private property shall not be taken by government, even if just compensation is paid, merely to give it to some pet of government, as Henry VIII, after the breach with Rome, gave monastic property to his favorites. It militates against taking property from A in order to give it to B—as commentators frequently put it. But this meaning would in no way limit, and could not have been intended to limit, transfer of private property into *public* ownership. The phrase, "public use," does not expressly exclude purchases intended as steps towards nationalizing some or all means of production.

In short, the takings clause as a whole was intended to preclude arbitrary exactions but not "orderly" exactions. Yet compulsory purchase, even when procedurally correct, cannot serve as a bulwark to capitalism or as a barrier to socialism, and could not rationally have been intended to serve as such.

The Commerce Clause

Aside from absolutely taking property, in the sense of acquiring title to it, government may, by regulating its use, deprive the private owner of some or much or all the benefit of property, though he continues to retain title to it. Obviously no government could function without some power to regulate the use of private property, otherwise, to say the least, a deliberate killer could exculpate himself by showing that he owned the gun, the use of which is immune, like any use of any private property, to regulation. But once this minimal requirement is conceded, the maximal limit on regulatory power remains in question.

To what extent did the Framers and their contemporaries intend to limit the regulatory power of the federal government? That power was conferred in Section 8 of Article I, authorizing Congress to "regulate commerce with foreign nations, and among the several States, and with the Indian tribes." On the face of it the commerce clause gives an unbounded power, except insofar as bounds may be implied by the terms "commerce" and "among." According to the monumental investigation by William Winslow Crosskey[7] into how the Framers and their contemporaries spoke and understood English, "commerce" could signify business or trade of every sort, including what we would now call production (primary, secondary, and tertiary). And "among" signified "within" as well as "between." Crosskey accordingly concluded that the commerce clause was intended to give Congress regulatory power over *all* economic activities anywhere in the United States (as well as between the United States and foreign nations and Indian tribes). But even if we take the conventional view—that the commerce clause was intended to give Congress power to regulate trade between the states but not economic activities confined within any given state—we must still conclude that within its reach the federal regulatory power is unbounded, at least by any terms in the text of the commerce clause. Under that power, Congress could legitimately limit the use of private property, in any degree, and could alter any of the conditions—such as unconstrained bargaining—that constitute a market economy.

But the matter cannot be allowed to rest there, for it might be that the commerce power was intended to be hedged in by other provisions of the Constitution. On inspection, however, no such hedges reveal themselves. Among the explicit limits set on Congressional power by Section 9 of Article I, only one pertains to the regulatory power, namely that it may not be exercised so as to give preference to the ports of one state over those of any other. Clearly this could not have been intended to preserve free markets; while insisting on even-handed regulation, it does not otherwise confine the scope of regulatory power. Next we may consider whether the Preamble was intended in any degree to limit the commerce power. Crosskey, though he argues that the Framers and their contemporaries always worked on the theory that a preamble lays out the rationale of an enactment, in the light of which the technical text must be read,[8] does not for a moment suggest that the Preamble of the Constitution was in any way intended to diminish the commerce power. In the Preamble the only clause that might be thought to aim at such an effect states that the Constitution is ordained to "secure the Blessings of Liberty to ourselves and our Posterity." But for reasons that will be made clear later, the Framers cannot be thought to have included in "Liberty" the idea of laissez-faire—that economic actors should be free from government intervention. Moreover, it may well be doubted whether the Preamble was really intended to control the interpretation of the Constitution's substantive provisions.

We can also dispose of the possibility that the commerce power was meant to be substantially limited by the due process clause of the Fifth Amendment. As we have seen, that clause requires only (aside from fair trial) that property be taken by authentic law rather than arbitrary fiat. This means that whenever Congress exercises the commerce power in the proper manner, it satisfies the intention built into the due-process requirement—no matter how deeply such laws might interfere with the free operation of markets.

The Contract Clause

Finally, we should consider what light the contract clause throws on our questions. Article I, Section 10 prohibits the states from passing any "Law impairing the Obligation of Contracts." Occasioning this, as is generally agreed, were a number of state laws passed or proposed after 1781 to relieve debtors and others of contractual obligations.[9] Insofar as this prohibition served to insulate contract from political intervention, it can certainly be construed as intended to guarantee the rights of private property-owners (including among these, of course, persons whose chief asset consisted of property in their own labor-power) and thus as underpinning a capitalist economy.[10]

But the contract clause prohibition applies only to state governments. Did the Framers intend any equivalent limit on the federal government? To be sure, Congress was empowered to pass uniform laws on bankruptcy and was given exclusive authority over money, but these confirmed the intent to deprive the states of such powers, which they had on occasion used with the effect of imparing obligations of contract. Again, although the Constitution denies to the federal government, as to the state governments, power to pass ex post facto laws, it is dubious whether this was meant to limit the federal government's power to impair the obligations of existing contracts. If prohibition of ex post facto laws had been intended to entail prohibition of laws impairing contracts, then the clause (Article I, Section 10) prohibiting the states from passing any "ex post facto Law, or Law impairing the Obligation of Contracts" would have to be regarded—contrary to a basic canon of constitutional interpretation—as containing redundant, lazy words. Moreover, the federal power to make laws on bankruptcy means nothing if not a power to impair the obligations which the bankrupt had incurred under previous contracts. And above all, if the Framers had intended that Congress should not pass laws impairing the obligations of contract, how can we explain why they failed to say so explicitly in spite of having explicitly said so about the states? All of these considerations drive one to conclude that the Framers intended to entrust to Congress the power, an exclusive power, to pass laws impairing the obligations of contract, perhaps because they expected Congress (unlike past state legislatures) to do so rarely and only when the need seemed inescapable.

Here, as in the other provisions of the Constitution, there is no apparent intention to close the door to any departure from either capitalism or laissez faire.

II. Evidence from Contemporary Writings

The Federalist

If the Framers had intended to foster capitalism and laissez faire, we should expect those intentions to have left traces in the *Federalist*. But in fact, what little those essays suggest about our subject has to be teased out delicately.

A suggestive comment occurs, for instance, in Madison's renowned *Federalist* No. 10. His central theme there is how to minimize the clash of private interests within a republican government. Because in such a government the representatives register the views of many electors, they inevitably speak in some degree for special interests, that are "adverse to the rights of other citizens, or to the permanent and aggregate interests of the community." Factions, that is, interest groups, cannot be expunged from a republic because each person's interests are largely determined by the amount and kind of property he owns, which in turn depends on the "diversity in the faculties of men." All that can be hoped for, accordingly, is to mitigate the clash of factions and to avoid tyranny by the faction that commands majority support. Madison concludes, for well-known reasons, that such a hope will best be realized in an "extensive" republic, the federal republic envisioned by the Constitution, "a Republican remedy for the diseases most incident to Republican Government."

In the course of this discussion, Madison remarks that the protection of men's "different and unequal faculties of acquiring property" is "the first object of Government." How he comes by this vital premise, Madison does not explain. It might have been drawn directly or indirectly from Locke's *Second Treatise*,[11] and on that account might be reckoned as an unquestioned assumption among Americans at the time. On the other hand, it flatly contradicts Montesquieu, whose influence on American thought was at least as strong as Locke's, for Montesquieu held that inequality of income and wealth is the source of faction and thus ruinous to a republic.[12] But leaving aside the question of whether what Madison was saying would have struck his contemporaries as probably true or false, his thesis—that the first end of government is to protect not merely private property but the unequal distribution of private property that might emerge from the diversity of individual capacities—certainly would seem to place him on the side of capitalism.

Another incidental comment in *Federalist* No. 10 suggests that Madison did not wholeheartedly support laissez faire. By way of illustrating the disruptive effect of faction, Madison offers the example of disagreement between "the landed and the manufacturing classes" about whether government should restrict imports of foreign manufactures in order to encourage domestic manufacturing. That question, says Madison, will be answered differently by both factions, "and probably by neither, with a sole regard to justice and the public good." This may be nothing more than a reflection, fairly commonplace, on the psychology of self-interest. On the other hand it may imply also a belief on Madison's part about the abstract merits of the argument, that the public good is furthered neither by absolute prohibition of imports nor by absolute freedom to import. Certainly a devout follower of laissez faire, however discreet, would scarcely have passed by such a question without a hint of his own view.

Hamilton, in his contributions to the *Federalist*, was equally elusive as far as our questions are concerned. In No. 11, for instance, he considers the virtue of a federal union from the standpoint of commerce. European powers, he says, are so frightened by American success in the Atlantic carrying trade that they are plotting against it. If united, the states will be able to counteract such plots by enacting "prohibitory regulations" that would force European governments to negotiate commercial treaties favorable to the United States. A strong American navy would have a similar effect.

In *Federalist* No. 12, Hamilton goes on to say that the "prosperity of commerce is now perceived and acknowledged, by all enlightened statesmen, to be the most useful as well as the most productive source of national wealth; and has accordingly become a primary object of their political cares." Commerce, he adds, rather than being antagonistic to the interests of agriculture, fosters them by extending the market for agricultural produce. To understand Hamilton's attitude we must place it in the context of what he described as "the often-agitated question, between agriculture and commerce." At the theoretical level, the issue stemmed from the Physiocratic theory that agriculture is the sole form of productive enterprise, on which commerce and manufacture are purely parasitical: they transform wealth but cannot create it. This position, of which Jefferson was a leading American spokesman, Hamilton denied. But Hamilton did so, and knowingly did so, on different grounds than those which Adam Smith had advanced in his famous refutation of Physiocratic doctrine in *The Wealth of Nations*. For Smith, while showing why that doctrine was fallacious, insisted that commerce and manufacturing are no less and no more productive than agriculture.[13] In contrast, Hamilton asserted that commerce is "the most useful as well as the most productive source of national wealth." Moreover, Hamilton lauded commerce partly for "promoting the introduction and circulation of the precious metals, those darling objects of human avarice and enterprise," an idea that Smith abhorred as the bullionist fallacy of mercantilism.[14] In short, if we use Smith as a yardstick, the Hamilton of the *Federalist* was far from devoted to laissez faire, as his later writings amply demonstrate.

Madison and Hamilton: Their Later Writings

The later writings of Madison and Hamilton make it far easier to identify their views about capitalism and laissez faire. This is not surprising. The *Federalist*, designed to serve the single purpose of supporting the ratification of the Constitution, focuses on broad questions of how the federal government should be constructed, leaving open—as did the Constitution itself—any question about what economic policies the federal government should adopt in the future. To have made these essays that comprise the *Federalist* a manifesto on economic policy might have jeopardized their success in procuring ratification. But later on, Madison, as secretary of state and president, and Hamilton, as secretary of the treasury, had ample opportunity to take stances on specific issues of economic policy, and every reason—within the bounds of political prudence—to disclose their views candidly.

Of Madison's commitment to capitalism—in the sense of a presumption in favor of private property—those writings leave no doubt.[15] He even subscribed to the proposition that private property ought to be "inviolable," which was one of the cant phrases of the time, the real thrust of which is clarified when he said, in an adjoining passage, that property should be secure against *"arbitrary restrictions, exemptions, and monopolies."*[16] To have believed strictly in the "inviolability" of private property would have been to deny to government any power to tax or regulate, in short to have made government impossible. To prohibit *arbitrary* interventions by government, on the other hand, is to erect procedural safeguards, which would not however preclude substantive interference by government in the use of private property. In short, then, Madison's commitment to private property and thus to capitalism was pragmatically realistic rather than as dogmatic as some of his words might suggest.

As for laissez faire, Madison's attitude emerges with great clarity from a letter written late in his life to the German economist, Frederick List. Concerning efforts by government to encourage domestic manufactures, a policy that List strongly advocated, Madison wrote:

> the true policy. . .will be found to lie between the extremes of doing nothing and prescribing everything; between admitting no exceptions to the rule of 'laissez faire,' and converting the exceptions into the rule. The intermediate Legislative interposition *will be* more or less limited, according to the differing judgments of Statesmen, and *ought to be so*, according to the aptitudes or inaptitudes of countries and situations for the particular objects claiming encouragement. . .[17]

This passage crystallizes what Madison said on various other occasions.[18] While specifically mentioning "the rule of laissez faire" it specifically disavows it in favor of an "intermediate" level of government intervention, a policy of intervention whenever politicians judge it to be probably beneficial. In short, at this stage in his life Madison neither rejected nor accepted laissez faire in principle; nor does the statement of his position suggest that this equivocal attitude toward the principle pertained only to encouragement to domestic manufactures. Therefore, it may be that Madison, in the capacity conferred on him by some historians as Father of the Constitution, intended that it should enshrine neither laissez faire nor the opposite, though it would be somewhat rash to infer this from what Madison said some forty years after the drafting of the Constitution, perhaps expressing what he had come to think at some time in between.

Hamilton also, in his later writings, assumed that productive property would continue to be held largely by private individuals.[19] That assumption, a fact too obvious to Americans to need explicit statement, pervaded the famous reports that Hamilton submitted to Congress while he served as the first secretary of the treasury. It is well illustrated by the axiom underlying his *Report on Public Credit* of 1790, that the new government must honor at par the certificates of debt which the Revolutionary governments had issued to private lenders. Even though heated dispute had broken out over how much of the debt should be repaid to the original lenders and how much to subsequent buyers of the certificates, nobody seemed to doubt that repudiation would indefensibly violate property rights.[20]

As to Hamilton's attitude toward laissez faire, it emerges vividly from his *Report on Manufactures* of 1791,[21] where he maintained that the government could and should stimulate the development of manufacturing. By way of preface he attacked Adam Smith's precept that all such artificial encouragement diminishes a nation's prosperity; in this brief duel, which Hamilton fought with the deftness to be expected of a great lawyer, he made one or two telling hits but failed to injure any vital organs.[22] Then, passing on to practical proposals, Hamilton advanced a bundle of measures of just the sort that Smith or any other protagonist of laissez faire would have found totally erroneous, measures that included protective duties, prohibition of imports, and subsidies.[23] Hamilton thus fueled protectionist sentiments, which had been present in the United States from the beginning, and became increasingly influential during the nineteenth century.[24]

Somewhat later Hamilton wrote of laissez faire that: "This favorite dogma, when taken as a general rule, is true; but as an exclusive one, it is false, and leads to error in the administration of public affairs."[25] From the phrasing we may infer that is was not his favorite dogma; he was at most a lukewarm votary, ready to renounce the faith whenever it stood in the way of better things. According to Clinton Rossiter's correct assessment, Hamilton subscribed to "no mystique of collectivism or individualism, of mercantilism or *laissez faire*, of protection or free trade, of liberty or authority.... He was a mixed-economy pragmatist..."[26]

The Views of Other Thinkers of the Period

What did other Framers and contemporaries think about the questions before us? Obviously they entertained a variety of views, and some of them held positions riddled with internal contradictions.[27] No survey could possibly detect where the bulk of American opinion lay in 1787. It is possible, however, to trace some of the widely held presuppositions of American thought at that time. Sample data is available to indicate which earlier writers Americans regarded as authoritative on questions that arose during the ratification controversy.

From three sources—the *Federalist, The Complete Anti-Federalist*, and the collection assembled by Hyneman and Lutz[28]—an unmistakable pattern emerges. Writers represented in these collections, of whom there are about 150, referred repeatedly to a small core of authorities and sporadically to a dozen or more others. Montesquieu tops the list by far, with Blackstone second, and Locke third. Prominent among the also-rans appear Hume, Grotius, and Pufendorf. Adam Smith is cited once, and then only as authority for the proposition that "Decency nowhere requires that any man should eat butcher's meat".[29]

Several important uniformities characterize the stars, Montesquieu, Blackstone, and Locke, as well as the supporting players. First, their texts figured prominently in the education of Americans concerned with law and politics during the late eighteenth century.[30] Second, the works of these authors had been published well before 1787. The most recent, Blackstone's *Commentaries*, had been printed in America in 1771-72.[31] The age of those works helps explain why Adam Smith could hardly have influenced the making of the Constitution. By 1776, when *The Wealth of Nations* was first published in London, the American colonies were actively at war with Britain; from then through 1782 Americans would not have been placing orders with London booksellers or receiving shipment. It is unlikely that, even after peace was arranged in 1783, many copies of *The Wealth of Nations* reached America; the first American printing did not appear until 1789.[32] Thus, it is unlikely that many Americans had seen the book by 1787. By contrast, the bulk of the works that sank deeply into the minds of educated Americans had established their preeminence up to a century earlier. Eighteenth-century illuminati, even in the New World, still believed that old philosophical texts were more venerable than new ones.

Third among the common characteristics of these authorities is that each of them relied on a theory of natural law. But too much significance should not be attached to this consensus, since various believers in natural law or natural rights differed substantially about what it is that natural law dictates, and also about the extent to which natural law could or should be realized in the positive laws made by men. Because the Framers and their contemporaries so regularly relied on natural-law theorists,[33] it is reasonable to surmise that specters of natural law lurked in some of the Constitution's interstices.[34] Yet, as natural law is not published in any statute book, its silent presence in the Constitution cannot readily be construed. To be sure, many Americans declared that natural law confers on men a right to liberty; but "liberty," in the absence of precise definition, serves better as a slogan than as a canon for explicating the Constitution.

Turning now to the most heavily cited authority, Montesquieu, what was his probable influence on the Framers and their contemporaries? Over and above the attractions, intellectual and aesthetic, that drew Europeans to his works and especially to *De l'Esprit des Lois* (1748), post-Revolutionary Americans were attracted to his theory of republics, because it was so pertinent to their circumstances.

A well-ordered republic, according to Montesquieu, is an admirable kind of government. It is animated by civic virtue, which induces each citizen to prefer the public good to his private interest, and by the recognition of the rulers (who represent the people) that they too must submit to the laws that they make and enforce. If civic virtue decayed, then the republic would degenerate into lawless chaos (III, 3).[35] Civic virtue tends to flourish in a republic that occupies a small territory, for there "the public good is better sensed, better understood, and closer to each citizen." (VIII, 16) A democratic republic, if it is to be sustained, depends also on the citizens' frugality, since approximate equality of wealth insures equality of power. (V, 3) Here in Montesquieu was to be found a vision of virtue, simplicity, and stable self-government that confirmed and informed the aspirations of many Americans who might very roughly be identified as Jeffersonians.

To other Americans, who might loosely be described as Hamiltonians, Montesquieu offered another variety of republic that was more to their taste. This was a "commercial republic," on the order of Athens, Venice, and the Netherlands. Although its stability too depends on civic virtue, such virtue does not depend on equality of fortunes. Some citizens may well amass great wealth, but this need not corrupt them, because the spirit of commerce encourages "frugality, economy, moderation, energy, prudence, tranquility, order, and system." (V, 6) Here then was a different republican vision, sharing the attribute of a virtuous citizenry, free in the sense of choosing their own rulers, but distinct in holding out the prospect of great and growing wealth.

Other features in Montesquieu's vision of commercial republics would have struck Hamiltonians as less palatable. For one thing, Montesquieu held it to be "almost a general rule" that commerce softens men's manners and makes nations pacific. (XX, 1-2) And what especially distressed nationalists was Montesquieu's maxim that a republic must be small, for in the American constitutional setting this argued against a strong central government.

Montesquieu's influence is demonstrated by the concerted efforts that the *Federalist* writers made to contradict those of his pronouncements that proved awkward for the Constitutional scheme that they were defending. Madison's tenth essay is a direct answer to Montesquieu. It is an effort to prove that a large republic, namely the United States, would more effectively control factions than could small republics, namely the separate states. In the same way, Hamilton's *Federalist* No. 6 directly answers one of Montesquieu's arguments. Hamilton summarized Montesquieu's position in this way:

> The genius of republics. . .is pacific; the spirit of commerce has a tendency to soften the manners of men, and to extinguish those inflammable humors which have so often kindled into wars. Commercial republics, like ours, will never be disposed to waste themselves in ruinous contentions with each other.

Hamilton proceeded to show that this rosy picture, embraced by the Antifederalists, was false. Various historical episodes suggested that the commercial republics in North America, that is, the thirteen states, might well fall into conflict with each other unless they were joined in a single union.

Given that Montesquieu held such sway that Americans received much of what he said as gospel and rejected bits of it only with great circumspection, it might be supposed that his ideas made their way into the Constitution. It is widely agreed that the separation of powers came from him, or at least through him. Did his ideas about economic policy penetrate the Constitution?

As to private property, Montesquieu constantly assumes that the citizens of a republic own property, exchange it, and bequeath it. Whether to call this an endorsement of capitalism is a fine point, for private ownership of productive property typified, in Montesquieu's historical examples, classical city-states and medieval cities, long before capitalism is normally thought to have arisen. Moreover, Montesquieu treats private ownership more nearly as a fact than as a value.

As to anything like laissez faire, on the other hand, Montesquieu's position was decidedly adverse. That he extolled frugality as a virtue is not material, even though doing so ran contrary to the Mandevillian strand in laissez-faire theory, according to which the self-indulgence of some stokes the engine of production that benefits all.[36] But he directly opposed a central tenet of laissez faire when he advocated that the laws of a republic should *enforce* frugality. He advocated, for instance, that as a safeguard against excessive accumulation, a republic should require a father's estate to be devised not as he might see fit but in equal shares to each child. (V, 6) He advocated that a commercial republic should from time to time redistribute fortunes, both for the benefit of the poor and to force the rich to continue their labors. (V, 6) And more broadly he advocated that all forms of "contracting"—by which, as the context suggests, he meant unilateral transfers—must be regulated by law. "For were it permitted to give property to whom one wished and how one wished, the will of each individual would disturb the order of the fundamental law." (V, 5)

Montesquieu took an equally interventionist stand on international trade. He upheld the policy of European empires that monopolized trade with their overseas colonies, on the ground that the disadvantage to the colonies was offset by the services rendered by the mother countries in governing and defending them. (XXI, 21) Furthermore, he endorsed mercantilism expressly:

> Freedom of trade is not a faculty accorded to merchants to do what they like. . . That which constrains the merchant does not thereby constrain trade. It is in free nations that the merchant encounters numberless obstacles, and he is never less crushed by the laws than in an unfree nation.
>
> England prohibits exportation of her wool; she insists that coal be transported to the capital by sea; she does not permit at all the export of breeding stallions; the ships of her colonies that trade with Europe must call in England. She troubles the merchant, but in favor of commerce. (XX, 12)

Although Montesquieu's many comments on economic policy fall far short of mapping out a coherent theory, their general flavor is interventionist. To the extent that the Framers and their contemporaries were influenced by Montesquieu, evidently a considerable extent, they too must have conceived of intervention as acceptable or necessary, and to have allowed for it when designing the powers of the federal government.

III. Evidence from the Public Policy of American Government

Makers of a constitution must be presumed to be familiar with the main facts of the political life that they mean to reshape. They must be presumed to be confirming or at least condoning those antecedent practices that their constitution does not reject or reform. Analysis of the Framer's intentions concerning economic policy must accordingly take into account the economic policies pursued by American governments—colonial, state, local, and congressional—down to 1787.

Broadly speaking, those policies were mercantilist in inclination. As a matter of course the colonists carried over to the New World the general habits of policy with which they had grown up in Britain, even though they adapted some of them to their new circumstances and grumbled about others (such as the restrictions imposed on the colonies by the Navigation Acts). In 1787, then, many of the economic policies enacted by American governments were closely akin to those that Smith had condemned the British government for practicing.

Few major aspects of economic life were immune from regulation by colonial assemblies and their dependent local governments or by their successors after 1776.[37] Labor markets were particularly unfree. Well over half of the Europeans who migrated to the colonies did so as indentured servants, whose bondage, lasting up to seven years, was enforced by law.[38] That this institution still persisted in 1787 is witnessed by the fact that the constitution distinguishes between "free Persons" and the sub-class of "those bound to Service for a Term of Years." (Article I, Section 2) Besides indentured servants (and "customary servants," "redemptioners," and convicts), an increasing number of slaves were held in servility by law. Nor were free laborers unfettered. Colonial legislators and magistrates often fixed their maximum wages and minimum hours of work. They regulated entry into various occupations, sometimes requiring apprenticeship, a license, or discretionary approval by magistrates. Thus, following complaints that porters in Boston and Charlestown were overcharging, it was ordained that the selectmen "shall have power to regulate in this case, and to state their wages, as in their understanding shall be most just, and equal, as also to determine what persons shall be employed therein."[39]

Similar restrictions applied to product markets. In many places, retail trade was confined to official market-places during officially sanctioned hours. Prices of many commodities were held down to levels that magistrates considered just or reasonable. Authorities inspected and regulated the quality of commodities important in domestic consumption, like bread, or in foreign trade, like tobacco and timber. Production of certain goods was prohibited or punitively taxed, whereas production of others was encouraged by payment of bounties. Such interventions obviously affected patterns of consumption, even if not always intentionally. But intentional regulation of consumption was not uncommon. In Massachusetts, for instance, selectmen were commanded to keep watch over people's dress, and to levy fines on those who wore apparel above "their rankes & abilities in the costliness, or fashion. . . especially in the wearing of Ribbons or great boots... lace, points... silk hoods or scarfes..."[40] And even during the Constitutional Convention, George Mason of Virginia proposed (with support of a minority) that in order to suppress extravagance and luxury Congress should be empowered to pass sumptuary laws.[41]

Apart from these and other ways in which governments controlled private economic activities, they themselves engaged in a variety of productive enterprises either by direct ownership or by participation in mixed enterprises. Thus, various governments operated harbors and wharves, public loan offices or land banks, postal services, export agencies, and offices for retail sale of public land. They also subsidized and invested in certain private enterprises, and fostered the development of private public-service companies by granting them monopolies.

Upon achieving independence, the states began to regulate their own external trade, partly by imposing duties on imports, partly by adopting measures imitating the British Navigation Acts, and partly by urging the Congress of the Confederation to adopt a national navigation act.[42]

Although the Congress of the Confederation lacked power to govern economic affairs, it did not lack inclination. In 1777 the New England states passed a series of parallel "regulating acts" that fixed the wages of farm workers, mechanics, tradesmen, and "other labour," as well as the prices of farm produce, manufactured goods, rum, sugar, and other imports, and the charges for various services. Having done so, they applied to the Congress to approve those measures and to recommend that the other nine states adopt similar ones. After some debate, Congress did so.[43] Far from being an extraordinary response to war-time emergency, this step merely extended a practice traditional among the colonial governments.

Debate over the "regulating acts" offers a curious side-light on attitudes toward economic intervention generally. During the debate John Adams was reported to have objected to the acts on the ground that "it is as plain as any demonstration in Euclid, that trade cannot be regulated, it must regulate itself."[44] Yet at almost the same moment he submitted to the Congress a set of resolutions urging state governments to "promote" and "encourage" agriculture, arts, manufactures, and commerce[45]—presumably by the elaborate variety of protections and subsidies that had previously been employed by American governments.

The Framers and their contemporaries must have known from their own experience what American governments at all levels deemed useful and proper in economic policy. Had the Framers regarded those established patterns as harmful and improper, they could have drafted constitutional provisions tending to inhibit or exclude them. But as we have seen, no such provisions can be found in the Constitution.

Conclusion

Some legal historians, eminent among them Bernard Siegan and Richard Epstein,[46] have traced the steps by which judicial interpretation transformed the Constitution so as to sanction the "new mercantilism," the welfare state, the redistributive state, "pluralism" in the pernicious sense of that term, or the "insurance state."[47] That Constitutional interpretation has long been drifting in this direction cannot be denied.[48] That it would be desirable to reverse this drift, I agree. But no desire about the future course of American economic policy should impair our understanding of what the Constitution meant when it was drafted and ratified.

The makers of the Constitution assumed that much and probably most productive property would be owned by private persons. They did not doubt, however, that public bodies could rightfully own and operate some productive property. Nor was it scandalous in their eyes that the greatest owners of land, albeit land as yet unsettled, should be governments. Neither could they doubt that private property in land was subject to prescriptive easements and other obligations in the interest not only of other proprietors but also of the public at large. [49] And they could not fail to recognize that the use of every sort of private property was in some substantial degree conditioned by law. Yet despite all such qualifications on the extent and implications of private ownership, cap-italism—in the sense that I have defined, as private ownership of the means of production—was certainly built into the Constitution. To be more precise, the Framers assumed the actual prevalence of private ownership, but that is very different from saying that the Constitution expressly or by necessary implication guaranteed that capitalism would continue unabated or even at all.

As to laissez faire, the Framers never experienced it in practice, were as a group unfamiliar with its theory, pledged it little or no faith, and certainly did nothing to embody it in the Constitution. Neither however did they write anything into the Constitution that could have prevented American govern-ments from pursuing a policy of laissez faire.

It may be a matter for regret that the Framers overlooked, or refrained from deliberately designing, so important an area of government activity as the making of economic policy. It may however be a source of some comfort that the Constitution's economic neutrality has contributed to its marvelous durability.

Notes

1. A thorough scholarly analysis is given in A. E. D. HOWARD, THE ROAD FROM RUNNYMEDE (1968).
2. *Id.* at 388.
3. 28 Edw. 3, c.3 (1354).
4. SOURCES OF OUR LIBERTIES 148 (R. Perry & J. Cooper eds. 1959).
5. Thus, the Declaration of Rights in the Constitution of North Carolina of 1776

(§ XII) reads: "That no freeman ought to be taken, imprisoned, or disseized of his freehold, liberties or privileges, or outlawed, or exiled, or in any manner destroyed, or deprived of his life, liberty, or property, but by the law of the land." *Id.* at 355. Similar passages occur in the 1776 constitutions of Pennsylvania, (§ 9), Maryland (§ 21), and North Carolina (§ 12). *Id.* at 330, 348, 355.

6. R. EPSTEIN, TAKINGS: PRIVATE PROPERTY AND THE POWER OF EMINENT DOMAIN (1985), *passim.*

7. W. CROSSKEY, POLITICS AND THE CONSTITUTION (1953), see especially Parts I and II.

8. 1 *Id.* at 365-379.

9. *Id.* at 324. *See also* Plattner, *American Democracy and the Acquisitive Spirit,* in HOW CAPITALISTIC IS THE CONSTITUTION? 14 n.33-36 (R. Goldwin & W. Schambra eds. 1982).

10. THE FEDERALIST No. 44 (J. Madison) (J. Cooke ed. 1961).

11. Locke maintained that in the state of nature "different degrees of Industry were apt to give Men Possessions in different Proportions..." LOCKE, TWO TREATISES OF GOVERNMENT 319 (P. Laslett ed. 1967). Once men in the state of nature consented to the use of money, they thereby "agreed to disproportionate and unequal Posession of the Earth." *Id.* at 320. Since the "great and *chief end...* of Mens uniting into Commonwealths, and putting themselves under Government, *is the Preservation of their Property...,*" (*Id.* at 368-369) it would seem to follow that government must preserve the inequality of possessions that existed before government was created. Although in other writings, Locke held that government might justly redistribute property, (*Id.* at 104) no such statement appears in the *Second Treatise.*

Madison's assertion parallels a statement by Adam Smith in 1766, when according to a student's lecture notes he said that "Till there be property there can be no government, the very end of which is to secure wealth and to defend the rich from the poor." SMITH, LECTURES ON JURISPRUDENCE 404 (R. Meek *et al* eds. 1978). Although Smith frequently referred to Locke's writings, there is no evidence to prove that Smith took this idea from Locke, nor evidence to prove that Madison took it from Locke or any subsequent writer.

12. MONTESQUIEU, DE L'ESPRIT DES LOIS, BK. VII, Chs. 1-2 (1748).

13. SMITH, THE WEALTH OF NATIONS BK. IV, Ch. 9 (1776).

14. *Id.* at BK. IV, Ch. 1.

15. E. BURNS, JAMES MADISON, PHILOSOPHER OF THE CONSTITUTION (1968), and especially at 203-205.

16. THE COMPLETE MADISON 268 (S. Padover ed. 1953). Emphasis added.

17. *Id.* at 274-275 (Madison to List, Feb 3, 1829).

18. *Id.* at 270-276, *cf.* at 291-293.

19. C. ROSSITER, ALEXANDER HAMILTON AND THE CONSTITUTION 163 n. 42 (1964).

20. 6 PAPERS OF ALEXANDER HAMILTON 51ff. (H. Syrett *et al.* eds. 1961-79). On the controversy about redemption, *see* E. FERGUSON, THE POWER OF THE PURSE (1961).

21. 10 Syrett, *id.* at 1-340. For an authoritative account of Hamilton's sources for the report, *see* J. COOKE, TENCH COXE AND THE EARLY REPUBLIC Ch. 9 (1978).

22. On Hamilton's handling of Smith's text, *see* Bourne, *Alexander Hamilton and*

Adam Smith, 8 QUARTERLY JOURNAL OF ECONOMICS 328-344 (1893-94).

23. Hamilton successfully rebutted the objection that Congress lacked constitutional power to grant subsidies; indeed, he had earlier maintained that this power was comprehended in the commerce clause. *See* 1 CROSSKEY, *supra* note 7, at 401 n.

24. C. NETTELS, THE EMERGENCE OF A NATIONAL ECONOMY 109-111 (1962).

25. Dec. 24, 1801. In 25 Syrett, *supra* note 20, at 467.

26. ROSSITER, *supra* note 19, at 180.

27. *See, e.g.*, the views of John Adams, discussed below.

28. THE COMPLETE ANTI-FEDERALIST (H. Storing ed. 1981), and AMERICAN POLITICAL WRITING DURING THE FOUNDING ERA, 1760-1805 (C. Hyneman & D. Lutz eds. 1983).

29. Hyneman, *id.* at 778 n.

30. L. FRIEDMAN, A HISTORY OF AMERICAN LAW 88 (1973); ROSSITER, *supra* note 19, at 118-120; A. CHROUST, 2 THE RISE OF THE LEGAL PROFESSION IN AMERICA 176, 184 n.48 (1965); G. GOEBEL *et al.*, A HISTORY OF THE SCHOOL OF LAW, COLUMBIA UNIVERSITY, Ch. 1 (1955).

31. FRIEDMAN, *id.* at 88.

32. THE VANDERBLUE MEMORIAL COLLECTION OF SMITHIANA 20 (1939) (Kress Library, Harvard Business School, Publication No. 2).

33. *See. e.g.*, ROSSITER, *supra* note 19, at 119, 123, *et passim*; and BURNS, *supra* note 15, at 6, 63, 154.

34. Corwin, *The Higher Law Background of American Constitutional Law*, 62 HARVARD LAW REVIEW 398 (1929).

35. Passages quoted from Montesquieu are translated from the text of DE L'ESPRIT DES LOIS (G. Truc ed. 1961). Citations in the form, III, 3, refer to Book III, Chapter III.

36. B. MANDEVILLE, FABLE OF THE BEES (1723).

37. My summary is documented in the following books and the sources they cite: J. MCCUSKER & R. MENARD, THE ECONOMY OF BRITISH AMERICA (1985), especially at 47-48, 242, 313-316, 333-344; J. HUGHES, THE GOVERNMENTAL HABIT, Ch. 2 (1977); and F. McDonald, *The Constitution and Hamiltonian Capitalism*, in Goldwin, *supra* note 9, at 49-62.

38. MCCUSKER, *id.* at 242.

39. HUGHES, *supra* note 37, at 40.

40. *Id.* at 30.

41. J. MADISON, NOTES OF DEBATES IN THE FEDERAL CONVENTION 488-489, 632 (1966).

42. NETTELS, *supra* note 24, at 72-75.

43. 1 CROSSKEY, *supra* note 7, at 179-186.

44. *Id.* at 182.

45. 2 J. ADAMS, DIARY AND AUTOBIOGRAPHY 234-235 (L. Butterfield ed. 1964).

46. *See* B. SIEGAN, ECONOMIC LIBERTIES AND THE CONSTITUTION (1980); and EPSTEIN, *supra* note 6.

47. W. Letwin, *Social Responsibility of Business in an Insurance State*, in RATIONALITY, LEGITIMACY, RESPONSIBILITY (E. Epstein & D. Votaw eds. 1979).

48. *Cf.* Letwin, *Economic Due Process in the American Constitution, and the Rule of Law,* in LIBERTY AND THE RULE OF LAW (R. Cunningham ed. 1979).

49. McDonald, *supra* note 37, at 51.

Contract Rights and Property Rights:
A Case Study in the Relationship between
Individual Liberties and Constitutional Structure

MICHAEL W. McCONNELL*

The natural inclination is to think that individual "rights" must be protected against "the state"—that is, against government in general. Political liberalism, in both its new and old varieties, is based on the generalized distinction between individual autonomy and governmental authority. Yet it is striking how many important rights in the Constitution of the United States are protected by their terms against one level or branch of government and not against the others. The provisions of the Bill of Rights apply only to the federal government and not to the states; the equal protection clause of the Fourteenth Amendment applies only to states and not to the federal government; the First Amendment applies to Congress and not, apparently, to the executive or judicial branches. It is also striking that the courts typically disregard these limits and protect rights against government action generally. Thus, most provisions of the Bill of Rights have been "incorporated" against the states;[1] the equal protection clause has been "reverse-incorporated" against the federal government;[2] and the apparent limitation of the First Amendment to legislative action has been ignored.[3]

One of the most puzzling, and thus most interesting, instances in which the constitutional text guarantees individual rights only against one level of government and not the other lies in the area of economic liberties—the rights of property and contract. The Fifth Amendment just compensation clause prohibits takings of private property for a public use without just compensation. But until its "incorporation" through the Fourteenth Amendment at the end of the nineteenth century, the just compensation clause applied only to

*I thank the Lynde and Harry Bradley Foundation for financial support during the preparation of this article, and Albert Alschuler, David Currie, Howard Dickman, Frank Easterbrook, Richard Epstein, Geoffrey Miller, Ellen Frankel Paul, Richard Stewart, Geoffrey Stone, David Strauss, and Cass Sunstein for helpful comments on an earlier draft.

the federal government.[4] States were free to take property without compensating, unless the taking happened to violate some other provision of law. On the other hand, Article I, Section 10, prohibits laws "impairing the Obligation of Contracts." This provision applies only to the states. The federal government may impair the obligation of contracts without constitutional restraint, unless the impairment is also a taking of property or a violation of some other provision of the Constitution.

A mere glance at the Constitution suffices to show that it is exceedingly improbable that this difference in treatment was inadvertent. Section 10 of Article I contains certain limitations on state powers; Section 9 of the same article contains parallel limitations on the powers of Congress. Section 10 provides that "[n]o State shall. . .pass any Bill of Attainder, ex post facto Law, or Law impairing the Obligation of Contracts." Section 9, which applies only to Congress, provides that "[n]o Bill of Attainder or ex post facto Law shall be passed." The omission of a contracts clause from Section 9 is too obvious to be anything but deliberate.[5]

The inconsistent treatment of these two overlapping economic rights has been occasionally commented upon,[6] never convincingly explained,[7] and most often ignored by scholars in the field.[8] My intention is to explore possible reasons for this disparate treatment of contract and property rights, and thus the connection, in the original constitutional scheme, between individual rights and the structure of government. I propose two different, but complementary, explanations loosely derived from comments made by Hamilton and Madison in the *Federalist*. The "Hamiltonian" explanation lies in the special role of contracts, as opposed to tangible property, in national commercial life. The "Madisonian" explanation lies in the relation between the threats to contractual and property rights and the problem of faction in state and federal government.

Section I of this paper will briefly summarize the textual problem posed by the contracts and just compensation clauses, as illuminated by the conceptions of property rights prevalent at the time of the Founding. Section II will review the history of the adoptions of the two clauses with attention to the question posed by this paper. Section III will offer a speculative and analytical account of the reasons for the constitutional provisions as written. Finally, Section IV will discuss some of the implications of these conclusions for constitutional analysis today.[9]

I. Contracts and Property: A Textual Puzzle

Critics as well as admirers frequently observe that the American constitutional scheme was designed, in large part, for the protection of private property. James Madison, writing in the *Federalist* No. 10, stated that "the protection of different and unequal faculties of acquiring property" is "the first object of government."[10] He wrote to Thomas Jefferson that the principal motivation for the Constitutional Convention was not (as is often thought) that the Confederation government was ineffectual, but that the rights of property were endangered by the unstable popular governments of many of the states.[11] Gouverneur Morris, also a leading draftsman, stated during the Constitutional Convention: "Life and liberty were generally said to be of more value, than property. An accurate view of the matter would nevertheless prove that property was the main object of Society."[12] These were not isolated statements or idiosyncratic views. It is fair to conclude that the protection of private property was as nearly unanimous and intention among the founding generation as any other element of a political creed.[13]

The Constitution is, in most respects, admirably suited to the protection of private property. We think immediately of the explicit restrictions against takings of property without due process and just compensation, against the impairment of the obligation of contracts, against bills of attainder, and against debased currency, all backed up by the institution of judicial review. Still more important, however, is the structure of government, which is designed to promote the stability and insulation from popular upheavals that economic life demands.

Discussions in the Convention show that the Framers were well aware of the dangers to property that are inherent in unchecked popular assemblies. Gouverneur Morris, for example, commented that "[e]very man of observation had seen in the Democratic branches of the State Legislatures, precipitation—in Congress changeableness—in every department excesses against personal liberty, private property, and personal safety."[14] The Convention's proposal of an extended union, deliberative representation, and checks and balances was the antidote to this problem. The structure of government was designed to promote "the permanent and aggregate interests of the community,"[15] and to reduce the "instability, injustice, and confusion" that had always plagued popular governments.[16] By making legislative change difficult to achieve, the system inclines toward limited government. It also provides procedural safeguards that settled expectations will not be upset by passing political passions. The underlying bias of the system is to preserve the status quo; this in turn protects the preexisting distribution of property.

The difference in application of the contracts and just compensation clauses, however, is difficult to square with this emphasis on the rights of property. If taking property without compensation is wrong, why is it permitted to the states? If impairing contract rights is unfair, why is it permitted to the federal government? A simple theory of the importance of property will not explain the matter; nor is it explicable on the ground that one level of government is inherently more trustworthy than the other. Unless we are to conclude that the Constitution is simply incoherent on these points—and the presumption should be to the contrary—the search for an explanation must go beyond the Framers' attitude toward property to the connection they saw between private rights and the structure of political institutions.

These reflections raise practical questions of interpretation. Should the contracts clause be interpreted broadly, so as to protect against the taking of property by a State? This depends, in large part, on whether there was a reason not to apply the just compensation clause to the states in the first instance. Should the just compensation (or possibly the due process or ex post facto) clause be interpreted broadly, so as to prevent the federal government from impairing the obligation of contracts? Again, this depends on one's view of the underlying purposes.

The nature of the problem, as well as its persistence, is illustrated by two Supreme Court decisions—one under Chief Justice Marshall, the first decision to construe the contracts clause, the other at the end of the Court's 1985 term and one of the more recent attempts to construe the just compensation clause. Both play upon the slender distinction between contract and property.

In *Fletcher v. Peck*,[17] the State of Georgia attempted to seize large land holdings from current owners who were, for the most part, bona fide purchasers, because the original grants had been procured by bribing the legislature. This attempt would appear to be a classic "taking," as Marshall's opinion for the Court implicitly acknowledged. Where are the "limits to the legislative power," he wondered, "if the property of an individual, fairly and honestly acquired, may be seized without compensation"?[18] But since the just compensation clause did not apply to the states, the Court had to look elsewhere for a basis to invalidate the action. Marshall's solution[19] was to hold that a "grant" was a "contract"; the grant of land by the State of Georgia "implied a contract" by the State "not to reassert" its right to the land in question.[20] Georgia's seizure of the lands thus violated not the just compensation clause, but the contracts clause.

The reasoning in support of the Court's conclusion, that a "grant" is also a "contract," is instructive for our purposes. It would be "strange," Marshall commented, "if a contract to convey was secured by the constitution, while an absolute conveyance remained unprotected."[21] This merely restates the problem: does it make any sense to protect contract rights without also protecting property rights? Marshall solved the problem in *Fletcher* essentially by ignoring the textual difference between the contracts and just compensation clauses.[22] If takings are also impairments of contract, and if impairments of contract are also takings, then the constitutional scheme seems to make little sense. But even if we overlook its textual improbability, Marshall's solution fails to eliminate the "strangeness" of the two clauses. Under his view, a purchaser of property is protected only where the state is the seller. Specifically, the State of Georgia could seize the property of any citizens who were not grantees from the state. Is this not also "strange," since it treats differently persons whose rights as against the world, including the government, are identical?[23]

Bowen v. Public Agencies Opposed to Social Security Entrapment[24] is the mirror image of *Fletcher v. Peck*. In *Bowen*, the federal government reneged on a written commitment to allow state and local governments to withdraw from the Social Security system at any time. The commitment had been made in exchange for the voluntary participation of those governments in the system. This would appear to be an impairment of the obligation of contract, if it is a constitutional violation at all. Because the contracts clause does not apply to the federal government, however, the respondent governments characterized the federal government's action as a taking of property. Marshall's logic in *Fletcher* could have been used in reverse: would it not be "strange" that the valuable right to withdraw from the Social Security scheme could be taken away without compensation, after the federal government had received its consideration, merely because the respondents had yet to receive the benefit of their bargain?

In *Bowen*, however, the Court did not follow Marshall's reasoning. Respondent's rights, however valuable, bore "little, if any, resemblance to rights held to constitute 'property' within the meaning of the Fifth Amendment."[25] The reason this was so, admittedly, was left somewhat unclear;[26] it does not seem to be because the right was contractual.[27] At heart, however, the right "did not rise to the level of 'property' "[28] because it was merely executory and the United States had given generalized notice, before the agreement was made, that it could alter the terms of the program.[29] This is contracts clause analysis, of the most grudging and positivistic sort, here applied to prove that the public employees had been denied no property right.[30] The end result may be correct, but it seems an indirect way to reach the conclusion that the federal government is not forbidden to impair the obligation of contracts.

Evidence from the founding period only complicates the puzzle. To the extent the terms were distinguished, "contract" seems to have been understood as a subcategory of "property." Blackstone, the Framers' leading authority on the common law, treats contract as "property in action."[31] His discussion of contract law appears in the *Commentaries* solely as one of the various means by which title to property may be acquired.[32] Contract would seem to have no higher status in justice or in law than title by gift, grant, marriage, or occupancy.[33] Property, according to Blackstone, is the essential concept—the "third absolute right, inherent in every Englishman."[34] This is not to say, however, that contract rights are therefore unimportant. Rather, they are subsumed in the larger concept of property. Blackstone's definition of property is compendious enough to comprise contract rights as well as more tangible forms of property. The right of property, he explains, "consists in the free use, enjoyment, and disposal of all his acquisitions, without any control or diminution, save only by the laws of the land."[35]

The concepts of property developed by the English common law were echoed and even expanded by the Framers. Madison, for example, wrote an essay on property in which he distinguished between the term "property" in its "particular application" and in its "larger and juster meaning."[36] The "particular application" he defined by paraphrasing Blackstone (without attribution): "that dominion which one man claims and exercises over the external things of the world, in exclusion of every other individual."[37] This meaning Madison associated with the just compensation clause.[38] In its "larger and juster meaning," the term embraces "every thing to which a man may attach a value and have a right," including "the free use of his facilities and [the] free choice of the objects on which to employ them."[39]

The main point of the essay was that property in both the narrower and broader senses warrants legal protection: "Government is instituted to protect property of every sort; as well that which lies in the various rights of individuals, as that which the term particularly expresses."[40] Madison's principal concern, it seems, was with the acquisition and transfer, rather than the mere possession, of property—that is, with contract rights as well as property rights. "That is not a just government, nor is property secure under it, where arbitrary restrictions, exemptions, and monopolies deny to part of its citizens that free use of their faculties, and free choice of their occupations, which...are the means of acquiring property."[41]

Gouverneur Morris was in agreement. As one scholar has commented:[42]

> [T]he rights of property Morris was so concerned with were those essential to a commercial society, the rights of property in transaction. Everyone knew that people's possessions should be secure from theft or arbitrary confiscation; Morris' arguments urged that in a commercial society the freedom of dispositon and the security of contractual agreements were at least as important as this physical security.

An emphasis on acquisition and transfer as well as possession was consistent with the development of a commercial republic.[43] An agrarian economy could be preserved on the basis of rights of property alone; commerce required exchange. The emphasis on contract was also connected with the distrust of a landed nobility and attendant aristocratic institutions.[44] The constitutional scheme tends toward a social system of economic mobility—of static inequality but expansive opportunity—rather than one of fixed concentrations of wealth.[45] At the same time, however, the need to protect rights of possession was seen to follow from the rights of acquisition. "The personal right to acquire property, which is a natural right," Madison stated late in life, "gives to property, when acquired, a right to protection, as a social right."[46]

None of this supplies an explanation of the differential treatment of contract and property rights in the Constitution. While contract rights were not seen as identical to property rights, they were a type of property right; it cannot be said that one was more valuable than the other. It remains to be seen why one category of rights should be protected against one level of government, and another against the other.

II. Framing of the Contracts and Just Compensation Clauses

The historical record of the events and debate at the time of adoption of the Constitution and Bill of Rights casts little direct light on the question here. Although Madison commented in a letter to Jefferson that the contracts clause, along with the two other prohibitions on state actions in Article I, Section 10, "created more enemies than all the errors in the System positive and negative put together,"[47] we have little record of this controversy. Records concerning adoption of the just compensation clause are even more sparse. Nonetheless, it is useful to canvass the available sources, as much to eliminate possible explanations that are inconsistent with the record, as to discover evidence as to why the rights of contract and property received such disparate treatment in the Constitution.

The Northwest Ordinance and the Treaty of Paris

Both clauses of the Constitution find their origin in Article 2 of the Northwest Ordinance, which was adopted by Congress under the Articles of Confederation on July 13, 1787, some six weeks after the Constitutional Convention had convened. The Northwest Ordinance's precursor to the just compensation clause provided:[48]

> [N]o man shall be deprived of his liberty or property but by the judgment of his peers, or the law of the land; and should the public exigencies make it necessary for the common preservation to take any person[']s property, or to demand his particular services, full compensation shall be made for the same. . . .

According to Richard Henry Lee, "It seemed necessary, for the security of property among uninformed, and perhaps licentious people as the greater part of those who go there are, that a strong toned government should exist, and the rights of property be clearly defined."[49] This suggests that the need for explicit, nationally-imposed definition and protection for property rights, going beyond the common law and local legislation, was associated with the lesser degree of sophistication of people on the frontier.

The Northwest Ordinance's precursor to the contracts clause, which followed immediately after the provision just quoted, provided:

> [A]nd in the just preservation of rights and property it is understood and declared; that no law ought ever to be made, or have force in the said territory, that shall in any manner whatever interfere with, or affect private contracts or engagements, bona fide and without fraud previously formed.

This provision had no counterpart in the state constitutions of that day, and no explanation for its appearance has been found.

The provisions are of interest to our inquiry for two reasons. First, the two

provisions were closely associated in the Northwest Ordinance, being successive clauses of the same article, connected by the conjunction "and."
Moreover, the contract provision was said to be for the purpose of "the just
preservation of rights and property," thus emphasizing the connection between
the rights protected. Second, the two provisions applied to the same unit of
government—the territory. Under what would soon become our Constitution,
territories are subject to the constitutional restraints applicable to the federal
government; but federal power over the territories in some ways more closely
resembles state governmental powers than federal powers.[50] The Northwest
Ordinance provisions could therefore have been precedent for the application
of their restraints to the federal government, to state governments, or to both.
These factors make it all the more striking that the Framers separated the two
concepts in the Constitution and applied each to a different level of
government.

Another potential precursor to the clauses, the treaty of peace with Great
Britain, similarly accentuates the oddity of the constitutional scheme. The
treaty protected British citizens both from "any lawful impediment" to the
collection of bona fide debts and from confiscation of property.[51] This language
required the United States to protect the contract and property rights of
British subjects from any legal impairment, an obligation logically coterminous
with the protections embodied by the just compensation and contracts clauses.
If the Framers had been concerned with enforcing these treaty obligations, it
would have been logical to prohibit both levels of government from
impairments of contracts and uncompensated takings. The two principles were
associated in treaty as well as in domestic legislation. The Framers' failure to
incorporate these protections of contract and property rights against both the
states and the federal government in the Constitution thus cannot be
explained by inadvertence: the obligations imposed by the Treaty of Paris
necessarily drew attention to the connection between these issues.

The 1787 Constitution and the Contracts Clause

The early drafts of the Constitution at the Convention contained no
contracts clause or equivalent provision. This may be explained by the fact that
the forces that later favored a contracts clause at first devoted their energies to
an attempt to invest Congress with the power to nullify any state law thought
to be unwise or contrary to the plan of union. Such a power was thought by its
advocates, including Madison, to be "necessary to secure individuals ag[ainst]
encroachments on their rights"; he thought specific restraints against violation
of contracts "not sufficient" because legislatures could evade them at will by
using "an infinitude of legislative expedients."[52] Only when that effort had
narrowly failed did the delegates turn to more precisely tailored protections
against the most common excesses of democracy in the states.

On August 28, 1787, Rufus King of Massachusetts moved to add a constitutional prohibition, applicable to the states alone, against interference with "private contracts."[53] The wording of the provision was to be that of the Northwest Ordinance. Gouverneur Morris spoke in opposition, stating that "[t]his would be going too far. There are a thousand laws relating to bringing actions—limitations of action & which affect contracts." He further noted that the federal judiciary would be "a protection in cases within their jurisdiction"—presumably cases involving citizens from different states. "[W]ithin the State itself," Morris said, "a majority must rule, whatever may be the mischief done among themselves." This suggests a principal concern for the impact of state legislation on interstate commerce, and relatively little concern, on Morris's part, for preventing depredations against contractual rights within the confines of the individual states. It also suggests that Morris believed that, in practicality, there could be no absolute prohibition on impairments of the obligation of contract.

Madison spoke in favor of the provision, while reiterating his view that only a general power of Congress to nullify state laws would be adequate protection. Nonetheless, in supporting the measure, he acknowledged that Morris was correct that "inconveniences might arise" from the absolute prohibition. "[O]n the whole," he said, "it would be overbalanced by the utility of it."

George Mason of Virginia picked up the theme. "This is carrying the restraint too far," he said. "Cases will happen that can not be foreseen, where some kind of interference will be proper, & essential." He gave as an example a statute of limitations for collecting on bonded indebtedness. In the Maryland House of Delegates, Luther Martin was later to make a similar argument that in times of "*great public calamities* and *distress*" it might become the "*duty of government*" to interfere with contractual obligations, mentioning the more pertinent examples of laws "*totally or partially stopping* the courts of justice, or authorizing the debtor to pay by *instalments*, or by delivering up his property to his creditors at a *reasonable* and *honest* valuation."[54]

James Wilson of Pennsylvania, who earlier had stated his support for the provision but without recorded reasons, now pointed out that the answer to the objections raised by Mason and Morris was that "*retrospective* interferences only are to be prohibited." This, of course, is the interpretation ultimately adopted by the Supreme Court in *Ogden v. Saunders*,[55] over the only dissenting opinion ever written by Chief Justice Marshall in a constitutional case. Wilson's point introduced a note of confusion in the proceedings. Madison asked whether protection of contract from retrospective interference was not "already done by the prohibition of ex post facto laws." But at that stage, the Convention had not yet adopted an ex post facto provision applicable to the states. The ex post facto clause to which Madison presumably referred, which had been debated six days before, was applicable only to Congress.[56] Apparently following up on this suggestion, Edward Rutledge then moved a substitute motion to prohibit the states from passing bills of attainder and ex post facto laws.[57] This motion carried.

The next day, John Dickinson of Delaware reported the results of his research in Blackstone, to the effect that "the terms 'ex post facto' related to criminal cases only; that they would not consequently restrain the States from retrospective laws in civil cases, and that some further provision for this purpose would be requisite."[58] Subsequently, the Committee on Style proposed the contracts clause in its present form, and on September 14, the Convention adopted it without further recorded debate.[59]

Immediately upon its adoption, Elbridge Gerry of Massachusetts moved to apply the newly-adopted contracts clause to the federal government as well as to the states. His reasoning is familiar: since the contracts clause protects against breaches of the public faith, Congress ought to be "laid under the like prohibitions."[60] No delegate seconded Gerry's motion, and it therefore failed. This further demonstrates that application of the contracts clause to the states and not the federal government was deliberate.

Both debate and historical context make clear that—whatever else it may mean—the contracts clause was intended to prevent the states from enacting laws retroactively relieving debtors from the payment of their private debts.[61] In the depressed economic conditions of the Confederation period, many states had passed debt moratoriums, installment laws allowing debts to be paid in gradual installments despite contrary terms of the contract, commodity payment laws allowing debts to be paid in commodities rather than hard currency, and laws requiring creditors to accept paper money (often of little value) as legal tender for the payment of debts.[62] These were the specific evils that inspired the contracts clause. It is important to bear in mind that the type of "contract" the Framers had most in mind was the contract of debt.[63]

The Fifth Amendment's Just Compensation Clause

The origins of the just compensation clause are well known, though there are few records bearing on the drafting and adoption of the constitutional provision itself.[64] Unlike the contracts clause, the principle of the just compensation clause was deeply embedded in both the common law and natural law traditions. Blackstone insisted that in cases where the legislature could require a landowner to surrender his property for the common good, it must also give him "a full indemnification and equivalent for the injury thereby sustained."[65] Grotius, Pufendorf, Burlamaqui, Vattel, and Van Bynkershoek were to similar effect.[66] With some exceptions (takings of undeveloped land for roads, wartime requisitions, and seizure of the property of Tory Loyalists), the regular practice in colonial America was to pay compensation when property was taken for public use.[67] Compensation was, however, made pursuant to specific statutory authorization or judicial decision, and not as a matter of constitutional right. As of 1789, only Vermont and Massachusetts had included just compensation requirements in their state constitutions.[68]

There is no stated explanation for the decision to apply the just compensation clause to the federal government and not to the states. At first blush, however, this may seem less puzzling than the decision to apply the contracts clause to the states and not the federal government. The entire Bill of Rights, of which the just compensation clause is a part, was a restriction on federal and not state power.[69] The just compensation clause was not unique in this regard. One reason why the clause was not applied to the states at this juncture, then, is simply that attention was drawn to limiting power at the federal level, sparked by fears of an overpowerful central government. This cannot be the full answer, however, for the principal draftsman of the Bill of Rights, Madison, proposed and the House of Representatives adopted three additional limitations on state power as part of the Bill of Rights.[70] Indeed, although they were rejected by the Senate,[71] Madison described these limitations on state power as "the most valuable" of his proposed amendments to the Constitution.[72] Conspicuously, the just compensation clause was not among the provisions Madison and the House would have applied to the states. This strongly suggests that the decision not to apply the just compensation clause to the states was deliberate.

So far as historical records show, none of the participants in the Constitutional Convention ever proposed that the 1787 Constitution include a just compensation clause, or any equivalent to it. Indeed, the 1787 Constitution contained no reference to the rights of "property" whatsoever.[73] Nor did any of the states petition Congress for inclusion of a just compensation provision in the initial amendments to the Constitution. Although the protection of property and the role of men of property in the government were major topics of discussion, the 1787 Constitution relied almost exclusively on institutional arrangements to accomplish its objectives.

The first recorded proposal for a just compensation provision for the United States Constitution was made by Madison, when he presented his draft amendments to the House of Representatives on June 8, 1789.[74] No letter or statement by Madison has been found to explain why he chose to make this proposal, or anything about the drafting. Nor is there any recorded discussion in the Congress or the state legislatures that casts light on why the just compensation clause was thought to be a necessary addition to the Constitution, or why, if necessary, it was not thought equally applicable to the states. Indeed, the clause was one the least controversial provisions in the Bill of Rights, occasioning no recorded substantive comment at all.

III. Possible Explanations for the Different Treatment of Contract Rights and Property Rights

Although the Framers of the Constitution provided no explicit explanation of the different protections afforded contractual and property rights, this treatment is broadly consistent with two different but complementary understandings of the rights involved and their relation to the constitutional system. The first relies on a conventional understanding of the difference between property and contract, and finds the latter of greater importance to the commercial life of the nation. The second relies on a more abstract understanding of the distinction between property and contract; it finds contractual rights relatively more secure in the hands of the federal government and property rights relatively more secure in the hands of the states. I find a suggestion of these explanations in the interestingly divergent accounts of the contracts clause offered by Hamilton and Madison in the *Federalist.* I will therefore call them the "Hamiltonian" and the "Madisonian" explanations.[75]

The "Hamiltonian" Explanation

In *Federalist* No. 7, Hamilton sets forth the various tendencies that might cause the states, in the absence of a more effectual union, to go to war against one another. One of these is the interference by the states with contractual obligations owed to citizens of other states. "Laws in violation of private contracts," he says, "amount to aggressions on the rights of those states whose citizens are injured by them."[76] Indeed, he points out that the "enormities perpetrated by the legislature of Rhode Island" had excited a "disposition to retaliation" in neighboring Connecticut. Hamilton argued, moreover, that "if unrestrained by any additional checks" there was no reason to expect any improvement in the individual state legislatures in the future.[77] In *Federalist* No. 22, he elaborated that the "interfering and unneighborly regulations of some States," if not "restrained by a national control," would become both "serious sources of animosity and discord" and "injurious impediments to the intercourse between the different parts of the Confederacy."[78]

The reason for the contracts clause, then, was not so much that laws impairing the obligation of contract are "atrocious breaches of moral obligation and social justice"—though Hamilton states that they are.[79] The principal motivating factor was the effect of such laws on citizens of other states, on commerce throughout the country, and even on peaceful relations among the states. Charles Pinckney shared this understanding. In the debate before the South Carolina ratifying convention, he described the limitations on the powers of the states, including the contracts clause, as "the soul of the Constitution."[80] "Henceforth," he said, "the citizens of the states may trade with each other without fear of tender-laws or laws impairing the nature of contracts. The citizen of South Carolina will then be able to trade with those of Rhode Island, North Carolina, and Georgia, and be sure of receiving the value of his commodities."[81]

There are echoes here of Gouverneur Morris's reaction to Rufus King's proposal of a contracts clause, as well as parallels to the Supreme Court's subsequent interpretation of the commerce clause. When the baneful effects of state legislation are visited upon the citizens of the state itself, it is reasonable to rely upon the political processes to correct it. And if they do not, as Morris pointed out, "within the State itself a majority must rule, whatever may be the mischief done among themselves."[82] Constitutional prohibitions are needed principally to protect against parochial legislation with effects on out-of-state business which disrupt the flow of national commerce.

This sounds a great deal like the Court's practice of striking down state laws that discriminate against interstate commerce under the so-called "negative" commerce clause.[83] The classic statement of this doctrine was made by Justice Jackson in *H.P. Hood & Sons v. DuMond*:[84]

> [The] principle that our economic unit is the Nation, which alone has the gamut of powers necessary to control the economy, . . .has as its corollary that the states are not separable economic units. . . . . Our system, fostered by the Commerce Clause, is that every farmer and every craftsman shall be encouraged to produce by the certainty that he will have free access to every market in the Nation.

The normal political processes, unless checked by a national authority, cannot be counted upon to resist legislation where the benefits of the legislation are largely felt within the state and the burdens largely felt without.[85]

Parallels might also be drawn to the privileges and immunities clause of Article IV and to some modern applications of the equal protection clause of the Fourteenth Amendment, which are also used to prevent discriminatory treatment by states of persons from other states. Together with the contracts clause and the prohibition on state issuance of paper money, these constitutional provisions serve the common purpose of preventing the states from obstructing interstate commerce, and thus fostering the development of the United States into an integrated commercial republic. Indeed, in *Federalist* No. 7, Hamilton treated discriminatory state trade regulations and laws violating private contracts as aspects of the same problem.

Under the "Hamiltonian" view, the contracts clause serves the same end as the Constitution's other economic provisions; however, it operates in quite a different way. The commerce clause applies by its terms only to commerce "among the several states"—that is, commerce that extends across state lines.[86] By contrast, the contracts clause applies to all contracts, not just to those with parties in different states. Accordingly, the "Hamiltonian" explanation might be called into doubt. If the protection of out-of-state obligees is the purpose, why not confine the clause to interstate contracts, as Morris obliquely suggested?

The explanation, I think, is that it is important to national commercial life that contractual rights—especially the quintessential contractual right, the contract of debt—be transferrable in the national market. If A borrows money from B in Philadelphia, B should be able to resell the debt instrument to C in

Baltimore without legal hindrance. If states were permitted to impair the obligation of interstate contracts, then a single contract could have one meaning if held by B and a different meaning if held by C. To confine the contracts clause to interstate contracts would introduce a serious element of uncertainty and confusion into commercial affairs. If debt instruments are expected to enter the national market, it must be clear at the outset that they cannot be nullified by state laws.

The reason for not applying the contracts clause to the federal government now becomes evident. Some impairments of the obligation of contract, it was generally agreed, would be necessary. Even supporters of the clause, like Madison, agreed that it would produce "inconveniences."[87] In particular, some form of insolvency legislation, which would inevitably impair the obligation of contract, might well be desirable. It was only natural to vest the authority to adopt such dangerous but potentially "proper, & essential" measures, insofar as they affected interstate commerce, in the Congress. The exercise of congressional authority would not be likely to disrupt national commerce or lead to interstate hostilities. Thus, Congress was given the express authority to establish "uniform Laws on the subject of Bankruptcies through-out the United States."[88] The constitutional provisions forbidding states to impair the obligation of contracts and granting Congress the power to pass bankruptcy laws are two sides of the same coin.

Under this explanation, the reason the Framers failed to apply the just compensation clause to the states must be because takings of property were thought to be less likely than impairments of contracts to have interstate consequences. This would explain why it was thought more important to protect contracts than property from state interference.[89] This conclusion rests, however, on an important, and questionable, presupposition about the nature of "property." Property, under this view, must be conceptualized as tangible property, located in one place. This is a conventional understanding of property: property as "thing ownership."[90] If property is viewed in the sense of modern financial property—corporate shares, electronic transfers, bank deposits, and so forth—then property is no less interstate in nature than are contracts. Indeed, in this sense, property is little more than a web of contractual commitments. When, however, the dominant concept of property is land and comparable fixed tangible "things," it is plausible to believe that the effects of state action on property will principally be felt within the state. It might be thought that the provision of federal diversity jurisdiction for the out-of-state claimant would be sufficient protection, without more.

It also seems plausible that contract, and not property in this conventional sense, is the principal concern of commerce across state lines. If, as Blackstone says, a contract is "property in action," then commerce, too, is property in action. Restrictions on the transfer of goods in the national market are more likely to take the form of interference with contracts than of seizure of tangible property. Although title to property can be transferred to another state, just as contractual rights can, it is not improbable that a rough empirical judgment at the time of the Founding would have been that contractual rights, especially debts, were much more likely to travel across state line.[91] It therefore seems reasonable—if the purpose of the contracts clause is to protect against interstate hostility and the disruption of interstate commerce—that the Framers would prohibit the states from passing laws impairing the obligation of contract, while leaving property rights to the protection of state law.

The Madisonian Explanation

Madison's explanation of the purpose of the contracts clause in *Federalist* No. 44 differs markedly from Hamilton's in No. 7. Madison explains that "[b]ills of attainder, *ex post facto* laws, and laws impairing the obligation of contracts, are contrary to the first principles of the social compact and to every principle of sound legislation."[92] The reason for the clause, then, is not its impact on interstate commerce, but the prevention of injustice. If so, it is difficult to see why laws impairing the obligation of contracts should not be forbidden at the federal as well as the state level, as are bills of attainder and ex post facto laws.

Madison himself posed, and answered, this very question. In a letter to Jefferson explaining why Congress should be given the authority to nullify state laws—a power explicitly aimed at such injustices as the "violations of contracts"—he noted: "It may be asked how private rights will be more secure under the Guardianship of the General Government than under the State Governments, since they are both founded on the republican principle which refers the ultimate decision to the will of the majority."[93] The full answer to this question would, he said, "unfold the true Principles of Republican Government";[94] the nub of the answer is that a larger, more extended republic would be less vulnerable to control by particular interest groups or coalitions.[95]

Madison's discussion of the contracts clause in *Federalist* No. 44, after the portion quoted above, proceeds:[96]

> The sober people of America are weary of the fluctuating policy which has directed the public councils. They have seen with regret and indignation that sudden changes and legislative interferences, in cases affecting personal rights, become jobs in the hands of enterprising and influential speculators, and snares to the more industrious and less informed part of the community.... They very rightly infer, therefore, that some thorough reform is wanting, which will...give a regular course to the business of society.

The source of the problem, therefore, is "fluctuating policy" and "sudden changes"—the instability of government that is to be found in small, unchecked popular assemblies like the state legislatures. The very design of the federal government was intended to bring stability—to "give a regular course to the business of society." It was the state governments, not the new federal government, which Madison believed most likely to endanger "personal rights."[97]

The "Madisonian" explanation for the application of the contracts clause solely to the states, then, is that the extended republic, deliberative representation, and checks and balances that characterize the federal scheme make further provision against interference with contracts unnecessary. And since an absolute ban on laws impairing the obligation of contracts would produce "inconveniences,"[98] it made sense to preserve flexibility by rejecting the application of the contracts clause to the federal government. Bills of attainder and ex post facto laws (assuming the latter are confined to criminal statutes) are unnecessary to good government, and thus could be banned at both levels.

The Madisonian explanation gains force when contract and property rights are distinguished not on the conventional ground but on a more sophisticated legal basis expounded by Professor Wesley Hohfeld.[99] Under his analysis, the distinctive feature of property is that it is a right "good against the world," while contract is a right good only as against determinate persons— those with whom one has made the contract. A particular object may give rise to both contractual rights and property rights. X may contract with Y for exlusive use and enjoyment of real property owned by Y. X has a contractual right as against Y; if Y enters the property he is in breach of contract. However, X also has obtained, by virtue of the contract, rights against the world, in the nature of property rights.

The principal danger addressed by the contracts clause is that the government will favor one determinate set of persons over another—the debtors over the creditors. The relationship in question is person to person. The principal danger addressed by the just compensation clause, on the other hand, is that the government itself will appropriate the property right. The relationship is government to individual. The distinction between the two constitutional provisions, under this view, is not between tangible and intangible rights, but between forced transfers to other individuals and forced transfers to the government.

I have spoken thus far of the *principal* dangers addressed by the contracts and just compensation clauses. Each has a secondary significance, of lesser legal weight, that cuts the other way. Ever since *Fletcher v. Peck* (1810)[100] and contrary to strong indications in the legislative history, the contracts clause has been held to apply to contracts entered into by the government itself, as well as to private contracts.[101] When so applied, the relationship in question is that between government and individual; the case is conceptually more like a takings case than the prototypical impairment of obligation of contract. The just compensation clause also has a second element—the "public use" requirement—that prohibits the taking of property, even with compensation, for other than a public use. The danger here is that one person's property will be taken for the private benefit of another. The relationship in question is person to person. Conceptually, cases arising under the "public use" limitation are more like contracts clause cases than prototypical takings.[102]

There is a close connection between the pricipal problems addressed by the contracts and just compensation clauses and the political evils Madison viewed as characteristic of the states and the federal government, respectively. As explained by Madison, there are two inherent weaknesses in republican government that give rise to two necessities of constitutional design: "to guard the society against the oppression of its rulers," and "to guard one part of the society against the injustice of the other part."[103] The first concern is the relation between the government and the individual. The fear is that government officials will rule in their own interest instead of the interest of the people. The second concern is that some persons will use the machinery of government to exploit others; the dominant faction, presumably the majority, will oppress minority interests.

Madison's celebrated argument in *Federalist* No. 10 is that the second of these concerns is best met at the federal level, where the multiplicity of factions will make it unlikely that any one group could summon the strength to exploit the others. His argument is familiar; I will not repeat it here.[104] His optimistic conclusion is that the "rage for paper money, for an abolition of debts, for an equal division of property, or for any other improper or wicked project, will be less apt to pervade the whole body of the Union than a particular member of it."[105]

It follows, however, that the first of these concerns—the fear of self-interested government—is best met at the state level. There, the officers of government will live among the people, be more numerous in relation to the population, and be more susceptible to popular control. The representatives at the federal level, by contrast, will live at a remote distance from their constituents; offices will tend to be held by the well-known but unrepresentative few; communication will be slow and difficult; and the intended ethos will be one of deliberation rather than mere representation of the interests and opinions of the constituents. These arguments were the stock in trade of the Antifederalists,[106] and they had force. Even Madison had to acknowledge (in a private letter) that "[a]s in too small a sphere oppressive combinations may be too easily formed ag[ainst] the weaker party; so in too extensive a one, a defensive concert may be rendered too difficult against the oppression of those entrusted with the administration."[107] The very faults Madison identified in the state governments arise from an excess of popular control rather than a lack of it. Thus Madison wrote to Jefferson that if it were not for the problem of faction, the "voice" of the majority "would be the safest criterion" of the public good, and that "within a small sphere, this voice could be most easily collected, and the public affairs most accurately managed."[108]

Under this view, it is understandable why the contracts clause should apply only to the states. Laws impairing the obligation of private contracts are an instance of injustice by "one part of the society. . .against. . .the other part."

Such laws are particularly likely to be adopted, and likely to be particularly egregious, at the state level, where factions (such as the debtor class) might well seize the machinery of government and use it to their advantage. At the federal level, however, such laws are not likely to pass unless they would further the public good. Indeed, the bankruptcy clause is evidence that the Framers believed national action impairing contractual rights might be necessary.

It is also understandable, under this view, why the just compensation clause was applied to the federal government. Since the federal government is more remote, and more likely to develop interests separate from and in tension with the people, it is important that private property not be exposed to confiscation for the benefit of the government. This had been the experience with military authorities during the revolution. St. George Tucker, writing in 1803, stated that the main purpose of the just compensation clause was "to restrain the arbitrary and oppressive mode of obtaining supplies for the army, and other public uses, by impressment, as was too frequently practised during the revolutionary war, without any compensation whatever."[109]

It is less apparent why the just compensation clause should not also apply to the states. The "Madisonian" explanation shows why such a provision might have been considered more vital at the federal than the state level, but it does not explain why the clause could not have been applied at both levels. It is possible that the clause was not applied to the states out of simple inadvertence: because no one suggested that it should be, perhaps because the common law was thought clear enough. The "inadvertence" explanation, though, has the difficulty that Rufus King, proponent of the contracts clause, explicitly lifted his proposal from a provision in the Northwest Ordinance. Since the first clause of that provision is a just compensation requirement, King's proposal must have directed the attentions of at least some of the delegates to the just compensation concept. And although the common law, as seen through Blackstone, was tolerably clear, in practice the courts had not always recognized just compensation as a judicially-enforceable priciple in the absence of specific legislation.[110]

Perhaps the better explanaton, along "Hamiltonian" lines, is that takings of property were viewed as an internal affair of the various states, unlike violations of contract, which were more likely to have effects in other states. But there is no record of any affirmative reason to restrict application of the clause to the federal level. Unlike the impairment of the obligation of contracts, which Madison believed necessary in some extreme circumstances, there is no evidence that the Framers believed property should ever be taken without compensation. There was no need to retain the power at the level of government least likely to abuse it. The most that can be said is that the clause applies to the level of government to which it is most appropriate.

IV. Implications for Interpretation of the Clauses

It would be rash to propose radical revisions in our understandings of the contracts and just compensation clauses on the basis of these conclusions. They are, indeed, more in the nature of speculations than of hard historical or legal conclusions. Nonetheless, they suggest certain directions for thinking about the constitutional issues raised by the clauses.

First, they suggest that efforts to give the contracts clause a broad application at the state level, so as to protect what might more conventionally be viewed as property rights, are less objectionable than efforts to give the just compensation clause a broad application at the federal level, so as to protect contract rights. Thus, to take the illustrative cases with which we began,[111] both the expansive approach of *Fletcher v. Peck* and the restrictive approach of *Bowen v. Public Agencies Opposed to Social Security Entrapment* would seem appropriate, whatever the merits of their specific holdings. This is because there was an affirmative reason to refuse to apply the contracts clause to the federal government, but no comparable affirmative reason to refuse to apply the just compensation clause to the states. By the same token, the Court's decision to incorporate the just compensation clause as an aspect of the Fourteenth Amendment due process clause[112] does little apparent violence to the constitutional scheme. This made broad interpretations of the contracts clause, as in *Fletcher*, less significant.

Second, these conclusions suggest that the modern thrust of contracts clause jurisprudence is precisely backwards. The Court has stated that "impairments of a State's own contracts would face more stringent examination under the contract clause than would laws regulating contractual relationships between private parties."[113] However, it is interference with private contracts that lies at the heart of the clause. The reason the states, rather than the federal government, were thought in need of this form of restraint is that they are especially susceptible to political factions that would use state power to favor their interests over the interests of other persons. This suggests particular vigilance against laws altering private contractual arrangements. Even assuming that public contracts are properly subsumed under the clause,[114] this should be viewed as a more marginal application. Violation of public contracts might indeed be better viewed, in most instances, as a takings problem, with compensation rather than an outright prohibition as the remedy.[115]

Third, the analysis casts doubt on the Court's willingness to allow states to impair the obligation of contracts merely on the showing that it is plausibly "necessary for the general good of the public."[116] The Framers well understood that there would be times when laws violating contractual rights would seem "proper, & essential" and that the restraint imposed by the Constitution would cause "inconveniences."[117] Their solution was to allow the laws to be enacted at the federal level. Only if the public need were pressing enough to procure congressional action, despite the safeguards of the federal system, did they think the laws should be enforced. The Framers relied, not on the ad hoc judgments of courts to determine when laws violative of contracts are desirable, but on the procedural mechanisms of representative government and checks and balances.

Finally, and most generally, this analysis suggests that it is not reliable to base constitutional interpretation solely upon broad principles of substantive political theory—such as the sanctity of private property. In the minds of the Framers, these issues were complicated by the overriding need to establish just and stable institutions of republican government. The Framers were too practical to think they could bind the nation to wise policy through constitutional language alone. Some of the more pernicious evils were forbidden, as against the organs of government most likely to violate them. Beyond that, they relied on structural features of the federal system to prevent oppression. The founding generation held property and contractual rights dear, and for good reasons. But they did not simply invest future judges with sweeping power to protect them. This, no doubt, was also for good reasons. Aggressive judicial review, when predicated on loose and discretionary standards of judgment, is, at best, in tension with republicanism. The study of the broad principles of public policy held by the Framers is important to our understanding of the design of the Constitution; but it cannot substitute for a careful study of the way in which those principles are expected to emerge through the structure of government, which was the principal concern of the Framers of the Constitution.

Notes

1. See Duncan v. Louisiana, 391 U.S. 145 (1968).

2. See Bolling v. Sharpe, 347 U.S. 497 (1954).

3. See, e.g., Cornelius v. NAACP Legal Defense Fund, 473 U.S. 788 (1985) (First Amendment challenge to executive action); Nebraska Press Ass'n v. Stuart, 427 U.S. 539 (1976) (First Amendment challenge to court order); see also Denbeaux, The First Word of the First Amendment, 80 N. W. L. Rev. 1156 (1986) (questioning the wide acceptance of the application of the First Amendment to the non-legislative branches in light of the historical purposes of the amendment).

4. Barron v. Mayor of Baltimore, 32 U.S. (7 Pet.) 243 (1833). The protections of the just compensation clause were held applicable to the states through the Fourteenth Amendment in Chicago, B. & Q. R.R. v. Chicago, 166 U.S. 226 (1897).

5. And see text at notes 51-58 infra.

6. See, e.g., Currie, The Constitution in the Supreme Court: State and Congressional Powers, 1801-1835, 49 U. CHI. L. REV. 887, 895 (1982); Hale, The Supreme Court and the Contract Clause, 57 HARVARD L. REV. 512, 512-13 (1944); Johnson, The Contract Clause of the United States Constitution, 16 KY. L. J. 222, 223-24 (1928); Hutchinson, Laws Impairing the Obligation of Contracts, 1 n.s. S. L. REV. 401, 409-10 (1875); and

McKinney, *The Constitutional Protection of the Obligation of Contracts*, 53 CENT. L. J. 44, 45 (1901).

7. The most serious attempt to explain this anomaly was made by Professor William W. Crosskey. *See* W. CROSSKEY, 1 POLITICS AND THE CONSTITUTION IN THE HISTORY OF THE UNITED STATES 352-60 (1953). For further discussion of Crosskey's view, *see* note 83 *infra*.

8. B. WRIGHT, THE CONTRACT CLAUSE OF THE CONSTITUTION (1938), the classic work in the area, mentions it only in a footnote. *See id.* at 172 note 237.

9. I will not address liberty of contract, which was a late nineteenth century aspect of substantive due process. The subject of this paper is rights arising from contract, not the right to make contracts. Nor will I deal, except tangentially, with the procedural due process protections for property under the Fifth Amendment.

10. THE FEDERALIST No. 10, at 78 (J. Madison) (New American Library ed. 1961).

11. 5 WRITINGS OF JAMES MADISON 27 (G. Hund ed. 1904) (letter composed Oct. 24, 1787). Other commentators of the period agreed. *See, e.g., Letters From the Federal Farmer*, No. 1 (Oct. 8, 1787), *rep. in* 1 P. KURLAND and R. LERNER, THE FOUNDERS' CONSTITUTION 258 (1987), and in 2 H. STORING, THE COMPLETE ANTI-FEDERALIST, § 2.8.6, at 226-27 (1981) ("[S]everal legislatures, by making tender, suspension, and paper money laws, have given just cause of uneasiness to creditors. By these and other causes, several orders of men in the community have been prepared, by degrees, for a change of government.")

12. 1 THE RECORDS OF THE FEDERAL CONVENTION OF 1787, at 533 (Farrand ed. 1911).

13. For greater elaboration and support for this conclusion, *see* J. Nedelsky, PROPERTY AND THE FRAMERS OF THE UNITED STATES CONSTITUTION: A STUDY OF THE POLITICAL THOUGHT OF JAMES MADISON, GOUVERNEUR MORRIS, AND JAMES WILSON, (Ph.D. thesis, Univ. of Chicago, 1977); Plattner, *American Democracy and the Acquisitive Spirit*, in HOW CAPITALISTIC IS THE CONSTITUTION? 14-17 (R. Goldman and W. Schambra eds., 1982); E. JOHNSON, THE FOUNDATIONS OF AMERICAN ECONOMIC FREEDOM 191-92 (1973); and Katz, *Thomas Jefferson and the Right to Property in Revolutionary America*, 19 J. OF LAW & ECON. 467 (1976).

14. 1 Farrand, *supra* note 12, at 512 (punctuation clarified). *See also* THE FEDERALIST No. 44, *supra* note 10, at 282-83 (J. Madison); 5 WRITINGS OF JAMES MADISON, *supra* note 11, at 27 (letter to Jefferson); *Letter From the Federal Farmer*, No. 1, *supra* note 11.

15. THE FEDERALIST No. 10, *supra* note 10, at 78.

16. *Id.* at 77; *see also* Madison, *Notes on the Confederacy* (April 1787), in 1 LETTERS AND OTHER WRITINGS OF JAMES MADISON 320, 324 (1865). On Madison's understanding of the connection between government instability and the invasion of property rights, see Nedelsky, *supra* note 13, at 85-90.

17. 10 U.S. (6 Cranch) 87 (1810).

18. *Id.* at 135.

19. Marshall's opinion is similar in its reasoning to a legal opinion earlier issued by Alexander Hamilton. *See* Wright, *supra* note 8, at 21-22. Hamilton's argument had been paraphrased by counsel for Peck. 10 U.S. (6 Cranch) at 123.

20. *Id.* at 136-37.

21. *Id.* at 137.

22. *See* J. SHIRLEY, THE DARTMOUTH COLLEGE CAUSES AND THE SUPREME COURT OF THE UNITED STATES 408-09 (1895); Currie, *The Constitution in the Supreme Court: State and Congressional Powers, 1801-1835*, 49 U. CHI. L. REV. 887, 895 (1982). Currie points out that Marshall's construction leaves some, albeit reduced, "independent field of operation" for the just compensation clause. *Id.* at 896. Marshall, however, made no attempt to reconcile his reading with the constitutional text. Contrast Watson v. Mercer, 33 U.S. (8 Pet.) 88, 109 (1834), in which Justice Story's opinion observed that no constitutional provision restrains states from taking property without compensation.

23. *See* Trickett, *Is a Grant a Contract?*, 54 AM. L. REV. 718, 729 (1920); Hutchinson, *supra* note 6, at 416.

24. 106 S. Ct. 2390 (1986).

25. 106 S. Ct. at 2398.

26. The Court reasoned that the right to withdraw from the Social Security system is not a "debt" or an "obligation. . .to provide benefits under a contract from which the obligee paid a monetary premium," and therefore could not come within precedents protecting federal debts and obligations as "property." 106 S. Ct. at 2398-99.

27. Indeed, the Court implied that a contractual term over which the respondents had "any bargaining power" or for which they had provided "independent consideration" might have been considered protected proprety. *Id.* at 2399. This demonstrates that, in the Court's view, some executory contracts create rights under the just compensation clause, although this language may be merely considered dicta.

28. *Id.*

29. *Id.* at 2398 n.19, 2399.

30. Under the contracts clause, a state can avoid restrictions under the contracts clause by the simple expedient of announcing, in advance, that it does not intend to comply with its contracts. *E.g.*, Greenwood v. Freight Co., 105 U.S. 13 (1882); *see also* Ogden v. Saunders, 25 U.S. (12 Wheat.) 212, 339 (1827) (Marshall, C.J., dissenting). By contrast, it is unconstitutional for the government to disturb a property interest abritrarily, even if it announces in advance its intent to do so. *See, e.g.*, Goldberg v. Kelly, 397 U.S. 254 (1970).

31. 2 W. BLACKSTONE, COMMENTARIES ON THE LAWS OF ENGLAND *440 (1766).

32. *Id.*, Ch. XXX.

33. *Contrast* Thomas Hobbes, who defined "Justice" as meaning that *"men performe their Covenants made."* T. HOBBES, LEVIATHAN, Pt. I, Ch. XV, at 71 (1651) (ital. in orginal).

34. 1 BLACKSTONE, *supra* note 31, at *134. The first two are personal security and personal liberty. *Id.* at *125, *130.

35. *Id* at *134.

36. 6 THE WRITINGS OF JAMES MADISON, *supra* note 11, at 101 (article entitled "Property," which appeared in The National Gazette, March 29, 1792).

37. *Id.; cf.* 2 BLACKSTONE, *supra* note 30, at *2.

38. 6 THE WRITINGS OF JAMES MADISON, *supra* note 35, at 103.

39. *Id.* at 101.

40. *Id.* at 102.

41. *Id.*

42. Nedelsky, *supra* note 13, at 33-34.

43. *See* THE FEDERALIST No. 11 (A. Hamilton).

44. *See, e.g.,* Pennsylvania Packet, March 11, 1780 (G. Morris), quoted in Nedelsky, *supra* note 13, at 30 ("Above all things government should never forget that restrictions on the use of wealth may produce a landed monopoly, which is most thoroughly pernicious.").

45. Hence the trend toward abolition of primogeniture and entail during the founding period. *See* 1 WRITINGS OF THOMAS JEFFERSON 58-60 (P. Ford ed. 1904); 1 I. BRANT, JAMES MADISON 300-301 (1941).

46. 9 WRITINGS OF JAMES MADISON, *supra* note 11, at 361 (Speech in the Virginia Constitutional Convention, Dec. 2, 1829); *compare* FEDERALIST No. 10, *supra* note 10, at 78. See Nedelsky, *supra* note 13, at 93-95 ("the protection of vested rights assumes supreme importance" to Madison because they are the result of "the exercise of the faculties for acquiring property").

47. 5 WRITINGS OF JAMES MADISON, *supra* note 11, at 271 (letter of Oct. 17, 1788).

48. Northwest Ordinance, Art. III, cl. 5, *repr. in* 32 JOURNAL OF THE CONTINENTAL CONGRESS 340 (R. Hill ed. 1936). It should be noted that the first portion of this provision is a prototype for the due process clause, and the second for the just compensation clause. The clauses follow in the same order in the Fifth Amendment.

49. Northwest Ordinance, *id.* at Art II, cl. 7. E. Burnett, 8 LETTERS OF MEMBERS OF THE CONTINENTAL CONGRESS 620, 620 (1936) (letter to George Washington transmitting text of the Northwest Ordinance, dated July 15, 1787).

50. Congress's power to make "all needful Rules and Regulations" for the governance of the territories (U.S. CONST., Art IV, § 3, cl. 2) is a source of plenary governing authority, rather than enumerated powers.

51. Treaty of Peace with Great Britain, Arts. IV, VI (Sept. 3, 1783), in COMMAGER, DOCUMENTS OF AMERICAN HISTORY 118, 119 (7th ed. 1963).

52. *See* 5 WRITINGS OF JAMES MADISON, *supra* note 11, at 27-28 (letter to Jefferson, Oct. 24, 1787). Among the "expedients" available to state legislators to defeat contracts were statutes of limitations, evidentiary rules, moratoriums on court jurisdiction, and requirements that creditors accept payment in something other than hard currency. A broad congressional power to nullify such laws would more effectively bar such expedients than would a specific prohibition.

53. 2 Farrand, *supra* note 12, at 439-40. The entire debate on this day is recorded on these pages of Farrand's RECORDS. The quotations in the following text will not be separately noted.

54. 3 *id.* at 214-15 (speech delivered Nov. 29, 1787) (italics in original). These sentiments were not unusual. New York's recommended amendments to the 1787 Constitution included allowing the states to pass insolvency laws for the relief of debtors other than merchants and traders. 1 J. ELLIOT, DEBATES IN THE SEVERAL STATE CONVENTIONS ON THE ADOPTION OF THE FEDERAL CONSTITUTION 330 (1881).

55. 25 U.S. (12 Wheat.) 213, 215-17 (1827).

56. *See* U.S. CONST., ART. I, § 9.

57. Madison's notes record that Rutledge used the language "retrospective laws." 2 Farrand, *supra* note 12, at 440. The printed journal recorded the motion as using the

language "ex post facto laws." *Id.* Marginal notes by George Washington and David Brearly corroborate the journal rendition, as does Dickinson's subsequent comment quoted in text. *Id.* at 440 n.19.

58. 2 Farrand, *supra* note 12, at 448-49. This definition of "ex post facto" was subsequently adopted by the Court in Calder v. Bull, 3 U.S. (3 Dall.) 386 (1798).

59. 2 Farrand, *supra* at 619. The committee initially proposed that no state shall pass laws "altering or impairing the obligation of contract." *Id.* at 597. The words "altering or" were later omitted.

60. *Id.* at 619.

61. *See* Sturges v. Crowninshield, 17 U.S. (4 Wheat.) 122, 204-06 (1819).

62. *See* B. Wright, *supra* note 8, at 4-6, 15-16, 32-33; A NEVINS, THE AMERICAN STATES DURING AND AFTER THE REVOLUTION 1775-1789 570-71 (1927); Ogden v. Saunders, 25 U.S. (12 Wheat.) 213, 353-55 (1827) (Marshall, C.J., dissenting).

63. For a recent comparison of the historical background to the current interpretation of the contracts clause, *see* Kmiec and McGinnis, *The Contract Clause: A Return to the Original Understanding*, 14 HAST. CONST. L. Q. 525 (1987).

64. For further elaboration of the historical background of the just compensation clause, *see* McDonald, *supra* note 13, at 10-36; Stoebuck, *A General Theory of Eminent Domain*, 47 WASH. L. REV. 553, 553-88 (1972); Note, *The Origins and Original Significance of the Just Compensation Clause of the Fifth Amendment*, 94 YALE L. J. 694 (1985). For differing views about the present significance of the clause, see R. EPSTEIN, TAKINGS: PRIVATE PROPERTY AND THE POWER OF EMINENT DOMAIN (1985); B. ACKERMAN, PRIVATE PROPERTY AND THE CONSTITUTION (1977).

65. 1 BLACKSTONE, *supra*, note 30, at *139.

66. H. GROTIUS, DE JURE BELLI AC PACIS, 385, 807 (1625) (F. Kelsey trans. 1925); 2 S. PUFENDORF, DE JURE NATURAE ET GENTIUM 1285 (1688 ed.) (C. & W. Oldfather trans. 1934); 2 J. J. BURLAMAQUI, PRINCIPLES OF NATURAL AND POLITICAL LAW, Pt. III, Ch. 5 XXV-XXIX (1747) (Nugent trans. 1807); E. DE VATTEL, THE LAW OF NATIONS, 171-72 (1758) (1829); C. VAN BYNKER-SHOEK, QUAESTIONUM JURIS PUBLICI 218-223 (T. Frank trans. 1930).

67. The evidence for this conclusion is assembled in Stoebuck, *supra*, note 61, at 579-83. A contrary conclusion is reached in M. HORWITZ, THE TRANSFOR-MATION OF AMERICAN LAW 63-64 (1977). The disagreement revolves largely around the significance to be attached to uncompensated takings of undeveloped or unenclosed land for roadbuilding. Stoebuck argues (*supra*, note 64, at 583-84) that compensation was not given in such instances because of a presumption that the value of the undeveloped land taken for the road was offset by the benefit of access to the road. *But see* YALE note, *supra*, note 61, at 695 n.6.

68. Vermont Constitution of 1786, Ch. I, § II, *rep. in* B. POORE, 2 FEDERAL OR STATE CONSTITUTIONS, COLONIAL CHARTERS, AND OTHER ORGANIC LAWS OF THE UNITED STATES 1868 (2d ed. 1878); Mass. Const. of 1780, Part the First, Art. X, *rep. in* B. POORE, *supra*, at 958; *see also*, Vt. Const. of 1777, Ch. I., § II, *rep. in* B. POORE, *supra*, at 1859.

69. Barron v. Mayor of Baltimore, 32 U.S. (7 Pet.) 243, 247-49 (1833). This remained true until provisions of the Bill of Rights, beginning with the just compensation clause in 1897, were held to be applicable to the states through the

medium of the due process clause of the Fourteenth Amendment. *See* Fairman, *The Supreme Court and the Constitutional Limitations on State Governmental Authority*, 21 U. CHI. L. REV. 40 (1953); Currie, *supra*, note 6, at 966-68; *but see* 2 W. Crosskey, *supra*, note 7, at 1067.

70. 1 ANNALS OF CONGRESS 452 (June 8, 1789) (J. Gales ed. 1834). The three proposed protections against state governments were the "equal rights of conscience," the "freedom of speech or of the press," and the "right of trial by jury in criminal cases."

71. *Id.* at 86 (Sept. 21, 1789).

72. *Id.* at 458 (June 8, 1789).

73. The only place the term "Property" appears in the 1787 Constitution is in Art. IV, § 3, where it refers to "Property belonging to the United States."

74. 1 ANNALS OF CONGRESS, *supra* note 70, at 434.

75. These "Hamiltonian" and "Madisonian" explanations must be understood as analytical constructs based on the thought of these Founders, and not as historical reconstructions of their actual views. As a historical matter, these constructs may exaggerate the degree to which Hamilton's and Madison's political theories differed at this period. *See, e.g.*, note 76, *infra*.

76. FEDERALIST No. 7, *supra* note 10, at 65. Madison made a similar observation in his *Notes on the Confederacy, supra* note 16, at 321, but did not develop the theme in his FEDERALIST essays.

77. FEDERALIST No. 7, *supra* note 10, at 65. Rhode Island was notorious at that time for its debtor relief legislation, *see* Nevins, *supra* note 62, at 570-571.

78. FEDERALIST No. 22, *supra* note 10, at 144-45.

79. *Id.* at 65 (No. 7).

80. 4 J. Elliott, *supra* note 54, at 333.

81. *Id.* at 335.

82. 2 Farrand, *supra* note 12, at 439 (Aug. 28, 1786); *see* text and notes at note 53, *supra*.

83. The commerce clause itself (U.S. CONST., Art I, § 8, cl. 3), is no more than a grant of power to Congress to regulate commerce among the states. The "negative" (also called the "silent" or "dormant") commerce clause is the judicial doctrine that the clause impliedly displaces some aspects of state regulatory power over interstate commerce, even in the absence of congressional action. *See, e.g.*, Lewis v. BT Investment Managers, 447 U.S. 27 (1980).

84. 336 U.S. 525, 537-38, 539 (1949).

85. *See* South Carolina State Highway Department v. Barnwell Bros., 303 U.S. 177, 184 n.2 (1938). This free trade understanding of the commerce clause is challenged by Professor Kitch in *Regulation and the American Common Market*, in REGULATION, FEDERALISM, AND INTERSTATE COMMERCE 9-55 (A. D. Tarlock ed. 1981).

86. U.S. CONST., Art. I, § 8, cl. 3. This is the traditional understanding of the reach of the commerce clause. This understanding has been disputed (*see* W. Crosskey, *supra* note 7, *passim*) but I will assume its validity for purposes of this discussion. While Congress's power to regulate commerce under the commerce clause now effectively extends to purely intrastate transactions (*see, e.g.*, Perez v. United States, 402 U.S. 146 (1971), the "negative" commerce clause retains the original emphasis on interstate movements. *See, e.g.*, CTS Corp. v. Dynamics Corp. of America, 107 S. Ct. 1637 (1987).

87. See text and notes at notes 51-52 *supra*.

88. U.S. CONST., Art I, § 8, cl. 4.

89. Under this view, Professor Crosskey's conclusion that the applicability of the contracts clause solely to the states demonstrates that the Congress intended to exercise plenary authority over commercial law seems less than inevitable. 1 Crosskey, *supra* note 7, at 355. His argument is as follows:

> The Contracts Clause...could not, therefore, have been intended as an interdiction of something the Federal Convention regarded as inherently evil; it was a provision, instead, for making some power, or powers, of Congress, *in so far forth*, exclusive.

Id. (ital. in original). The contracts clause thus becomes an argument in favor of Crosskey's central theme: that the commerce power of Congress is not limited to interstate commerce. The alternative reading of the contracts clause, presented in the text, is fully consistent with the conventional assumption that the principal concern of the Framers in this area was to provide federal authority over commercial matters with interstate effects.

90. *See* United States v. General Motors Corp., 323 U.S. 373, 377-78 (1945); Grey, *The Disintegration of Property*, in PROPERTY (NOMOS XXII) 69, 71-73 (J. Pennock & J. Chapman eds. 1980); ACKERMAN, *supra* note 64, at 97-100, 116-167.

91. The interstate nature of debt was the subject of contemporary comment. *See*, *e.g.*, Madison, *Notes on the Confederacy*, *supra* note 62, at 570-72. I have encountered no significant discussion of problems arising from interstate ownership of property. Interestingly, New York's ratifying convention proposed confining federal bankruptcy power to the debts of merchants and traders, leaving the state free to enact insolvency legislation on behalf of others. 1 J. ELLIOTT, *supra* note 54, at 330. This suggests that some debts were thought to have more of an interstate character than others.

92. THE FEDERALIST No. 44, *supra* note 10, at 282.

93. 5 WRITINGS OF JAMES MADISON, *supra* note 11, at 28.

94. *Id.*

95. *See id.* at 31.

96. FEDERALIST No. 44, *supra* note 10, at 282-83.

97. *See also* 1 ANNALS OF CONGRESS, *supra* note 74, at 458. Madison stated that the restrictions on state power in Article I, § 10, were "wise and proper restrictions in the Constitution. I think there is more danger of those powers being abused by the State Governments than by the Government of the United States." *Id.*

98. See text at notes 51-52 *supra*.

99. Hohfeld, *Some Fundamental Legal Conceptions As Applied in Judicial Reasoning*, 23 YALE L. J. 16 (1913); Hohfeld, *Fundamental Legal Conceptions As Applied in Judicial Reasoning*, 26 YALE L. J. 710 (1917). Professor Hohfeld's views on the nature of property rights have been influential. *See*, *e.g.*, Cohen, *Dialogue on Private Property*, 9 RUTGERS L. REV. 357, 373-74 (1954); Grey, *supra* note 84, at 71; Cormack, *Legal Concepts In Cases of Eminent Domain*, 41 YALE L. J. 221 (1931). For a related explanation of the distinction between property and tort, see Calabresi and Melamed, *Property Rules, Liability Rules, and Inalienability: One View of the Cathedral*, 85 HARV. L. REV. 1089 (1972).

100. 10 U.S. (6 Cranch) 87 (1810).

101. The Northwest Ordinance provision and Rufus King's initial proposal were expressly limited to "private" contracts. See text and notes at note 51 *supra*. Debate in

the Convention centered entirely on whether this proposal "would be going too far"; no one criticized it for failing to go far enough. The later deletion of the reference to "private" contracts was not explained. There is no necessary reason to infer that it was intended to broaden coverage. Charles Pinckney interpreted the clause as preventing states from "interfering in private contracts." 4 J. ELLIOTT, *supra* note 54, at 334. The only unequivocal statements that the clause applied to public contracts were made by opponents of the Constitution and of the clause. 4 *id.* at 190 (statement of James Galloway); 3 *id.*, at 474 (statement of Patrick Henry). One of them, Patrick Henry, appeared to be answering an unrecorded assertion to the contrary by Madison, and both were immediately contradicted by participants in the Convention. See 4 *id.* at 191 (statement of W. R. Davie); 3 *id.* at 478 (statement by Edmund Randolph). Professors Wright and Corwin have concluded that the clause was not intended to apply to public contracts. B. WRIGHT, *supra* note 8, at 3-16; E. CORWIN, JOHN MARSHALL AND THE CONSTITUTION 167-68 (1919).

102. The "public use" aspect of the Fifth Amendment is of little present-day significance. EPSTEIN, *supra* note 64, at 161-62; Note, *The Public Use Limitation on Eminent Domain: An Advance Requiem,* 58 YALE L. J. 599 (1949); *see, e.g.,* Hawaii Housing Authority v. Midkiff, 467 U.S. 229 (1984) (upholding a state statute condemning land for purpose of sale to the tenants).

103. THE FEDERALIST No. 51, *supra* note 10, at 323; *see also* Madison, *Notes on the Confederacy, supra* note 11, at 325-28 (ascribing unjust laws to self-interested legislators and to the influence of "factions").

104. Probably the best summary and analysis is found in Diamond, *The Federalist, in* HISTORY OF POLITICAL PHILOSOPHY 631 (L. Strauss & J. Cropsey ed., 2d ed. 1972). For an application of modern public choice theory to Madison's arguments, see V. OSTROM, THE POLITICAL THEORY OF A COMPOUND REPUBLIC (2d ed. 1987).

105. THE FEDERALIST No. 10, *supra* note 10, at 84.

106. *See* H. STORING, WHAT THE ANTIFEDERALISTS WERE FOR 17-19, 48-52 (1981).

107. 5 WRITINGS OF JAMES MADISON, *supra* note 11, at 30. For a modern statement of this view, *see* A. Rapaczenski, *From Sovereignty to Process: The Jurisprudence of Federalism After Garcia,* 1985 SUP. CT. REV. 341, 380-91; *see also* McConnell, *Federalism: Evaluating the Founders' Design,* 54 U. CHI. L. REV. 1484, 1500-07 (1987).

108. *Id.*

109. ST. G. TUCKER, BLACKSTONE'S COMMENTARIES ON THE LAWS OF ENGLAND 305-06 (appendix) (Philadelphia, 1803); compare John Jay's essay, *A Freeholder, reprinted in,* 5 P. KURLAND and R. LERNER, *supra* note 11, at 312-313 (objections to impressment of horses and other property by military officials without proper authority).

110. *See* Respublica v. Sparhawk, 1 Dall. 357 (Pa. 1788) (denying compensation for wartime taking); Lindsay v. Commissioners, 2 S. C. L. (2 Bay) 38, 47-51 (1796) (denying compensation for taking of unimproved land).

111. See text and notes at notes 17-29, *supra.*

112. Chicago, B & Q R.R. v. Chicago, 166 U.S. 226 (1897).

113. Allied Structural Steel Co. v. Spannus, 438 U.S. 234, 244 n.15 (1978); United States Trust Co. v. New Jersey, 431 U.S. 1, 22-23 (1976). For a critical appraisal of these cases, *see* Merrill, *Public Contracts, Private Contracts, and the Transformation of the Constitutional Order,* 37 CASE W. RES. L. REV. 597 (1987).

114. See note 95, *supra*.

115. *See*, McConnell, *Why Hold Elections? Using Consent Decrees to Insulate Policies from Political Change*, 1987 U. CHI. L. FOR. 295 (1987) (discussing constitutional remedies for violation of government procurement contracts, nonprosecution agreements, and consent decrees).

116. Allied Structural Steel Corp. v. Spannaus, at 241, quoting Manigault v. Springs, 199 U.S. 473, 480 (1905). *See also* Home Bldg. & Loan Ass'n v. Blaisdell, 290 U.S., 398, 438 (1934) ("The question...is whether the legislation is addressed to a legitimate end and the measures taken are reasonable and appropriate to the end.").

117. See text at notes 51-52, *supra*.

Contributors

ELLEN FRANKEL PAUL is Deputy Director of the Social Philosophy and Policy Center and professor of political science. She received her doctorate from the Government Department at Harvard University in 1976. She is the author of numerous scholarly articles and is, also, the author or editor of thirteen books. She has written three books: MORAL REVOLUTION AND ECONOMIC SCIENCE (1979), PROPERTY RIGHTS AND EMINENT DOMAIN (1987), and EQUITY AND GENDER: THE COMPARABLE WORTH DEBATE (1988). She is the editor, with Philip Russo, of PUBLIC POLICY: ISSUES, ANALYSIS, AND IDEOLOGY (1981); and editor, with Dan Jacobs, of STUDIES OF THE THIRD WAVE: RECENT MIGRATION OF SOVIET JEWS TO THE UNITED STATES. She has also co-edited eight books published by Basil Blackwell: HUMAN RIGHTS (1984), LIBERTY AND EQUALITY (1984), ETHICS AND ECONOMICS (1985), NUCLEAR RIGHTS/ NUCLEAR WRONGS (1985), MARXISM AND LIBERALISM (1986), PHILOSOPHY AND LAW (1987), EQUAL OPPORTUNITY (1987), and THE NEW SOCIAL CONTRACT (1988).

HOWARD DICKMAN is a Research Associate at the Social Philosophy and Policy Center. He received his Ph.D. in history from the University of Michigan in 1977. He was Research Director of the Manhattan Institute for Policy Research, and Senior Editor of HARPER'S magazine. He has written many scholarly articles and is the author of the book INDUS-TRIAL DEMOCRACY IN AMERICA: IDEOLOGICAL ORIGINS OF NATIONAL LABOR RELATIONS POLICY (1987).

GORDON WOOD received his Ph.D. in history from Harvard in 1964. He is the author and editor of several important books on the development of the United States Constitution, such as THE CREATION OF THE AMERICAN REPUBLIC, 1776-1787, and THE CONFEDERATION AND THE CONSTITUTION; and many articles, including *The Democratization of Mind in the American Revolution, The American Revolution and the World,* and *Conspiracy and the Paranoid Style: Causality and Deceit in the Eighteenth Century.* He is the winner of such prestigious prizes as the John H. Dunning Prize of the American

169

Historical Association, and the Bancroft Prize. Professor Wood was nominated for the National Book Award in History and Biography in 1970.

MICHAEL KAMMEN received his Ph.D. from Harvard University in 1964. He has taught at Harvard and was first holder of the chair in American History at Ecole des hautes Etudes en Sciences Sociales, Paris, France, 1980-81. He has been awarded numerous fellowships including being named a Constitutional Fellow by the National Endowment for the Humanities. he is the author and editor of numerous books. His authored works include A ROPE OF SAND: THE COLONIAL AGENTS, BRITISH POLITICS, AND THE AMERICAN REVOLUTION (1968); DEPUTYES AND LIBERTYES: THE ORIGINS OF REPRESENTA- TIVE GOVERNMENT IN COLONIAL AMERICA (1969); EMPIRE AND INTEREST: THE AMERICAN COLONIES AND THE POLI- TICS OF MERCANTILISM (1970); PEOPLE OF PARADOX: AN INQUIRY CONCERNING THE ORIGINS OF AMERICAN CIVILI- ZATION (1972); COLONIAL NEW YORK: A HISTORY (1975); SPHERES OF LIBERTY: CHANGING PERCEPTIONS OF LIBERTY IN AMERICAN CULTURE (1986); and A MACHINE THAT WOULD GO OF ITSELF: THE CONSTITUTION IN AMERICAN CULTURE.

ANDREW RECK received his Ph.D. from Yale University in 1954. He is the author or editor of six books: RECENT AMERICAN PHILOSOPHY 1964), INTRODUCTION TO WILLIAM JAMES (1967), THE NEW AMERICAN PHILOSOPHY (1968), SPECULATIVE PHILOSOPHY (1972), SELECTED WRITINGS OF GEORGE HERBERT MEAD (1964, 1981), and KNOWLEDGE AND VALUE: ESSAYS IN HONOR OF HAROLD H. LEE (1972). Professor Reck is also the author of 100 articles (including chapters in books), and 50 book reviews. He is currently a member of the Advisory-Editorial Board of the journal PHILOSOPHI- CAL TOPICS. He is professor of philosophy at Tulane University.

EDWARD ERLER received his Ph.D. from the Claremont Graduate School in 1973, and is now a professor of political science at California State University, San Bernardino. He has published extensively on United States Constitutional history and interpretation. Articles such as *The Problem of the Public Good in the Federalist* (1981), *The American Tradition* (1975), and *Equal Protection and Personal Rights: The Regime of the 'Discrete and Insular Minority'* (1973) have appeared in such leading journals as POLITY and THE GEORGIA LAW REVIEW. Erler is also a contributor to THE ENCYCLOPEDIA OF THE AMERICAN CONSTI- TUTION, published by Macmillan. He was director of the Office of the Bicentennial of the Constitution for the National Endowment for the Humanities (1983-84).

JEAN YARBROUGH received her Ph.D. from the New School for Social Research in 1974. She has published numerous articles on constitutional political thought, among them *Federalism in the Foundation and Preservation of the American Republic* (PUBLIUS: THE JOURNAL OF FEDERALISM, 1976); *Some Thoughts on the Federalists' View of Representation* (POLITY, 1979); *Representatives and Republicanism: Two Views* (PUBLIUS: THE JOURNAL OF FEDERALISM, 1979); and *Rethinking 'The Federalists' View of Federalism'* (PUBLIUS: THE JOURNAL OF FEDERALISM), (forthcoming). Professor Yarbrough was a member of the National Endowment for the Humanities Planning Grant for the Bicentennial of the Constitution in 1983, and was an NEH Bicentennial Fellow in 1984-85. She is professor of political science at Loyola University, Chicago.

CHARLES HOBSON received his Ph.D. from Emory University in 1971. He is the author of several articles on early Constitutional history and interpretation, among them *The Negative on State Laws: James Madison, the Constitution, and the Crisis of Republican Government* (WILLIAM AND MARY QUARTERLY, 1979), *The Virginia Plan of 1787: A Note on the Original Text* (QUARTERLY JOURNAL OF THE LIBRARY OF CONGRESS, 1980), and *The Recovery of British Debts in the Federal Circuit Court of Virginia, 1790-1797* (VIRGINIA MAGAZINE OF HISTORY AND BIOGRAPHY, 1984). Dr. Hobson has been associated with the publication of THE PAPERS OF JOHN MADISON. He served as Assistant Editor from 1972-73; Associate Editor from 1973-77; Co-Editor from 1977-79; and was editor of the twelfth and thirteenth volumes of Madison's correspondence, published by the University of Virginia Press in 1979 and 1981, respectively. He is curator of John Marshall's papers at the Institute for Early American History and Culture.

BERNARD SIEGAN is director of Law and Economic Studies at the University of San Diego and a leading scholar of constitutional law. He received his J.D. from the University of Chicago Law School in 1950. Professor Siegan is the author or editor of eight books, including LAND USE WITHOUT ZONING (1972), OTHER PEOPLE'S PROPERTY (1976), ECONOMIC LIBERTIES AND THE CONSTITUTION (1981), and THE SUPREME COURT'S CONSTITUTION (1987). He edited and contributed to PLANNING WITHOUT PRICES (1977) and REGULATION AND ECONOMY (1980). He has also written numerous articles published as chapters in books or in journals, newspapers, and magazines. Professor Siegan was a member of President-elect Reagan's Task Force on Housing (1980-81) and also a member of the President's Commission on Housing (1981-82) where he chaired its Regulations Committee. He currently seves as a member of the National Commission on the Bicentennial of the U.S. Constitution.

WILLIAM LETWIN is professor of political science at the London School of Economics and Political Science. He received his Ph.D. from the University of Chicago in 1951. Professor Letwin has taught at the University of Chicago, MIT, and has served as Chairman of the Board of Studies in Economics at the University of London. He has published extensively in the area of American economic theory and policy. His books include FRANK KNIGHT: ON THE HISTORY AND METHOD OF ECONOMICS (1956), SIR JOSIAH CHILD (1959), DOCUMENTARY HISTORY OF AMERICAN ECONOMIC POLICY (1961, 1972), ORIGINS OF SCIENTIFIC ECONOMICS 1660-1776 (1953), LAW AND ECONOMIC POLICY IN AMERICA (1965), and AGAINST EQUALITY (1983).

MICHAEL McCONNELL received his J.D. from the University of Chicago Law School in 1979. McConnell has served as Law Clerk to Justice William J. Brennan, Jr., United States Supreme Court (1980-81); Assistant General Counsel, Office of Management and Budget (1981-83); and Assistant to the Solicitor General, Department of Justice (1983-85). He has argued six cases in the United States Supreme Court and has drafted numerous briefs in other matters in the Supreme Court on behalf of the United States. His scholarly articles include *Accommodation of Religion* (SUPREME COURT REVIEW), *Affirmative Action After Teal: A New Twist or a Turn of the Screw?* (REGULATION), *The Politics of Returning Power to the States* (HARVARD JOURNAL OF LAW AND PUBLIC POLICY), and Comment, *The Appealability of Orders Denying Motions for Disqualification of Counsel in the Federal Courts* (UNIVERSITY OF CHICAGO LAW REVIEW). He teaches law at the University of Chicago Law School.

Index